MW01286976

FIJI

1st Edition

**Where to Stay and Eat
for All Budgets**

**Must-See Sights
and Local Secrets**

Ratings You Can Trust

Fodor's Travel Publications New York, Toronto, London, Sydney, Auckland
www.fodors.com

FODOR'S INFOCUS FIJI

Series Editor: Douglas Stallings

Editors: Alexis C. Kelly, Christina Knight

Editorial Production: Carolyn Roth

Writers: Richard Brenner, Carrie Miller

Maps & Illustrations: David Lindroth, *cartographer*; Bob Blake, Rebecca Baer, and William Wu, *map editors*

Design: Fabrizio LaRocca, *creative director*; Guido Caroti, *art director*; Ann McBride, *designer*; Melanie Marin, *senior picture editor*

Cover Photo: (Raranitingga, Fiji): Chris A. Crumley/Alamy

Production/Manufacturing: Matthew Struble

COPYRIGHT

1st Edition

ISBN 978-1-4000-0685-4

ISSN 1941-0263

SPECIAL SALES

This book is available for special discounts for bulk purchases for sales promotions or premiums. Special editions, including personalized covers, excerpts of existing books, and corporate imprints, can be created in large quantities for special needs. For more information, write to Special Markets/Premium Sales, 1745 Broadway, MD 6-2, New York, NY 10019, or e-mail specialmarkets@randomhouse.com.

AN IMPORTANT TIP & AN INVITATION

Although all prices, opening times, and other details in this book are based on information supplied to us at press time, changes occur all the time in the travel world, and Fodor's cannot accept responsibility for facts that become outdated or for inadvertent errors or omissions. **So always confirm information when it matters,** especially if you're making a detour to visit a specific place. Your experiences—positive and negative—matter to us. If we have missed or misstated something, **please write to us.** We follow up on all suggestions. Contact the Fiji editor at editors@fodors.com or c/o Fodor's at 1745 Broadway, New York, NY 10019.

PRINTED IN THE UNITED STATES OF AMERICA

10 9 8 7 6 5 4 3 2 1

Be a Fodor's Correspondent

Your opinion matters. It matters to us. It matters to your fellow Fodor's travelers, too. And we'd like to hear it. In fact, we *need* to hear it. When you share your experiences and opinions, you become an active member of the Fodor's community. Here's how you can help improve Fodor's for all of us.

Tell us when we're right. We rely on local writers to give you an insider's perspective. But our writers and staff editors also depend on you. Your positive feedback is a vote to renew our recommendations for the next edition.

Tell us when we're wrong. We update most of our guides every year. But things change. If any of our descriptions are inaccurate or inadequate, we'll incorporate your changes in the next edition and will correct factual errors at fodors.com *immediately*.

Tell us what to include. You probably have had fantastic travel experiences that aren't yet in Fodor's. Why not share them with a community of like-minded travelers? Share your discoveries and experiences with everyone directly at fodors.com. Your input may lead us to add a new listing or a higher recommendation.

Give us your opinion instantly at our feedback center at www.fodors.com/feedback. You may also e-mail editors@fodors.com with the subject line "Fiji Editor." Or send your nominations, comments, and complaints by mail to Fiji Editor, Fodor's, 1745 Broadway, New York, NY 10019.

Happy Traveling!

Tim Jarrell, Publisher

CONTENTS

ABOUT THIS BOOK

Our Ratings

We wouldn't recommend a place that wasn't worth your time, but sometimes a place is so experiential that superlatives don't do it justice: you just have to be there to know. These sights, properties, and experiences get our highest rating, **Fodor's Choice,** indicated by orange stars throughout this book. Black stars highlight sights and properties we deem **Highly Recommended,** places that our writers, editors, and readers praise again and again for consistency and excellence.

Credit Cards

Want to pay with plastic? **AE, D, DC, MC, V** following restaurant and hotel listings indicate whether American Express, Discover, Diners Club, MasterCard, and Visa are accepted.

Restaurants

Unless we state otherwise, restaurants are open for lunch and dinner daily. We mention dress only when there's a specific requirement and reservations only when they're essential or not accepted—it's always best to book ahead.

Hotels

Unless we tell you otherwise, you can assume that the hotels have private bath, phone, TV, and air-conditioning. We always list facilities but not whether you'll be charged an extra fee to use them, so when pricing accommodations, find out what's included.

Many Listings

★	Fodor's Choice
★	Highly recommended
✉	Physical address
⊕	Directions
⌂	Mailing address
☎	Telephone
🖷	Fax
⊕	On the Web
✍	E-mail
🖾	Admission fee
☉	Open/closed times
Ⓜ	Metro stations
⊟	Credit cards

Hotels & Restaurants

🏨	Hotel
🛏	Number of rooms
⚭	Facilities
⑩	Meal plans
✕	Restaurant
⚘	Reservations
⟍	Smoking
🔊	BYOB
✕🏨	Hotel with restaurant that warrants a visit

Outdoors

🏌	Golf
⛺	Camping

Other

🛈	Family-friendly
⇨	See also
✉	Branch address
☞	Take note

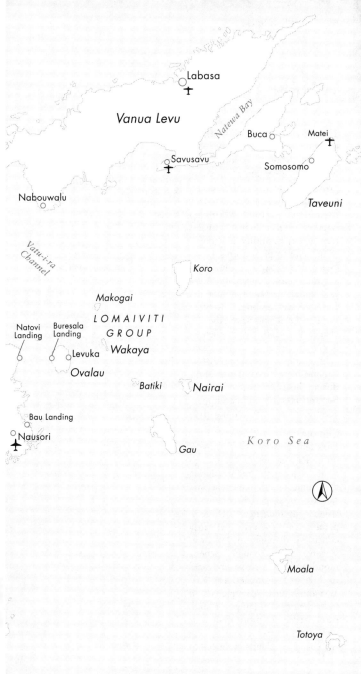

WHEN TO GO

The two treasures of Fiji—paradisiacal landscape and friendly people—are always in season but, as with every destination, there are pros and cons to visiting at certain times. The "tourist season" is from May to October, when Fiji's weather is at its mild best, with less rain, lower humidity, and fewer chances for tropical storms. However, expect to pay for the privilege, as airfare and accommodation rates peak during the months of June and July. Fiji's wet season is November through April, and there's the odd chance of a weather phenomenon, like hurricanes or tropical cyclones. School holidays for Fiji, Australia, and New Zealand also occur during this time, usually December and January and can impact accommodation availability.

Climate
Fiji's temperature usually hovers around a pleasant 77°F, although it can creep into the mid-80s during the summer months (December and January), or drop to the mid-60s in winter (July and August). The temperature of the ocean stays fairly consistent throughout. Fiji's wet season averages around 12 inches a month and its dry season averages to three or four inches. The Yasawa and Mamanuca regions tend to be the driest in Fiji year-round, rarely receiving more than four inches of rain per month. As Fiji is a cluster of islands in the South Pacific Ocean, there are the occasional cyclones or hurricanes, but catastrophic storms are rare.

Information Fiji Meteorological Service (⊕www.met.gov.fj).

Suva, Viti Levu

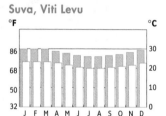

Savusavu, Vanua Levu

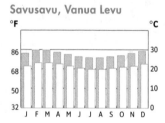

Welcome to Fiji

WORD OF MOUTH

"Take the opportunity, if it arises, to travel off island to any of the many reefs that are dotted between the islands. At these you will get the opportunity to see a lot more than you would straight off the beach."

—Kiwi_acct

Written by Robert Brenner & Carrie Miller

FROM THE MOMENT YOU SET EYES ON FIJI through cabin-pressured windows, the country promises to be more than just another pretty beach. The main island's mountainous, un-ignorable green landscape seems to rise to meet you, a reflection of the extraordinary hospitality of its people. Among its 333 islands are rain forests and sparkling cobalt-and-white shores. Resorts of every size and caliber comprise the sumptuous playground of sun worshippers, spa-goers, water-sports enthusiasts, golfers, foodies, and most everyone in between. Were there a vacation fairy, you can imagine she'd sprinkle Yasawa Islands sand in place of fairy dust.

Behind the gorgeous facade, the country's history runs deep. Captain William Bligh sailed for his life through these islands shortly after the mutiny on the *Bounty,* narrowly avoiding capture by pursuing cannibals. The tiny town of Levuka, the nation's first capital, remains frozen in time, a living relic of 19th-century British colonial rule. In the premier South Pacific capital city of Suva, a silent Parliament house is testament to a country quietly grappling with its political demons.

Adventurous, exceptionally friendly, environmentally conscious, in-part cultured and in-part wild and, of course, extraordinarily good-looking, Fiji is as well-rounded a tropical destination as you're likely to set barefoot on.

HISTORY

The first Fijians arrived on the mainland around 1500 BC—shards of intricate pottery called "Lapita" discovered at the Sigatoka Sand Dunes date to around this time. The population spread throughout many of Fiji's islands, eventually developing mutually unintelligible dialects and frequently warring over territory and influence. The Fijians were a merciless people, killing women and children as readily as men in war, burying men alive as they filled in the holes dug for the foundations of houses, and launching their large, masterfully crafted *drua* (war canoes) over the bodies of slaves used as rollers. They ate the flesh of their murdered enemies and rivals; "Eat me" was a phrase commonly used by villagers to humbly greet their godlike chiefs. Fiji was nicknamed "the Cannibal Isles" by Europeans, who were informed by the Tongans of their ways.

1

This reputation caused both the Dutch explorer Abel Tasman and Englishman Captain James Cook to resist landing on the islands in 1643 and 1774, respectively. Days after the mutiny on the *Bounty* in 1789, Captain Bligh was the first to glimpse the mainland.

In 1808 muskets were introduced by the shipwrecked Charles Savage, who later became notorious for his politicking among the Fijian chiefs and was eventually killed and eaten. The United States Exploring Expedition charted Fiji in 1840 and the first missionaries arrived later that decade. Ratu Cakobau, an ambitious chief, began consolidating power among the islands, appointing himself *Tui Viti* (King of Fiji) in 1854 without authority over most of the country. The following year he was aided by King George I of Tonga in suppressing a large resistance, further consolidating power but giving the Tongan leader entrée to influence in Fiji. Levuka, in the Lomaiviti Group, began to swell with settlers and Cakobau declared it the capital.

The U.S. consul held Cakobau responsible for a theft, and over the coming two decades he fell into debt with the U.S. government. *See Chapter 4, Lomaiviti, in Settling a Score*; a confederacy of chiefs he established fell apart after just two years and Levuka grew into a raucous stronghold of conmen, fugitives, and drunks. A short-lived Ku Klux Klan was established by Europeans at one point to challenge his rule. He tried once to cede the Fiji Islands to Britain while maintaining the title of King of Fiji, but this, combined with the fact that he did not control most of the territory, led Britain to reject the offer. In 1874 he tried again to cede control to the Queen, this time unconditionally, and his offer was accepted.

In 1877 the capital was moved to Suva. Two years later, the first ship with indentured laborers from Calcutta arrived. They harvested cotton, world prices of which had skyrocketed owing to the American Civil War, and grew sugarcane. About 70,000 Indians arrived over the next five years, with most choosing to remain in Fiji after their service was completed. Fijians served in both world wars, although they were accepted with less difficulty in the second. Fijian guerrilla-commandos fought behind Japanese enemy lines on Guadalcanal in the Solomon Islands. It's said they were so adept at guerrilla warfare that, rather than Missing In Action (MIA), Fijian soldiers who were unaccounted for were labeled NYA—Not Yet Arrived.

FIJI'S TOP 5

A Warm Welcome. Fijians have a talent for making guests feel welcome. Whether you meet locals at your resort, in a village, or on a public bus, the encounter is sure to thaw even the frostiest big-city commuter.

Pampered Luxury. Speaking of friendly, most resorts are quiet and intimate, housing no more than 40 guests, and the staff will remember your name the first time you meet and know your favorite drink by the third day. You'll be blown away by your lush, comfortable surroundings as well.

Soft Coral Capital. Both seasoned and first-time divers and snorkelers will delight in the coral's shapes, sizes, and colors. Some reefs are only a short swim from the beach, so even those made timid by deep water can take a peak.

Beautiful Beaches. The blanket-soft, blindingly white beaches of the western island groups easily rival those of the Caribbean, and many have a sexy volcano-and-rain-forest setting to boot.

Natural Riches. Fiji's pristine natural riches are by no means limited to its coasts. There are kayaking and hiking in Viti Levu's rain forest and swimming beneath breathtaking waterfalls in Taveuni's Bouma National Heritage Park, just to name a few.

In 1968 Fiji was granted independence and established a parliamentary government, the first elections of which were held in 1972. A bloodless coup in mid-1987 was followed by a second in September, which broke ties with the British government. In 2000 civilian George Speight and a group of followers stormed the Parliament building in response to the election of an Indo-Fijian led government. He took the prime minister and 35 others hostage for nearly two months before releasing them under the promise of asylum by military leader Commodore Bainimarama, who then arrested and sentenced him to life imprisonment. In December 2006 Commodore Bainimarama orchestrated a bloodless coup largely in response to proposed legislation to pardon Speight and others responsible for the 2000 coup attempt. At the time of writing, he remained the country's self-appointed prime minister and had promised general elections by the end of March 2009.

CLOSE UP

What You Need in Fiji

1

A warm smile and a sense of humor. Fijians are serious contenders for the friendliest people in the world. They are curious, warm, and giving. They are also so relaxed about time that they have their own time frame, Fiji Time, which is more constant than a clock. Be prepared (mentally and practically) for unconcerned delays.

Insect repellent. Mosquitoes outnumber Fijians 50 to 1, and they know it. These buzzing armies are fierce and unrepentant, so prepare for battle by packing repellent and mosquito coils, which you can find in major cities like Nadi and Suva. Stock up before hitting the outer islands.

Reef shoes. Most people consider flip-flops or sandals to be adequate reef shoes, but travelers to Fiji need to take it to the next level as most of the islands are surrounded by coral and reefs. Even the sandy shallows have sinkholes that will suck flimsy footwear off the unsuspecting travelers. Make sure you have well-fitted, industrial strength reef shoes and walk where the locals walk.

A list of emergency contacts. This includes embassies, state departments, airlines, your hotel(s), your bank, and family: Fiji likes to coup. Best to be prepared if you find yourself caught in a political earthquake.

Snorkel, mask, and underwater camera. Fiji is a tropical paradise with uncounted underwater wonders. After a while, you'll tire of ill-fitting rental masks, or remote beaches where rentals are unavailable. Bring your own well-fitting gear and enjoy the view.

A tropical wardrobe. This should include—for both men and women—shorts, T-shirts, breathable rain gear, a warm jacket or fleece, sturdy footwear, and the local sulu or lavalava (wrap).

Swimsuits and sunscreen. You will spend a lot of time near the water, in the water, or on the water. Make certain you bring a couple of swimsuits and plenty of sunscreen.

Seasickness tablets. If you're island-hopping, or even traveling to one of the outer islands for a prolonged stay, most likely you'll be spending time on a boat. The comfort level in Fijian boats varies, and the ocean is always unpredictable, so plan ahead.

Reading material. Remember Fiji Time? You may face a few long waits, so arm yourself with pleasant distractions. The major cities in Fiji have bookstores, but the outer islands don't.

GETTING AROUND

The islands of Fiji have a few major cities like Nadi and Suva on Viti Levu and Levuka in Lomaiviti, but mainly there are small villages scattered over the islands. Travel times, therefore, can often be double what you'd expect due to the lack of infrastructure. You can get around by car and bus on the main islands, but in the outer islands like Kadavu, there's even less infrastructure. Travel is primarily by boat, or for those in a real hurry, plane.

Island-hopping is a great way to see the archipelago, and interisland ferry trips and sightseeing tours have increased because of this. There's regular ferry service from Viti Levu to Vanua Levu, Ovalau and Taveuni, and not-so-regular service among the smaller, outlying islands. Ferries transport just about everything from people to cargo and are often on Fiji Time—a slower, more laid-back approach to time and schedules often encountered on the islands.

CRUISING THE ISLANDS

Fiji is one giant port of call. Cruises of all sizes and variety flourish in this island nation, and seeing Fiji by water is one of the best ways to experience its diversity and beauty. A few major cruise lines, like the Holland America Line and Princess, do call into Suva, but if you're planning on visiting Fiji as a destination, the best value for money is to go with one of the many local options. Cruises are available from nearly every location (Nadi, Suva, Savusavu, Yasawa, etc.), and can be priced from $80 to $1,750 per day, depending on luxury, uniqueness, and privacy.

LOCAL CRUISE LINES

Blue Lagoon Cruises (☎877/252–3454 *in U.S.* ⊕*www. bluelagooncruises.com*) specializes in three- to seven-day boutique island cruises. **Beachcomber Cruises** (☎666–2600 ⊕*www.beachcomberfiji.com*) offers day trips to and from Beachcomber Island Resort, one of the most popular island resorts in Fiji. **Captain Cook Cruises** (☎670–1823 ⊕*www. captaincook.com.au*) has a fleet of small cruise ships and windjammers that offers everything from seven-day excursions to dinner cruises. **SeaHawk Yacht Charters** (☎885–0787 ⊕*www.seahawkfiji.com*) has a charter yacht for hire, complete with captain and crew, for overnight, day, or picnic cruises. **South Sea Cruises** (☎675–0500 ⊕*www.ssc.com.fj*) offers resort transfers to catamaran day cruises past uninhabited islands. **Tui Tai Adventure Cruises** (☎253/777–4290 *in U.S.* ⊕*www.tuitai.com*) specializes in off-the-beaten-path seven-night luxury cruises.

INTERNATIONAL CRUISE LINES

Holland America Line's (☎*206/281–3535* ⊕*www.hollandamerica.com*) *ms Amsterdam* briefly stops off in Suva on the Grand Asia and Australia Voyage or the South Pacific Odyssey trips. Itineraries range from 20 to 67 days at sea and depart from ports like Sydney, Seattle, or Singapore. **Princess** (☎*800/774–6237* ⊕*www.princess.com*) offers the Fijian Jewels Cruise, a roundtrip voyage from Sydney that visits the ports of Suva, Lautoka, and Dravuni Island.

FIJIAN FARE

Viti Levu is a great place to try traditional Fijian cuisine, the staple ingredients of which are fresh fish and coconut milk. Were the country to declare a national dish, it would be *Kokoda*—raw fish marinated in coconut milk and lime juice, spiced with pepper, onion, and tomato (often described as Fijian ceviche). Most fish dishes are cooked, often char-grilled to a crispy texture, and accompanied by local vegetables such as cassava (a potatolike starch), a leafy root vegetable called dalo (also known as "taro"), and rou rou (similar in taste and texture to spinach).

The vast majority of resorts offer a weekly *lovo*, a traditional Fijian feast of fish, chicken, and sometimes pork, wrapped in banana leaves and cooked on heated rocks in an underground oven. For dessert, Fijians traditionally enjoy fruits such as pineapple and bananas, which grow here in abundance and have an unusually sweet taste.

IF YOU LIKE

There are lots of things to like about Fiji and plenty of things to do while you're here.

NATURAL WONDERS

Everywhere you look, you'll be blown away by the beauty this island nation possesses. Viti Levu alone has landscapes that are unmatched anywhere else. There are the 300-foot-high black volcanic rock walls of Navua Gorge; the 1,106 acre Sigatoka Sand Dunes that were designated a UNESCO World Heritage site in 1999 and are home to Fiji's earliest recorded prehistoric sites; and the Colo-I-Suva Forest Park,

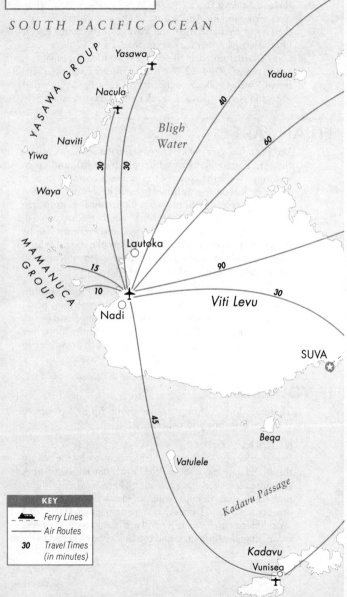

Flight & Ferry Times for Fiji

SOUTH PACIFIC OCEAN

YASAWA GROUP

Yasawa

Nacula

Naviti

Yiwa

Waya

MAMANUCA GROUP

Bligh Water

Yadua

40

60

Lautoka

15

10

90

Nadi

30

Viti Levu

SUVA

45

Vatulele

Beqa

Kadavu Passage

Kadavu

Vunisea

30

30

KEY

🚢 Ferry Lines

— Air Routes

30 Travel Times (in minutes)

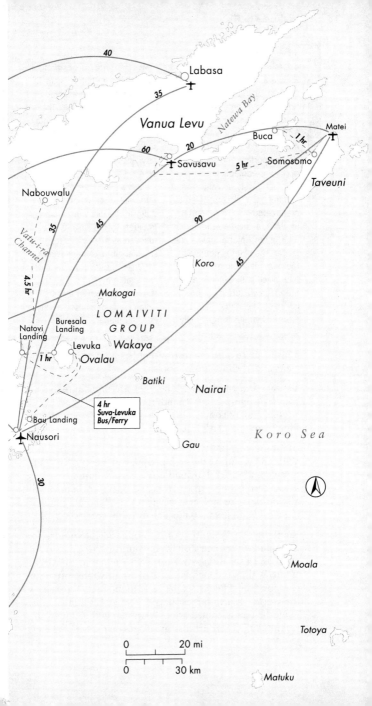

The Kava Ceremony

Known as *yaqona* ("yangg-ona") in Fijian and also simply referred to as grog, kava is a mildly narcotic drink made from the pepper plant (piper methysticum). It's used on both important and social occasions—notably in acceptance of guests or visitors—and is traditionally accompanied by great ceremony. Those partaking sit in a circle on the floor, a large bowl placed before the leader. The plant is pounded, the pulp placed in a cloth sack and mixed with water in a *tanoa* (bowl), turning a brownish color. The leader then soaks it up and strains it repeatedly using the cloth before a small bowl is filled and presented to be drunk in one swig. The drinker claps in appreciation a certain number of times before and after drinking, the number varying by region. Most people experience a slight numbing of the lips and tongue, and those who drink a lot generally feel sluggish the following morning. Traditionally the kava itself is supplied as a *sevusevu* (ceremonial gift) by the guests or party seeking favor of the chief and should be laid before the chief upon arrival at a village. Kava can be purchased at any open-air market.

a lush square mile rain forest that has numerous walking trails and several natural pools.

Yasawa and Mamanuca's beaches are undisputedly the country's finest. Mana Island has a particularly beautiful stretch, and, of course, there are the Yasawa's magnificent Blue Lagoon and it's fascinating coves.

DIVING & SNORKELING

With 333 islands in the archipelago, you'll find great spots to dive and snorkel around every bend in Fiji, as well as PADI–certified dive instructors and operators. There will also be plenty to look at since Fiji is the soft coral capital of the world and home to more than 1,000 species of fish.

Rainbow and Vuna, two of the South Pacific's top reefs, are found off the coast of Taveuni and are rich in colorful coral and fish. Rainbow Reef is also home to the Great White Wall, so named because of its all white soft coral composition. The Astrolabe reef, found near Kadavu, is the world's fourth-largest barrier reef at 120 km (75 mi) long; the reef is named after a ship that collided with the reef in 1827. There are also great sites on the fringing reef, mostly off the southern coast of the island, including shallow spots ideal for snorkeling just off-shore.

Looking for more snorkeling options? The lack of weather around Yasawa and Mamanuca make the visibility over the area's coral exceptionally clear and the sites are usually just a short swim from the beach.

WORD OF MOUTH. "As far as sea life is concerned, it is all before you. Tropical fish abound as well as small sharks—usually harmless—octopus, giant clams, eels, etc." –Kiwi_acct

OUTDOOR ACTIVITIES

You don't have to dive or snorkel to have fun in the sun while visiting Fiji. There are a whole slew of outdoor activities, including surfing, bird-watching, fishing, and kayaking, to occupy your hours.

Even though Fiji has world-class breaks, the country has yet to develop a surf culture, which means little or no wait to ride the huge waves at Viti Levu's Frigates and Wilkes Passages; it also means long, uninterrupted rides, but only for intermediate and expert surfers.

Taveuni is bird-watcher heaven with the famed Orange Dove, stunning Silktail, and Red Shining Parrot flitting about the island's lush rain forest. If you're looking to hook "the big one," head to Kadavu, where you can also kayak. The island's rugged terrain, lack of roads, and fantastic water-based views make it easy to head to the water to explore.

RESORTS

Fiji's lodging options range from small pensions and village stays to hotels and resorts. But, if you really want to pamper yourself, consider booking one of the resorts on Taveuni's northern end. You can expect to have a staff that knows your name within the hour, as well as personalized activities and private beachfront dining at your fingertips. If you find yourself on Vanua Levu and are looking for a great experience for the family, check out Namale and Jean-Michel Cousteau. These two small resorts house the South Pacific's most lavish spas as well as upscale yet family-appropriate surroundings.

Maybe you're looking for an all-inclusive that won't break the bank. The Yasawas, and increasingly the Mamanucas, are famous for their inexpensive options. The true beach bum can relax in an unspoiled setting, rest his or her head comfortably, and dine on three meals for less than $100 per day. "Paradise" is available at any price range in Fiji.

FIJI IN FILM & LITERATURE

Like many a sun-kissed, rock-hard body with dazzling blues, the Fiji islands have featured prominently in entertainment media. *Castaway* (2000), starring Tom Hanks as a FedEx executive stranded on a deserted island, was mostly filmed on tiny Monuriki island in the northwest corner of the Mamanucas. The far-less Oscar-contentious *Anacondas: The Hunt for the Blood Orchid* (2004) was shot around Viti Levu's Pacific Harbour, despite being set in Borneo, and was the first Hollywood film to have its premiere in Fiji.

At least seven books and three films are based on the true events famously known as the "mutiny on the Bounty," in which Fletcher Christian and others mutinied against Captain William Bligh aboard the ship *The Bounty* on April 29, 1789. Shortly after the mutiny, Bligh and 18 loyal crew members narrowly escaped cannibals who pursued them north of the Yasawas; had they been caught, they would have most likely been eaten. The most recent film, *The Bounty* (1984), stars Mel Gibson as Christian and Anthony Hopkins as Bligh.

American author James Michener grew well-acquainted with Fiji while a naval officer stationed in the South Pacific. His book *Rascals in Paradise* devotes a chapter to Cleveland-native William H. Hayes, known as the "last buccaneer" and notorious for kidnapping indigenous people in the mid-1800s and selling them into slavery on islands including Fiji.

The Yasawa Islands has a hold on a franchise. *The Blue Lagoon* (1949) starring Jean Simmons, tells the story of two shipwrecked children growing up and falling in love on a deserted island. It was largely filmed in the pristine lagoon between Nanuya Lai Lai and Tavewa in the middle of the island group. Its 1980 remake starring Brooke Shields and Christopher Atkins was also filmed here and at locations throughout Fiji. The 1991 *Return to Blue Lagoon* starring Milla Jovovich was largely filmed on Taveuni.

Viti Levu

WORD OF MOUTH

"Learn at least one word—'bula.' This is a general greeting for all occasions, meaning 'hello—welcome—or whatever.' Everybody you pass will say 'bula' to you - so you might as well be the first to say it."

—LDameson

Written
by Robert
Brenner

THE HEART OF FIJI'S 333 ISLANDS (106 are inhabited) is a 4,020-square-mi island of verdant mountainsides encasing volcanic peaks and lush river valleys running out to barrier reefs. The English-speaking former British colony is home to 75% of the country's population and Fiji's only two cities. The inhabitants are a unique mix of Melanesian Fijians (about 51%), Indo-Fijians, whose ancestors came from India as indentured laborers (about 44%), and a small number of Europeans, Chinese, and other Melanesians. Although not heavily industrialized, Fiji is a nation of "shop-keepers," with an eager, white-collar economy epitomized by storefronts, table service, and taxi cabs. The country as a whole is seeing a trend toward urbanization; cities and larger towns tend to have large Indo-Fijian populations while most Melanesians remain in the same close-knit villages and even the same houses inhabited by their families since long before European contact. Fiji's Melanesians have a strong tradition of hospitality in complement to their communal lifestyle and are considered to be among the friendliest people in the world.

The indigenous people called their land "Viti" but Europeans first learned of the islands from Tongans, who referred to it as "Feejee." Viti Levu translates as "Great Fiji," and as the mainland, it has the economic and intellectual epicenters of the South Pacific in its cosmopolitan capital of Suva and that city's branch of the University of the South Pacific. The sugarcane-and-sugar-train-crossed Lautoka-Ba area is one of the country's two major sugar-producing regions (Fiji's second-largest industry). Fiji's tourism hub rests in quirky Nadi, point of entry for virtually every traveler. A two-lane highway conveys chatty locals on open-air buses between Nadi and Suva and the mellow, inviting villages they call home.

The island's southern half is full of magnificent natural wonders, each within a few hours' drive of every hotel. You can climb millennia-old sand dunes and then surf from the beach, raft, or kayak through a prehistoric setting capped by 300-foot black volcanic rock walls, and swim with sharks as they're fed within one of the world's largest barrier reefs, in Pacific Harbour. You can recount the experience by one of the multiple bars or pools at a huge resort on the Coral Coast. On the urban side, you can have your pick of handicrafts in Nadi, fine-dine on a bevy of cuisines in Suva, feel the local Indo-Fijian vibe by the waterfront in

VITI LEVU'S TOP 5

Shark Diving. Observe the sea's greatest predator feasting in its natural environment.

Firewalking. Natives of Beqa Island villages stroll over smoldering coals in dramatic performances of this ancient ritual at resorts and in Pacific Harbour.

Wine & Dine in Suva. Savor the capital's fine cuisine, whether above a brewery, in a lavish Italian dining room, or afloat on the harbor.

Surf Frigates Passage. Rip through a barrel and ride for 100 yards or more at this world-class break.

Village Visits. Give a sevusevu (ceremonial gift) and take in a kava ceremony among some of the friendliest people on earth.

Lautoka, and discover the Melanesian lifestyle around a kava bowl in a village anywhere along the way.

You won't find Fiji's best beaches on Viti Levu, but excursions to the Mamanuca group's lovely sands leave daily from Denarau Island, near Nadi, returning you back in time for Fiji's best restaurants and five-star hotels. Other easy trips are to one of the smaller off-shore islands, where you can watch islanders walk across smoldering coals or just sink your own toes into a warm stretch of sand.

EXPLORING VITI LEVU

The big joke on Viti Levu is that the buses are the only things that run on time, which, like many humorous things, is also mostly true. Taxis abound and buses run frequently between the Nadi area and Suva during the day. The latter are a good way to meet locals, who are almost always happy to chat, and some public buses have luggage storage. The mainland is also a great place to rent a car, with only the paved two-lane Queens Road in the south and rougher Kings Road in the north. Travel times can vary considerably depending on road conditions and how long you have to wait before overtaking a public bus that may be slowing you down. Along the southern coast, there's plentiful parking in towns and at resorts of the Coral Coast and Sunset Strip. For the most part, attractions and hotels along Queens Road announce themselves and are evenly spaced; "If you haven't seen it yet, keep going" is a safe motto for those renting a car, although bus and taxi drivers are well-acquainted with the island. Distances given for resorts in this chapter are in kilometers from the Nadi International Airport. Depending on how much you want to see and do, a scenic cross-island road trip could take three weeks or three hours.

ABOUT THE HOTELS & RESTAURANTS

Viti Levu is notable among the Fiji islands for its abundance of large four- and five-star resorts. Families in search of a one-stop holiday with in-room amenities, plenty of space for the kids to explore, and numerous dining options need look no further than Denarau Island and the Coral Coast (though be aware there are very few channels on TV). Nearly all hotels welcome nonguests to book into their spa, and some permit use of the pool, beach, and other facilities with the purchase of lunch. Pristine Beqa Lagoon has upscale resorts in a setting to match anything found in the Mamanucas, but note that its beaches are more noticeably subject to tides. Many resorts offer a range of accommodations, from private beachfront bures to shared-bathroom dorms, with a restaurant and facilities that meet a standard somewhere between budget and upper-mid-range. Some quoted hotel rates may not include taxes of up to 17.5%. Check with your hotel before booking.

Seafood is Fiji's star ingredient. Countless locals make their livings as divers and fishermen, keeping the local restaurants and open-air markets stocked with prawns, lobsters, scallops, walu, tuna, and *ika* (fish) of the day. Some even go door-to-door in the mornings, peddling the day's catch. Due to a lack of steady tourism, many mainland restaurants offer what appears to Westerners a ridiculously wide range of cuisines in order to appeal to locals. It's common to see curries, Chinese-style dishes, seafood, and pizzas all crowding the same menu. Because most chefs are Indo-Fijian, curries are generally your best bet.

Suva, the nation's capital, has far and away the country's biggest restaurant scene, with a couple of outstanding venues on or near its attractive harbor. Its diversity, however, is rivaled by the large resorts of the Coral Coast that have up to four dining venues with globe-spanning menus. Virtually all hotels welcome non-guests to dine at their restaurants.

Viti Levu

*SOUTH PACIFIC
OCEAN*

Naviti

Bligh Water

Vomo

Vatia Pt.

Tavua

Malake

Rakiraki

Matawailevu

Namarai

Lautoka
see detail
map

▲ *Mt.
Koroyanitu*

Navala

Natovi
Landing

Lomolomo

VITI LEVU

Korovou

Kumi

Malolo

*Malolo
Lailai*

▲ *Mt. Koroba*

▲ *Mt. Monavatu*

Kasavu

Nadi
see detail
map

Tuvu

Mt. Tuvutau ▲

Wainimakatu

Lami

Suva
see detail
map

Sigatoka Sand Dunes

Nabukelevu

*SIGUTAKA
VALLEY*

Sigatoka

Korolevu

Korovisilou

Navua

Pacific Harbour
see detail map

Coral Coast
see detail
map

Beqa Passage

Beqa

Vatulele

GREAT ITINERARIES

From the cascading waterfalls of its rain forest to the vibrancy of its capital, Viti Levu is a place of motion, a place to explore. The mainland's infrastructure makes some of its breathtaking peaks and stunning valleys accessible while its magnificent lagoon is at your beck and call. This island does not lend itself to inactivity although its amenity-laden hotels and boutique hideaways encourage that, too.

IF YOU HAVE 3 DAYS

Head straight for Pacific Harbour. Try to arrange a village visit in advance through your hotel for that morning or afternoon. If that's not possible, take in a show at the Arts Village, peruse the shops, and have lunch. Check into your accommodation and book tomorrow's white-water rafting trip, shark-diving excursion, or waterfall tour. Spend the rest of the day by the pool or on the beach before having dinner at the hotel restaurant. The next day, rise early for your excursion or day-trip. On Day 3, head to Suva early, check in, and visit the Fiji Museum or Colo-I-Suva Forest Park. Afterwards, savor lunch at Old Mill Cottage. In the afternoon, shop at the Curio & Handicraft Market and check out the scene at the Suva Municipal Market along Stinson Parade. Have dinner at one of the city's top restaurants, with the possibility of a nightcap at Traps Bar.

IF YOU HAVE 5 DAYS

Spend Day 1 unwinding at a resort on the Coral Coast. On Day 2, visit the Sigatoka Sand Dunes and/or Kula Eco Park. Rearrange the above three-day itinerary so that your Pacific Harbour excursion picks you up on Day 3 from the Coral Coast and drops you at your Pacific Harbour hotel afterwards. On the fourth day, visit the Arts Village and relax as above before taking in Suva on Day 5.

IF YOU HAVE 7 DAYS

Tack two more days onto your stay in either the Coral Coast or Pacific Harbour. Consider a day cruise out to Robinson Crusoe Island and a second day-trip into the magnificent interior. Conversely, this amount of time is ideal for a vacation-long escape, including snorkeling, diving, and a village visit, at an island resort off Suva or in Beqa Lagoon, off Pacific Harbour.

WHAT IT COSTS			
$	$$	$$$	$$$$
RESTAURANTS			
under F$10	F$10– F$20	F$20– F$30	over F$30
HOTELS*			
$90–$140	$140–$200	$200–$260	over $260
HOTELS**			
under F$300	F$300–F$500	F$500–F$800	over F$800

*EP, BP, CP **AI, FAP, MAP; Restaurant prices are per person for a main course at dinner. Hotel prices are per night for a double room in high season and may not include a 12.5% Value-Added Tax (V.A.T.) or a 5% hotel turnover tax. Hotel prices are in U.S. dollars where noted

NADI

The main drag is 9 km (6 mi) from the airport, 187 km (116 mi) from Suva.

Nadi is Fiji's third-largest center and its gateway town. Most budget and mid-range accommodations as well as the vast majority of shops and restaurants are in or just north of the town center. A 20-minute drive over a short bridge to the east lies Denarau Island, home to six international luxury hotels (and counting), the Port Denarau shopping complex and marina, and large private homes. From the country's major international airport, one can be whisked to a five-star resort or catch an open-air public bus to a lively hostel, and most accommodations in-between. On Denarau Island, a shared beachfront and free shuttle bus makes it easy to access the restaurants and spas of each hotel. Many excursions to the Mamanucas and Yasawas islands leave from Denarau Marina.

Owing to its relatively large commercial center, Nadi Town is one of the best places in Fiji to shop for souvenirs amid chatty Indo-Fijian shopkeepers, or to try a local restaurant. Yet it's a bit rough around the edges and decidedly lacking in major attractions for visitors, many of whom spend just one night here before catching a ferry from Denarau Island to the white-sand beaches of the island groups to the west.

IF YOU LIKE

NATURAL WONDERS

Viti Levu's magnificent landscapes are unmatched anywhere else. You can raft or kayak between the 300-foot-high black volcanic rock walls of "Fiji's Grand Canyon," Navua Gorge; climb the Sigatoka Sand Dunes, an archaeological treasure-trove; bird-watch and swim amid rain forest in the natural pools of Colo-I-Suva Forest Park. The gorge is accessible by well-organized day tours and the dunes and park have good visitor centers.

SURFING

Fiji has yet to develop a surf culture in spite of its world-class breaks. This means little or no line-ups for big barrels at Frigates Passage, the world-class right-hander at Wilkes Passage, and long rides just about everywhere. Due to their size and the fact that many break over reefs, most of these waves are for intermediate and expert surfers only, and almost all are subject to the tides. You'll have to stay at Tavarua Island Resort off the west coast of Viti Levu in order to surf the epic left-handers Cloudbreak (featured in the movie *Endless Summer 2*) and Restaurants.

ALL THE AMENITIES

The mainland is the place for those looking to have four restaurants within walking distance of multiple swimming pools, the largest range of facilities to keep children occupied, and 24-hour room service. Most of Viti Levu's four- and five-star hotels are within a two-hour drive of Nadi Airport. You'll find large, family-friendly resorts in the more pristine setting of the Mamanuca Islands, but none offer amenities quite on the scale of Denarau Island and the Coral Coast.

CURRY

Roughly 40% of the island's population is Indo-Fijian and a far higher percentage of them makes up its chef pool. From fresh lobster and prawn to classic chicken and beef, you'll find restaurants throughout serving excellent curry platters complete with rice, roti, dhal soup, vegetable curry, papedum, and a diced vegetable chutney.

EXPLORING NADI AND THE AREA

An afternoon's shopping and hunger cravings can be satisfied by a stroll down the Main Street section of Queens Road. If you start in the north, just south of the bridge, you'll have the whole main strip before you, culminating in the beautiful Hindu temple where the road forks. The Martintar area, a two-minute taxi ride north of the Main

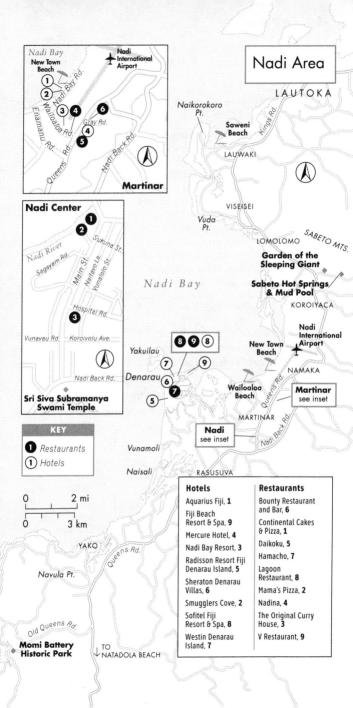

Nadi Area

Nadi Center (inset)

Nadi River
Sukuna St.
Sagayam Rd.
Main St.
Nattevo La.
Vunatolo St.
Hospital Rd.
Vunavau Rd.
Koroivolu Ave.
Nadi Back Rd.

Sri Siva Subramanya Swami Temple

Martinar (inset)

Nadi Bay
New Town Beach
Nadi International Airport
Nadi Bay Rd.
Wailoaloa Rd.
Enamanu Rd.
Queens Rd.
Gray Rd.
Nadi Back Rd.

Nadi Area (main map)

LAUTOKA
Naikorokoro Pt.
Saweni Beach
LAUWAKI
Kings Rd.
VISEISEI
Vuda Pt.
LOMOLOMO
SABETO MTS.

Garden of the Sleeping Giant
Sabeto Hot Springs & Mud Pool
KOROIYACA
Nadi International Airport
New Town Beach
NAMAKA
Wailoaloa Beach
Martinar see inset
MARTINAR
Nadi Back Rd.
Queens Rd.
Nadi see inset

Nadi Bay
Yakuilau
Denarau
Vunamoli
Naisali
RASUSUVA

Queens Rd.
YAKO
Navula Pt.
Old Queens Rd.
Momi Battery Historic Park
TO ↓ NATADOLA BEACH

KEY

1 *Restaurants*
1 *Hotels*

0 — 2 mi
0 — 3 km

Hotels

Aquarius Fiji, **1**
Fiji Beach Resort & Spa, **9**
Mercure Hotel, **4**
Nadi Bay Resort, **3**
Radisson Resort Fiji Denarau Island, **5**
Sheraton Denarau Villas, **6**
Smugglers Cove, **2**
Sofitel Fiji Resort & Spa, **8**
Westin Denarau Island, **7**

Restaurants

Bounty Restaurant and Bar, **6**
Continental Cakes & Pizza, **1**
Daikoku, **5**
Hamacho, **7**
Lagoon Restaurant, **8**
Mama's Pizza, **2**
Nadina, **4**
The Original Curry House, **3**
V Restaurant, **9**

Street section, is worth a separate visit for the town's best bar and a couple of its best restaurants. Although street numbers are slowly becoming en vogue in Nadi, so few businesses have them that they remain largely arbitrary. Nearly every restaurant is within a few blocks on Main Street and has a clearly marked sign.

Sri Siva Subramanya Swami Temple. This pastel-color Hindu temple cuts an impressive figure at the southern end of the main strip. Its many vivid ceiling murals and intricate patterns are the work of a single artist, C. Gopalakrishnan of Madras, India, who, at the time of writing, was repainting the entire 13-year-old structure. The open-air temple includes a number of shrines with ornate statues and doors imported from India, and is the site of weddings virtually every weekend. Its more than 1,000 devotees come to pray bearing fruit and other offerings throughout the day. Admission includes a casual tour—you may have to prod your guide with questions if you want more detail. Remove your shoes once inside the gates. ⊠*Queens Rd.* ☎*670–0977* ⊠*$3.50* ⊙*Daily 9–5.*

NEED A BREAK? The white bakers' uniforms only confirm what you
★ knew the moment your nose passed through the door of **Continental Cakes & Pizza** (⊠*Shop 2/511 Main St.* ☎*670-3595*): This is a serious bakery. In addition to the cakes, there are pizzas, croissants, and popular light-lunch deli sandwiches on freshly baked rolls. Floral tablecloths, flower centerpieces, and a shiny tile floor make this an ideal place to recoup from shopping or recharge for a second round.

Garden of the Sleeping Giant. Founded by the late Raymund Burr in 1977 to house his own orchids, the garden now displays more than 2,000 kinds of orchids across its 50 acres. Visitors can also tour Burr's holiday shack, which still contains a few personal items including photographs, his favorite chair, and his walking cane. Admission is an additional $8 and includes afternoon tea. The garden is a half-hour's drive north of Nadi, in the foothills of the Sabeto Mountains. ⊠*Wailoko Rd.* ☎*672–2701* ⊠*$12* ⊙*Mon.–Sat. 9–5, Sun. 9–noon.*

Sabeto Hot Springs and Mud Pool. For a naturalistic bathing experience north of town, you can take a dip in these underdeveloped thermal bathing and mud pools in the lush Sabeto River Valley. They're best enjoyed as the air cools later in the day. There are basic changing and shower facilities. Those looking for a Canyon Ranch substitute will be disappointed. ⊠*Wailoko Rd., past the Garden of the Sleeping Giant, Waikataka* ☎*No phone* ☜*$3.50–$5* ⊘*Mon.–Sat. 8–5.*

Momi Battery Historic Park. Guns and bunkers were set up here during World War II to protect Nadi from a potential attack by the Japanese. One of the bunkers has been turned into a museum with photographs documenting its history. The site offers spectacular views over Momi Bay and the Mamanuca Islands. The turnoff for Old Queens Road is about 20 km (12 mi) south of Nadi; the battery is about 8 km (5 mi) farther along. ⊠*Old Queens Rd., Momi Bay* ☎*670–0977* ☜*$3* ⊘*Daily 9–5.*

OFF THE BEATEN PATH. While its character is certain to change with the resort development spearheaded by InterContinental, **Natadola Beach** remains arguably the mainland's best beach. You can ride horses provided by the locals (if they're not there, this can be arranged through the Natadola Beach Resort (☎*672–1001*), swim without fear of stepping on coral, soak up the sun and eat at the beachfront resorts. The beach is at the end of Maro Road, which appears just past the police post on Queens Road, near Km 45. ⊠*Maro Rd.*

WHERE TO EAT

NADI

FIJIAN

$$$ ✕**Nadina.** Whole fish and prawns (and we do mean whole fish and prawns) are among the specialties at this picturesque and authentic Fijian restaurant. Some may consider the fish overcooked (so order a sizzling stir-fry) while others will enjoy the flavor of char-grilled walu or Naqu (catch of the day) dipped in the provided bowls of coconut milk and lemon-chili sauce. All traditional dishes are served with local vegetables. Deck seating overlooks a front garden and the small inside dining room features traditional local artwork for sale. ⊠*Lot 6, Khalil St., Martintar* ☎*672–7313* ▤*No credit cards.*

INDIAN

$$ ✕**The Original Curry House.** Practically a Nadi institution, this
★ restaurant has weathered nearly 20 years of stiff competi-

tion and expanded to a second storefront on the strength of its Indian fare. Seafood is the specialty and big-ticket items such as lobster and prawn curries come fresh from nearby Momi Bay. All are served with rice, dhal soup, vegetable curry, papadum, salad, and chutney. Crab Vakalolo—fresh whole mud crab poached and served with Chinese cabbage, cassava, and salad—is another top dish. Choose the porch on a cool night or the ocean-themed, air-conditioned main dining room as the setting for your feast. It's also open for breakfast. ⊠*Corner of Main St. and Hospital Rd.* ☏*670–0798* ▭*MC, V.*

JAPANESE

$$$ ✕**Daikoku.** The quick tableside knife-work at this two-story shrine to teppan-yaki never fails to please locals and tourists alike. Nor does the succulent flavor of locally caught tuna, Australian beef, and New Zealand salmon expertly sliced, diced, and cooked before patrons' eyes. The traditional look of the restaurant and professional service make it a marvel of international cuisine in Fiji and a great experience for families. A decent wine list completes the festive atmosphere for those old enough to know not to touch the hot metal cooking surface. There's also a Suva location. ⊠*Queens Rd., Martintar* ☏*670–3622* ▭*AE, DC, MC, V* ⊙*Mon.–Sat. 12–2, 5:45—10. Closed Sun.*

PIZZA

$ ✕**Mama's Pizza.** No frills here and none are needed: Mama's serves up tasty, good-value pizzas in a cool, comfortable setting on the main drag. Rock music from the past five decades pumps into the dimly lighted, wood-furnished interior and air-conditioning means there's no need for the giant, rusty fan threatening to turn overhead. Gourmet combos such as chicken, pineapple, and onion or smoked walu, red onions, capers, and chives are delivered to the table along with dressings by the friendly staff. Although the size diagram on the wall may appear a bit meager, rest assured: a "solo" makes for a filling lunch. There's a second location north of town and a third at Port Denarau. ⊠*Main St.* ☏*670–0221* ▭*No credit cards.*

STEAK

$$$ ✕**The Bounty Restaurant and Bar.** After 9 PM, expats and tourists get the karaoke going at this fun seafood joint and steak house. Yet most guests come to hear the imported rib eyes and T-bones sizzle on their way from the kitchen to the

beer garden. Prawn dishes and the Bounty Burger are also highly in demand, as is the steak sandwich at lunchtime. "Bula Hour" (5–6 PM) sees prices on the tropical cocktail menu drop 20%. A mural of the restaurant's namesake ship plus stacked wooden barrels at the maitre 'd stand and good-natured, buxom servers complete the feel-good atmosphere. It's also open for breakfast. ⊠ *79 Queens Rd, Martintar* ☎*672–0840* ⊟*AE, MC,V.*

DENARAU ISLAND

ECLECTIC

$$$$ ✕ **V Restaurant.** The Sofitel's signature restaurant does not
★ disappoint as it uses local produce in contemporary, French-influenced cuisine. Popular local crab may take the form of crab cakes with coriander, chile jam, and meyer lemon soubise, while Nadi bay prawns might be flambéed with French brandy, garlic, and chive butter. Well-spaced tables and comfortable leather-upholstered chairs exclude stuffiness, and desserts such as green tea iced soufflé with berry compote are equally light. Private beach dining from a set menu can be arranged and executive chef Brendon Coffey anticipates having an optional set menu in the dining room. ⊠ *Sofitel Fiji Resort & Spa* ☎*675–1111* ⊟*AE, DC, MC, V* ⊗*No lunch.*

JAPANESE

★ **Fodor'sChoice** ✕ **Hamacho.** Set apart on the grounds of the
$$$–$$$$ Westin in a Japanese-style house with a raked-sand garden, independently managed Hamacho offers a dining experience of quality and ambience beyond that found in most international resorts. The classic menu includes shabu shabu and sukiyaki (you cook your own thin slices of beef and vegetables) as well as teppan-yaki prepared tableside by a chef with characteristic flare. Sushi, sashimi, and tempura are delectably fresh and beautifully presented. The restaurant's numerous rooms and delicate service allow for an intimate atmosphere. ⊠ *The Westin* ☎*675–0177* ⊟*AE, DC, MC, V* ⊗*No lunch.*

SEAFOOD

$$$$ ✕ **Lagoon Restaurant.** Diners come from around Denarau
★ to this casual restaurant for the legendary seafood buffet Wednesday and Saturday nights. Dubbed Ika Levu (Fijian for "Great Fish"), the buffet features the restaurant's characteristic live cooking stations and artful presentation, only with an extravagant array of Fiji's freshest. Indoor and out-

door tables are well-spaced. Buffet themes on other nights include Indo-Fijian, native-Fijian, BBQ, and Asian-Pacific, and there's always a children's buffet. It's on the ground floor of the resort's main building, and you can walk up from the beach. ⊠*Sofitel Fiji Resort & Spa* ☎*675–1111* ⊟*AE, DC, MC, V* ⊘*No lunch.*

WHERE TO STAY

NADI

$ 🖥**Aquarius Fiji.** This cozy, quiet option is to jetlag what
☾ chicken soup is to the common cold: Just sink into a ham-
★ mock beyond the pool on the grey-sand beach or even into
a couch in front of the big TV in the open-plan lounge.
While most of the eight private rooms are on the small
side, Room 5 is a spacious corner with a great view and a
larger bathroom. Each of the clean, air-conditioned dorms
shares a bathroom; a couple on a short stay and a budget
may want to snag the bunked two-bed one. You won't have
to reach far beyond the TV remote for a good meal from
the eclectic restaurant (try its Indian fare) or a drink from
its bar. **Pros:** Helpful staff; relaxing atmosphere. **Cons:**
Mediocre beach; smallish rooms. ⊠*17 Wasawasa Rd.,
Wailoaloa, Newtown* ☎*672–6000* ⊕*www.aquariusfiji.com*
⊸*8 rooms, 12-bed, 6-bed, and 2-bed dorms* ⟁*In-room: no
phone, no TV. In-hotel: restaurant, bar, pool, beachfront,
water sports, no elevator, laundry service, public Internet,
airport shuttle* ⊟*AE, MC, V* ⦿*EP.*

$ 🖥**Mercure Hotel.** What you see is what you get at this reli-
able if impersonal member of the international Accor chain,
which isn't half bad. All rooms face the pool area: Superior
rooms have double and single beds and a bit of the motor
inn feel with parking spaces at their doors while Deluxe
rooms are away from the lot and have queen beds and larger
bathrooms. Meeting rooms and event services satiate busi-
nesspeople, a second pool and newly upgraded playground
occupy the kids. The restaurant, which the hotel promotes
shamelessly, offers an aspiring but predictable international
menu in either a spacious dining room or under gas lamps
on a deck. **Pros:** Professional service; close to nightlife.
Cons: Impersonal; generic atmosphere. ⊠*Queens Rd.,
Martintar* ☎*672–2255* ⊕*www.accorhotels.com.fj* ⊸*85
rooms* ⟁*In-room: refrigerator. In-hotel: restaurant, bar, 2
pools, spa, laundry service, public Internet, airport shuttle*
⊟*AE, MC, V* ⦿*EP.*

2

$ ⊞**Nadi Bay Resort.** For those who associate hostels (or
★ "backpackers") with cordial staff and making fast friends
with fellow travelers, this large resort will not disappoint.
Its labyrinthine campus includes two pretty pools, two
decent restaurants, a movie theater with free screenings,
a modest spa, and game room. Live music brings guests
together nightly for alcohol-fueled carousing (don't settle
for a room near the main restaurant if you plan to sleep
before 1 AM). The value here is in the clean, air-conditioned
dorms: Gardenia overlooks one of the pools and has the
best lounge area. Some dorms and guestrooms are cooled by
fans, not air-conditioning, and share bathrooms. The number of beds in dorms range from three to ten. **Pros:** Warm
staff; party goes late. **Cons:** Party goes late; iffy hot water.
⊠ *Wailoaloa Rd.* ☎ *672–3599* ⊕ *www.fijinadibayhotel.
com* ⋑ *7 apartments, 38 rooms, 13 dorms* ⏚ *In-room:
no a/c (some), no phone (some), no TV (some), refrigerator (some). In-hotel: 2 restaurants, bars, 2 pools, spa, no
elevator, laundry service, public Internet, airport shuttle*
⊟ *AE, MC, V* ⊙| *EP.*

$ ⊞**Smugglers Cove.** "Smugglers" captures the twenty- to
fortysomething set with American hotel-style amenities, a
large dorm, and a host of facilities. Rooms are clean and
sensible, though don't expect a view worth mentioning
unless it's from an "Oceanfront Suite." A family suite on
the top floor sleeps five and has a full kitchen. Kayaks and
volleyball are available on the hammock-dotted beach,
which borders Aquarius Fiji's. A viewless, extremely tight
34-bed dorm rounds out the sleeping options. The restaurant draws guests from neighboring hotels with its eclectic
selection of mostly American and Asian standards; there's
a cheaper bar menu. Nightowls should be warned that the
bar closes at 11. **Pros:** Creature comforts; good restaurant.
Cons: Mediocre beach; early-closing bar. ⊠ *Wasawasa Rd.,
Wailoaloa, Newtown* ☎ *672–6578* ⊕ *www.smugglersbeach
fiji.com* ⋑ *22 rooms, 1 suite, 1 dorm* ⏚ *In-room: safe,
refrigerator. In-hotel: restaurant, bar, pool, spa, beachfront,
water sports, laundry facilities, public Internet, airport
shuttle* ⊟ *AE, MC, V* ⊙| *CP.*

DENARAU ISLAND

$$$–$$$$ ⊞**Fiji Beach Resort & Spa.** From the BMW airport-transfer to
★ the ultramodern amenity-loaded rooms, this Hilton-man-
aged property does not compromise. All have DVD players,
Playstations (movies and games for rent), flat-screen TVs,
stand-alone bathtubs, walk-in showers, Molton Brown

bath products, and ocean views. Villas include a living area, kitchen, outdoor BBQ grill, Bose sound system, washer and dryer, and larger bathroom, with two- and three-bedroom versions piling on the square-footage. The deluxe versions of studios and one- and two-bedroom villas are the same but share plunge pools. Equally modern "infinity pools" surround the restaurant ($$$$), and bar service extends to a string of daybeds just short of the sand. While some find the style of rooms a bit cold, all guests are warmed by Nadi's most polished service. A second phase of the resort will add 91 villas and 146 rooms and see it take the Hilton name. **Pros:** Denarau's-best room amenities; great on-site coffee shop. **Cons:** Spa lacking in ambience; a single, pricey restaurant. ⊠ *Denarau Island* ☎ *675–6800* ⊕ *www.fijibeachresortbyhilton.com* ➴ *108 studios, 52 1- to 3-bedroom villas* ⟁ *In-room: kitchen (some), refrigerator, DVD, ethernet. In-hotel: restaurant, room service, bar, pool, gym, spa, beachfront, water sports, children's programs (ages 3–12), laundry service, airport shuttle* ▭ *AE, DC, MC, V* ꙳ *EP.*

★ **Fodor's**Choice ▧ **Radisson Resort Fiji Denarau Island.** This resort
$$–$$$ made a big splash when it opened in mid-2007 with a mag-
☾ nificent rock waterfall as a centerpiece and the wow-fac-
tor, too, flows throughout. Guest rooms are spacious and stylish, while suites have full kitchens including all utensils and a large fridge. There's a kids' pool with impressive waterslide, an adults-only one and, set before the beach, a third lagoon-style pool with a swim-up bar fringed by imported white sand. All this creates a less stuffy atmosphere than that of some neighboring resorts. **Pros:** Spacious rooms with extra amenities; multiple large pool areas. **Cons:** Spa somewhat lacking in ambience. ⊠ *Denarau Island* ☎ *675–1246* ⊕ *www.radisson.com/fiji* ➴ *135 rooms, 135 suites* ⟁ *In-room: safe, kitchen (some), refrigerator (some), DVD, Wi-Fi. In-hotel: 3 restaurants, room service, bars, 3 pools, spa, beachfront, water sports, children's programs (ages 4–12), laundry service, concierge, public Wi-Fi* ▭ *AE, DC, MC, V* ꙳ *EP.*

$$$–$$$$ ▧ **Sheraton Denarau Villas.** These villas offer resort amenities in a more casual, choose-your-own-adventure atmosphere. Guest rooms, which sleep two, have stereos and mini-fridges while the three-person villas are fully self-contained; a lockable outside door allows groups to link the two. Many guests stock up from the coffee shop and general store out front, but neighboring resorts' restaurants, as well as all Sheraton and Westin facilities, are just as easily accessed

WHAT'S NEW UNDER THE SUN

The Intercontinental Hotel Group plans to open its 1,500-acre **Natadola Marine Resort** (⊕ *www.natadolafiji. com*) on what is arguably the mainland's best beach on the south coast, about 45 km from the Nadi airport. It will include a 275-room Intercontinental Hotel, a Navo Island Resort with 100 luxury villas, and private beaches on an island facing the Natadola Beach. The budget Yatule Beach Resort will offer 50 rooms with shared facilities. Nearby will be a "village" with shops, restaurants, a market, cultural entertainment center and corporate space. Fiji-born superstar Vijay Singh is planning to oversee the 7,400-yard championship 18-hole golf course with seven holes edging the ocean, a driving range, and a short-game area.

If you're ready for a big plunge, hold your breath a bit longer for the **Poseidon** (⊕ *www.poseidonresorts.com*) which will be 40 feet beneath the crystal water of a lagoon. Made of 70% acrylic glass, you'll have a superb view of the coral reef without donning scuba gear. At the time of writing, the setting was still a secret, referred to only as "Poseidon Mystery Island." One-week packages will include air transfer, two nights in the underwater accommodations (which will include library, fitness center, and restaurant), and four terrestial nights on a beach. The price tag for the experience: expect to pay upwards of $15,000 for one person.

along the beachfront. There's a large, winding central pool and a beachfront version with swim-up bar and BBQ menu, both of which can be overrun by kids during Aussie school holidays (July and December to mid-January). **Pros:** Spacious villas; access to Sheraton and Westin facilities. **Cons:** No organized activities on-site. ⊠*Denarau Island* ☎*675–0777* ⊕*www.starwoodhotels.com* ⤳*81 rooms, 82 suites* ⚐*In-room: kitchen (some), refrigerator, safe, ethernet. In-hotel: room service, bar, 2 pools, beachfront, water sports, laundry service* ⊟*AE, DC, MC, V* �𝄐*EP.*

$$$ ⚑**Sofitel Fiji Resort & Spa.** From its cavernous lobby to its massive lagoon-style pool, the Sofitel does things big. Standard rooms, while not to the same scale, are well-appointed with a king or two queen beds and particularly stylish bathrooms. Studio suites have Jacuzzis on their balconies and walk-in closets while ultra-exclusive executive and presidential suites also have living areas, refrigerators,

and microwaves; presidentials also have a dining area. The Zen-like Elemis spa includes seven bures with dual treatment tables, a steam room, and spa bath, and specializes in hot stone and four-hand massages. Among the dining options, the buffet-style Lagoon restaurant's seafood nights are renowned throughout the island and the V Restaurant is a serious gastronomic affair (*see Where to Eat, above*). **Pros:** Good dining options; Roger & Gallet bath products; great spa. **Cons:** Sprawling property with only one pool; particularly pricey food. ⊠*Denarau Island* ☎*675–1111* ⊕*www.sofitelfiji.com.fj* ➷*272 rooms, 10 suites* ⚐*In-room: safe, refrigerator, ethernet. In-hotel: 3 restaurants, room service, bars, pool, gym, spa, beachfront, water sports, children's programs (ages 2–12), laundry facilities, laundry service* ⊟*AE, DC, MC, V* ⊙|*EP.*

$$$$ ⊡**Westin Denarau Island.** Mood-lighting, dark wood-furnished rooms, and the island's best spa give this resort a sexy if somewhat incongruous feel. The vaguely Asian-inspired lobby leads straight through to a large, comfortable lounge before opening up to a highly styled, bi-level pool area. Rooms are equally fashionable with views from their bowl sink area through to the Westin's incredibly comfortable beds; deluxe rooms have dual sinks and Bose stereos. Tropical Gardenview rooms are in a wing away from the main building, which some guests prefer. Also set apart is the gorgeous spa with its individual treatment thatched-roof bures beside a hot tub spilling into a beautiful lap pool, and a small but well-equipped gym. The Japanese restaurant, Hamacho, stands out among the dining options. **Pros:** One of Fiji's best spas; mature atmosphere; access to Sheraton facilities. **Cons:** Moody decor; mediocre steak house and pasta restaurants. ⊠*Denarau Island* ☎*675–0000* ⊕*westin fiji.com* ➷*266 rooms, 7 suites* ⚐*In-room: safe, refrigerator (some), Wi-Fi (some). In-hotel: 3 restaurants, room service, bars, 2 pools, gym, spa, beachfront, water sports, laundry service, public Wi-Fi* ⊟*AE, DC, MC, V* ⊙|*EP.*

NIGHTLIFE

Central Nadi has one or two nightclubs but these are not safe places for tourists. Because the resorts generally have good restaurants and bars, most visitors stay within reach of their room come nightfall.

If you feel like entertaining yourself (or others), head to the the **Bounty Restaurant and Bar** (⊠*79 Queens Rd., Martintar* ☎*672–0840*), where expats and tourists man the bar and, after 9 PM, are on the mike for karaoke. Fijians and tourists drink, dance, and shoot pool until 1 AM at **Ed's Bar** (⊠*Lot 1, Kennedy St., Martintar* ☎672–4650), where the fun, personable staff makes everyone feel like a local. All four bars are open Friday and Saturday nights and the Top 40 music packs the dance floor. Just be aware it can get quite smoky here, and tourists should be wary of pickpockets. Consider swinging by early for the $8.50 King burger or a $24.50 sirloin, or return to the scene of the crime for the good-value breakfast.

SPORTS & THE OUTDOORS

From Nadi, you can make a day trip to many of Viti Levu's best sights and attractions. Virtually every hotel and resort has a tour desk happy to book everything from village visits to shark-diving and white-water rafting excursions. The following activities are all Nadi-based. Activities listed in other Viti Levu destinations in this chapter can also be accessed from Nadi.

DAY TRIPS & CRUISES

Whether you're staying in Nadi or a Coral Coast resort, you can get farther into or off the island by joining an organized day trip.

☾ Two tour options with Fijian-owned **Adventures in Paradise**
★ (⊠*Coral Coast* ☎652–0833 ⊕*www.adventuresinparadise fiji.com*) offer a balance of natural, cultural, and educational components; both are six to seven hours depending on where you come from. The separate waterfall and cave tours begin with a traditional kava ceremony and storytelling in a village, and include lunch. The waterfall tour takes you to an idyllic natural swimming lagoon with a 120-foot waterfall where you feed fish and learn how to husk a coconut; tours are offered Monday, Wednesday, and Friday.

The cave tour includes a short *bilibili* (bamboo raft ride) that leads to the Naihehe Caves where you see priest chambers and a cannibal oven among the stalactites and other formations. A second, longer bilibili ride, with a chance for swimming in the river, returns you to the bus; tours are offered Tuesday, Thursday, and Saturday.

Mala Mala Island Day Cruises (☎670–5192) leave twice daily for the uninhabited, 6½-acre Mala Mala, about a one-hour trip from Denarau. While there you can snorkel, fish (catch-and-release only), take a glass-bottom boat tour, and play volleyball and rugby. A BBQ lunch is served, beer and wine are available for purchase, and unlimited soft drinks, tea, coffee, and water are included. "Early Bird" trips (8–3) and half-day trips (10–3) are slightly cheaper than full-day trips (10–5) . The boat departs from Denarau Marina. Transportation from Nadi area hotels is included and Coral Coast transfers cost a little extra.

The **Robinson Crusoe Island Day Cruise** (⊠*Robinson Crusoe Island* ☎*628–1999*) offers a taste of the island-resort experience on a 25-acre island just off the coast of Viti Levu. A traditional lovo feast is accompanied by a Pacific Islander-style fire-dance and show. There are live music and a trek to a 3,500-year-old pottery site as well as opportunities to sea kayak and snorkel. Tube rides, waterskiing, jet boat rides, hair braiding, and massages are available at an extra charge. The island also has budget-style accommodations. Trips run Tuesday, Thursday, and Saturday.

FISHING, SAILING & MOTORIZED WATER SPORTS

With activity desks and staff at all Denarau Island resorts, it's hard to miss **Adrenalin Water sports** (⊠*Denarau Island* ☎*675–1288*). The company offers parasailing, jet ski rentals, hovercraft rides, and much more. An Adrenalin Water sports Pass includes jet-skiing, parasailing, a flying-fish ride, and sailing for $170.

GOLF & TENNIS

Denarau Golf and Racquet Club (⊠*Denarau Island* ☎*675–9710*) includes a picturesque 7,150-yard, par-72 championship golf course with water hazards on 15 of 18 holes. There are four floodlighted synthetic tennis courts and six natural grass courts, as well as a pro shop and restaurant. The green fee is $110 for guests staying on Denarau Island, $125 for nonguests, and $20–$25 per hour for a tennis court. Lessons and packages are available.

Nadi Airport (⊠*Newton, Nadi* ☎*672–2148* ⊕*www.nadi golffiji.com*) is favored by many locals for its 18-hole, 5,882-yard, par-70 championship course. Most parts of the course command stunning views over the ocean and off-shore islands. The course's claim to fame is that hall-of-famer and Nadi native Vijay Singh caddied and practiced here. You're welcome to join the club competitions held each Saturday. The clubhouse includes a modest bar, restaurant, and beachside dining area.

CLOSE UP

Mamanucas & Yasawas for a Day

For a taste of the Mamanuca and Yasawa island groups and its resort experience, you can choose one of many day trips offered by **South Sea Cruises** (☎675–0500 ⊕www.ssc.com.fj). All departures are from Denarau Marina. The Mamanucas are a closer destination and trips there include the island resorts of South Sea, Castaway, Mana, Malolo Treasure, Bounty, and Amanuca. Each includes lunch ranging from a BBQ buffet with salads and fruit, to two-course table-service depending on the resort, use of the resort facilities, snorkel equipment, and transfers from Nadi and Coral Coast hotels. Trips depart at 9 and return at 6. Prices range $125–$135 for adults and $65–$95 for kids.

The Yasawas are farther north than the Mamanucas. On its way to **Botaira Beach Resort** on Naviti island, the cruise picks up at the Mamanuca resorts of Bounty, Treasure, and Beachcomber Island. Once at Botaira, you'll have about 2½ hours to swim, snorkel, sunbathe, and kayak on the island in addition to having a leisurely two-course seafood lunch with the option of lobster for a bit more money. The trip departs from Denarau Marina at 8:30 and returns at 5:45. It costs $130 for adults and $75 for children, or $155 and $95 including a lobster lunch. The **Waya Island** day trip is distinguished by a village tour but there's also time to snorkel, swim, and relax on Waya Island (part of the Yasawas) and have a BBQ lunch at a hostel. The trip departs from Denarau Marina at 8:30 and returns at 5:45 with additional pickups at Bounty, Treasure, and Beachcomber Island resorts. It costs $125 for adults and $65 for children and includes pickup from Nadi hotels.

JET-BOAT RIDE
Adrenaline-junkies will enjoy the twists and turns of a high-horsepower 30-minute spin up the Nadi River with **Jet Fiji** (✉*Port Denarau* ☎675–0401).

SCUBA DIVING
Based just outside of Nadi, **AquaBlue** (✉*Wailoaloa Beach* ☎672–6111 ⊕*www.aquabluefiji.com*) visits more than 20 sites in the Mamanucas using a 30-foot (30 meters) custom-built dive boat. Pickups can be arranged from most Nadi-area hotels.

SKY DIVING
Tandem Skydive Fiji (✉*Nadi Airport* ☎992–4079) offers tandem skydives of 8,000–14,000 feet (2,438–4,267 meters)

over Denarau Island with freefalls of 15–60 seconds followed by 5- to 6-minute parachute glides. You can arrange to land on the beach of your resort.

SHOPPING

As in many third-world destinations, you'll find virtually the same stock in every store aimed at the tourist trade. Since nearly all Nadi's handicraft stores are within a few blocks of each other on the Main Street section of Queens Road, it's easy to compare prices. Be aware that some of the items for sale may be from neighboring South Pacific countries. Naturally, the places lacking in air-conditioning and glass shelves, such as the rustic outdoor stalls of the Handicraft Market, are likely to yield the best deals. Throughout town, you'll find the salespeople amusingly eager or overbearing, depending on your mood.

★ Competition is fierce at the **Handicraft Market** (⊠*Corner of Main St. and Koroivolu Ave.*), where locals fill their stalls with all manner of wood-carvings, jewelry, and other souvenirs produced by members of their villages (or so they claim) and local Indo-Fijians peddle a similar range of goods. Bargain here and you can likely bring prices down by half, if not more.

The successful retail chain **Jack's of Fiji** (⊠*Main St.* ☎*670–0744*) has locations throughout the mainland including those at numerous resorts. In addition to high-end traditional handicrafts and other souvenirs, it sells perfume, jewelry, watches, clothing, and other duty free–style goods.

Nad's (⊠*Main St.*) rivals Jack's in selection, with a similar array of weapons and large, imposing centerpieces among other items downstairs. You'll find T-shirts, some generic artwork, and watches on the second floor. **Nadi Handicraft Centre** (⊠*Main St.* ☎*670–2357*) is one of the more refined retailers offering a range of handicrafts from Fiji and neighboring island nations, as well as jewelry and other international items.

An open-air mall of sorts, **Port Denarau** (⊠*Denarau marina*) has all manner of retail and dining options. Retailers include a Marina General Store specializing in clothing and accessories and a Jack's of Fiji outlet. The well-stocked Xpress Mart is among the more reasonable places to buy groceries on Denarau and the Hot Bread Kitchen, part of a nation-wide chain, is a good place to pick up a hot pastry before the early ferry; the Esquire coffee shop is next door. Cardo's steakhouse, the Indigo fine-dining restaurant, and Hard Rock Cafe are also here. The complex includes the departure point for all Mamanuca and Yasawa Islands boat transfers and is accessible by the free "Bula Bus" shuttle from all Denarau Island resorts.

You'll find gear for nearly every sport at **Sports World** (⊠269 *Main St.* ☎670–5910), which is a good place to pick up a high-quality snorkel or bathing suit, or that pair of swim goggles you left at home.

LAUTOKA

15 mi (25 km) north of Nadi

North of Nadi through sugarcane plantations and past the Sabeto Mountains is Lautoka, nicknamed the Sugar City for the local agriculture and its big processing mill. With a population of around 50,000, it's the only city besides Suva and, like the capital, has a pleasant waterfront. It's the sailing point for Blue Lagoon and Beachcomber Cruises but is otherwise unremarkable for tourists, itself having few hotels and fewer good restaurants. Locals recommend the city as a less-expensive place to shop for clothing, but note that it can take as long as 45 minutes to drive here. Legend has it that Lautoka acquired its name when two chiefs engaged in combat and one hit the other with a spear. He proclaimed "lau toka" (spear hit) and thus the future town was named.

EXPLORING LAUTOKA

Numbers in the margin correspond to points of interest on the Lautoka map.

❷ **South Pacific Distilleries.** This large distillery uses molasses from the local sugar mill to produce the country's ubiquitous Bounty Rum. It also makes whisky, vodka, and gin and offers free plant tours. ⊠*Navutu Rd., 1.5 km (1 mi) southwest of town center, ½ km (.3 mi) south of sugar mill at western end of town* ☎666–2088 ⊡*Free* ⊙*Weekdays 9–5. Call to arrange tour.*

❶ **Sugar Mill.** One of the largest sugar mills in the southern hemisphere, this one was founded in 1903 and employs around 1,300 people. While tours are not offered, a good view of the operation is available from the main gate, under a prominent black smoke stack. Sugar is the country's largest industry after tourism and some 370 km (595 mi) of narrow-gauge rail serve the mills in Lautoka and Ba. ⊠*Mill View Rd., 1 km west of town center, 2 blocks from waterfront at western end of town* ☎666–0800.

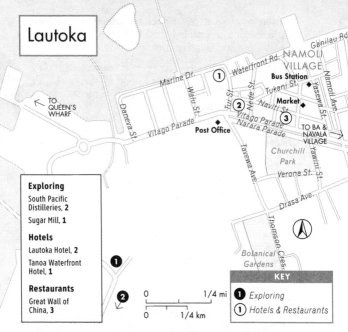

Lautoka

← TO QUEEN'S WHARF

Marine Dr.

Waterfront Rd. NAMOLI VILLAGE

Ganilau Rd.

Bus Station

Tukani St.

Market

Naviti St.

Vitago Parade

Narara Parade

TO BA & NAVALA VILLAGE

Post Office

Danera St.

Watu St.

Tui St.

Yasewa St.

Namoli Ave.

Vitago Parade

Churchill Park

Verona St.

Tavewa Ave.

Yawini St.

Drasa Ave.

Thomson Cres.

Botanical Gardens

Exploring
South Pacific
Distilleries, **2**

Sugar Mill, **1**

Hotels
Lautoka Hotel, **2**

Tanoa Waterfront
Hotel, **1**

Restaurants
Great Wall of
China, **3**

❶

❷

0   1/4 mi
0   1/4 km

KEY
❶ Exploring
① Hotels & Restaurants

OFF THE BEATEN PATH. Navala Village. Set amid mountains and on a river, this charming authentic village includes more than 200 thatch bures aligned in the shape of a cross around a rara, or village green. Beside the village is a rural school and a Catholic church. Visitors are required to present a sevusevu (literally "presentation," a ceremonial gift), traditionally a bundle of yaqona or kava, to the village chief. They might then have the chance to take part in a traditional kava ceremony before being led on a village tour. The village is in the Navala Valley roughly 26 km inland from the town of Ba, a winding hour's drive away (buses run daily). ✉ *Navala Valley* ✛ *64 km from Lautoka by Kings Rd. to Ba, and then via Rarawai Rd.* 🚍 *$15.*

WHERE TO STAY & EAT

CHINESE

\$\$ ✕ **Great Wall of China.** Both the chef and owner come from the Canton region and it appears that they brought their recipe books with them. Locally supplied seafood is whipped into the likes of steamed fish in soy sauce and steamed crab with glass noodles. Imported king prawns are put to good use in a garlic-ginger sauce. Rotating platforms at the tables make it easier to share the family-style portions amid the tasteful Asian decor. On some afternoons, there's not a seat to be had as locals pack in for the lunch specials. ⊠*Naviti St.* ☎*666–4763* ▤*No credit cards.*

2

$ ☷**Lautoka Hotel.** While not much to look at, Deluxe rooms at this basic hotel a block from the waterfront have decent amenities and sliding glass doors that open up onto a pool. In the older, main building there are even cheaper standard rooms as well as rooms with shared bathrooms and 10-bed dorms, but these are extremely basic and some are subject to noise from the nightclubs downstairs weekend nights. The in-house restaurant ($), popular with locals, serves everything from burgers and steaks to Chinese food and pizza, but can be quite smoky as fans circulate the smoke from the bar. ⊠*Naviti St.* ☎*666–0388* ✑*ltkhotel@connect. com.fj* ⇆*34 rooms, 1 dorms* ⌂*In-room: no phone (some), refrigerator (some), no TV (some). In-hotel: restaurant, bar, pool* ▤*No credit cards* ��⊙*EP.*

$ ☷**Tanoa Waterfront Hotel.** Lautoka's best hotel, part of a New Zealand–based chain, has a new wing (completed in late 2007) with modern dark-wood furnishings and LCD wall-mounted TVs. While the bathrooms could be larger, they feature stylish bowl sinks on marble countertops and glass-atrium showers. Most rooms in the new wing face the well-lighted pool area; those on the second floor also have good views of the harbor across the street. This is the only place in town most expats and businesspeople will stay; it's common to hear three or four languages while digging into the restaurant's international fare ($$$). **Pros:** International-standard rooms; one of Lautoka's better restaurants. **Cons:** Impersonal, corporate feel. ⊠*Main St.* ☎*666–4777* ⊕*www.tanoahotels.com* ⇆*70 rooms, 2 suites* ⌂*In-room: safe, refrigerator, ethernet, Wi-Fi. In-hotel: restaurant, room service, bar, 2 pools, gym, laundry, public Internet* ▤*AE, DC, MC, V* ⰰ⊙*EP.*

SIGATOKA

61 km (38 mi) southeast of Nadi.

The start of the Coral Coast is heralded by this dense commercial center. Sigatoka has little tourist infrastructure apart from a couple of hostels and centers on a municipal market. The bus station is usually crowded with commuting locals and taxis in between fares. It's an excellent place to pick up provisions if you're self-catering in the area.

Sigatoka Sand Dunes. Archaeologists continue to uncover shards of pottery and human remains up to 2,000 years old at these dunes, a tentatively listed UNESCO World Heritage site. The dunes are more than 60 feet (20 meters) high on average, with some climbing to more than 150 feet (50 meters). The views here, in Fiji's first national park, are impressive. Look for the visitor center on the roadside just west of Sigatoka. ⊠ *Queens Rd., Km 64* ☎ *652–0243* ⚏ *$5* ⊙ *Daily 8–6.*

WHERE TO EAT

INDIAN

$$ ✕ **Raj's Curry House.** Raj's isn't much to look at with its iron gate, but it's a local favorite for good reason: Kamlesh Lata and her husband have been making delicious curries here for more than a decade. There's a disconcerting mix of Chinese and fast-food options geared to the quick-lunch local trade, but you should take a seat in the air-conditioned, dimly lighted room and skip right to the seafood curries. The plastic placemats don't do much for the atmosphere, but let your tastebuds judge. The restaurant is beside the first roundabout in town if coming from Nadi. ⊠ *Queens Rd., Km 70* ☎ *650–1470* ⊟ *No credit cards.*

CORAL COAST

7 km(4 mi) southeast of Sigatoka

This is the tourism heart of Viti Levu, with clusters of resorts scattered between the towns of Sigatoka, Korotogo, and Korolevu. The huge Outrigger on the Lagoon resort is across the street from Kula Eco Park and is a focal point of the area, entertaining guests from the nearby "Sunset Strip" resorts as well. Because most of the beaches here are highly subject to tides and have sharp coral rocks close to shore, the emphasis at these resorts tends to be on pools and sports facilities. While a few resorts are located over bumpy ridgelines down to the beach, none is truly isolated. Many hotels are next to villages and offer tours introducing guests to the warm communal center of Fijian life.

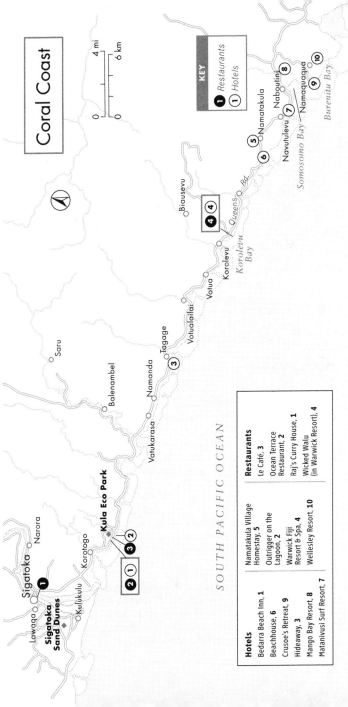

Coral Coast

KEY

● Restaurants
① Hotels

SOUTH PACIFIC OCEAN

Hotels
Bedarra Beach Inn, **1**
Beachhouse, **6**
Crusoe's Retreat, **9**
Hideaway, **3**
Mango Bay Resort, **8**
Matanivusi Surf Resort, **7**

Namatakula Village
Homestay, **5**
Outrigger on the
Lagoon, **2**
Warwick Fiji
Resort & Spa, **4**
Wellesley Resort, **10**

Restaurants
Le Café, **3**
Ocean Terrace
Restaurant, **2**
Raj's Curry House, **1**
Wicked Walu
(in Warwick Resort), **4**

EXPLORING THE CORAL COAST

Queens Road runs along the coast, making for easy access to almost all the Coral Coast's resorts and attractions. The "Sunset Strip," just west of Korotogo is a 1-km stretch of low- and mid-range accommodations in a neat row and a pleasant walk along the beach from Outrigger on the Lagoon. You can also walk along the beach from Crusoe's Retreat to Wellesley Resort and, at low tide, from Namatakula Village to Mango Bay Resort. Public buses stop at all resorts on the main road.

Kula Eco Park. The highlight of the park experience comes early on, when visitors have the opportunity to handle lizards and even a young boa constrictor, if one is on hand (bring your camera). But even the skittish will enjoy the walk-through bird sanctuary and informative descriptions of the many native and non-native bird species and the fruit bats (or "flying foxes") on display. The boardwalk loop concludes with an elevated walk through untouched rainforest and a native Fijian tools display. The park is directly across the street from Outrigger on the Lagoon. ✉*Queens Rd., Km 80, Coral Coast* ☎*650–0505* ⊕*www. fijiwild.com* ☑*$20* ☉*Daily 10–4:30.*

WHERE TO EAT

ECLECTIC

$$ ✕**Le Café.** Hamburgers, pizzas, steaks, and the occasional seafood item prepared by local chefs are the order of the day at this cool garden café. Swiss owner Jean Pierre Gerber, a certified chef, ran the ranges until he retired from the kitchen and began catering to Aussies visiting from the Outrigger on the Lagoon megaresort just down the beach. When Gerber isn't sailing, you might find him seated at the full bar, enjoying a pepper-steak sandwich. Stereo music and views of the ocean 60 ft. (18 meters) away make this a pleasant place to vacation from the Outrigger's menu prices. There's also a Sigatoka location. ✉*Sunset Strip, Old Queens Rd., Coral Coast* ☎*652–0877* ▭*No credit cards.*

PACIFIC RIM

$$$ ✕**Ocean Terrace Restaurant.** Formerly third-in-command at
★ the renowned Jean-Michel Cousteau Resort, chef Sushil Chandra has brought his talents to the Bedarra Beach Inn. Take a seat on the balcony overlooking the pool and ocean and enjoy masterful seafood dishes at reasonable prices.

Try the mahimahi in coconut milk, lemon, caper, and garlic butter or the Fijian specialty Ika Vakalolo—cooked fish in coconut milk with tomato and onion. The curries, too, are outstanding. The space is intimate, the service casual, and the cuisine well worth diving into. ⊠*Bedarra Beach Inn, Sunset Strip, Old Queens Rd., Km 78, Coral Coast* ☎*650–0476* ⊟*AE, MC, V* ⊘*No lunch.*

SEAFOOD

★ **Fodor's**Choice ✕**Wicked Walu.** At the end of a jetty extending
$$$$ into a lagoon, a sand floor and thick wooden tables furnish the setting for outstanding seafood. Among the restaurant's six types of fish, all but Coral Trout can be steamed, grilled, baked, panfried, crumbed, or battered and served with a trio of tartare sauce, soy sauce, and garlic butter. The pièce de résistance is a $155 seafood platter for two that includes oysters, mussels, scallops, shots of lobster bisque, baby octopus, calamari, prawn cocktails, parrot fish, mahimahi, tuna, and a whole lobster, all beautifully presented on a wooden board. You can dine under the hand-carved, traditional high ceiling or alfresco and take in the views some couples choose to accompany their wedding vows. ⊠*Warwick Fiji Resort & Spa, Queens Rd., Km 80, Coral Coast* ☎*653–0555* ⊟*AE, DC, MC, V* ⊘*No lunch.*

WHERE TO STAY

$ ▦**Beachhouse.** Days turn into weeks for unfussy backpackers of all ages at this picturesque miniresort. Quirks such as erratic hot water and occasional 6 AM bird cacophonies are offset by a tranquil beach setting, good food, and self-catering facilities, and comraderie among guests and staff. A pretty, heart-shaped pool and comfy lounge bar—set remnants of a 2006 British reality show "Celebrity Love Island"—add a touch of class but clean, smart six-bed dorms and a free light breakfast are the main draws. There are also Garden Rooms with shared facilities as well as a camping option. Dinner menus include two to four hearty, well-priced options. **Pros:** Great self-catering facilities; pretty beach; friendly staff. **Cons:** Towels cost extra for dormers; early-morning bird chirping. ⊠*Queens Rd., Km 104, Coral Coast* ☎*800/653–0530 in Vitu Levu* ⊕*www.fijibeachhouse.com* ⊷*12 rooms, 6-bed dorms, women's dorm, camping* ⚇*In-room: no a/c, no phone, no TV. In-hotel: restaurant, bar, pool, spa, beachfront, waters ports, bicycles, laundry service, public Internet, airport shuttle* ⊟*MC, V* ⊠*CP.*

★ **Fodor's** Choice 🏨 **Bedarra Beach Inn.** Across the street from the
$ ocean, the Bedarra has the cheerful atmosphere of people
enjoying great value in a place where everyone knows their
names. The bright rooms in the two-story L-shaped mini-
resort have plentiful white-tile floor space, a king or two
twin beds, a simple bathroom with ample counter space,
and a balcony with seating. Rooms 17, 18, and 19 have
views to the sea while the rest face the small pool; the two
cheaper rooms are directly off the bar area. Guests become
fast friends and this is a fantastic base for day trips to waterfalls, villages, and even the Mamanuca Islands. The café
is good and the delicious Ocean Terrace Restaurant (*see
above*) is excellent. **Pros:** Excellent; personal service; reasonably priced restaurants; central location. **Cons:** No on-site
activities; size inhibits privacy. ⊠*Sunset Strip, Old Queens
Rd. Km 78, Coral Coast* ☎*650–0476* ⊕*www.bedarrafiji.
com* ⇨*24 rooms* △*In-room: no phone, refrigerator, no
TV. In-hotel: 2 restaurants, room service, bar, pool, water
sports, laundry service, public Internet* ⽥*EP.*

$$ 🏨 **Crusoe's Retreat.** Friendly, sincere staff and an authentic
experience are the trademarks of this laid-back resort. All
bures are spacious with generous porches: Deluxe Sea-
sides are traditional wood-and-thatched-roof structures
while non-Deluxe are more modern with larger bathrooms.
Seaview bures, the least expensive, are smaller but set back
into the hillside where they offer better views and more
privacy. A generous beach and pool are the focal points
of most guests' stays and free fishing is a wink and a nod
toward getting on "Fiji Time." The restaurant mixes à la
carte nights in between theme buffets, including curry,
lovo, Mongolian stir-fry, and BBQ nights. It's a consider-
able ride over a long ridge top from the main road: Excur-
sions are doable, but many guests only walk to the nearby
village. **Pros:** Personal service; secluded setting, complete
relaxation. **Cons:** Relaxed service; make your own fun.
⊠*Off Namaquaqua Rd., Queens Rd., Km 108, Coral
Coast* ☎*650–0185* ⊕*www.crusoesretreat.com* ⇨*29 suites*
△*In-room: no a/c, refrigerator, no TV. In-hotel: restaurant,
room service, bar, tennis court, pool, beachfront, diving,
water sports, no elevator, laundry service, public Internet*
⊟*AE, MC, V* ⽥*BP.*

$$ 🏨 **Hideaway.** It won't win any design awards but then
� again, no one comes to this relaxing, mid-size resort to
★ be blown away by anything, let alone decor. All bures are
spacious and feature indoor and outdoor showers; stroll
along the ocean wall and you'll see guests of the Oceanview

bures pasted facedown to lounge chairs on their private lawns. Frangipani Bures are set farther back and have small porches. Kids sometimes take over the pool with its waterslide, but a kids' club keeps them busy outside of meal times. The spa, featuring a pair of outdoor treatment tables overlooking the ocean, is simple but it works. Kids under 12 stay and eat free from a certain menu at certain times and a full-buffet breakfast is included for all. Telling is the fact that there's one computer for guest-use and rarely anyone waiting in line. **Pros:** Great food; good nightly entertainment; warm staff. **Cons:** Small beach; underwhelming grounds. ⊠*Queens Rd., Km 92, Coral Coast* ☎*650–0177* ⊕*www.hideawayfiji.com* ⇱*106 bures* ⌂*In-room: safe, refrigerator, no TV. In-hotel: 2 restaurants, bar, pool, gym, spa, beachfront, diving, water sports, children's programs (ages 5–12), public Internet* ⊟*MC, V* ⊺⚪*CP.*

$–$$ ⌧**Mango Bay Resort.** Rustic, ecofriendly accommodations meet mid-range facilities at this social miniresort. The highlight here is the beach, where the mostly young crowd lazes in hammocks before joining a game of volleyball on the regulation-size court or in the pool. Fishing here is run by the operation of one of the resort's co-owners and is top-notch. Bures are smallish but have attractive outdoor showers; numbers 1–5 are first off the beach and farther from the dining room. Safari tents were imported directly from South Africa and face into the rainforest but numbers 1, 2, and 3 have partial ocean views. A state-of-the-art nightclub gets going some nights. There are also dorms. **Pros:** Great beach; excellent fishing; good restaurant. **Cons:** Particularly bad mosquitoes; poor dorm bathroom facilities; early-morning light in bures. ⊠*Queens Rd., Km 108, Coral Coast* ☎*653–0069* ⊕*www.mangobayresortfiji.com* ⇱*20 rooms, 7-bed and larger, bunked dorms* ⌂*In-room: no a/c, no phone, safe, no TV. In-hotel: restaurant, bar, pool, spa, beachfront, diving, water sports* ⊟*AE, MC, V* ⊺⚪*CP.*

★ **Fodor'sChoice** ⌧**Matanivusi Surf Resort.** Gorgeous, modern
$$ bures, great cuisine, and an infinitely relaxing atmosphere make this secluded, Australian couple–owned boutique resort a choice escape. The airy, unconnected and eco-friendly units, designed by Australian architect Paul Uhlmann, have plantation mahogany floorboards, a king-size bed, and stylish, spacious bathrooms; each has a porch leading down to the sand. An elevated boardwalk winds past untouched rain forest to the dining room and bar, fronted by a pool, hot tub, and leather-covered lounge chairs. A boat and crew take surfers to two right-hand breaks with

up to six-foot waves (a 10-minute boat ride away) or to renowned Frigates Pass, 20 km (12 mi) distant. Diving and day tours can be arranged. The all-inclusive meal plan features entrées such as chicken fillets stuffed with banana, excellent curries, and you won't see a menu repeated during your stay. Rates include round-trip two-hour transfers from Nadi. Three-night minimum. **Pros:** Great beach; personalized service. **Cons:** Communal setting; limited choices at each meal. ⊠*Turn in at Vunaniu Village, Queens Rd., Km 107, Coral Coast* ☎*992–3230* ⊕*www.surfingfiji.com* ⌁*6 suites* ⚐*In-room: no a/c, no phone, safe, no TV. In-hotel: restaurant, bar, pool, spa, beachfront, water sports, public Internet* ⊟*MC, V* ⊙*FAP.*

$ ⊠**Namatakula Village Homestay.** You probably won't find more rustic digs in Fiji, but you certainly won't find any that bring you closer to local life. Guests buy kava and present it to the chief at the community center on the first night, after which they are ceremonially accepted into the village. They can then mingle with locals as much as they please. Rosa Batibasaga prepares three meals a day incorporating native fruits and vegetables from the home's own garden, chicken, and fish speared by her husband. A lovo feast is prepared for guests who stay three nights. It's a two-minute walk to the pretty but tidal beach and snorkeling equipment is available. The basic accommodations include rooms sleeping three to four in combinations of double and single beds with shared bathrooms. ⊠*Queens Rd., Km 105, Korolevu* ☎*653–0189* ⊕*www.fijibure.com* ⌁*8 rooms* ⚐*In-room: no a/c, no phone, no TV. In-hotel: restaurant, laundry service* ⊟*No credit cards* ⊙*FAP.*

$$$ ⊠**Outrigger on the Lagoon.** A perennial favorite with Aussie families, this large resort is a one-stop holiday for most. Parents and kids alike appreciate the American-style room amenities (request a newly renovated room) and selection of four restaurants, although kids complain that their menu doesn't change. The beautiful, lily pond–dotted grounds encompass tennis courts, a decent gym, and a golf driving range, as well as a huge pool. An intimate, adults-only fine dining restaurant serves Continental-meets-South Pacific fare, while a Kids' Club takes the load off mom and dad 10–9. All rooms face the ocean but those on the first floor can't see it through the garden. **Pros:** Five-star rooms; extensive facilities; Kula Eco Park across street. **Cons:** Notoriously overpriced food; battles for poolside seats; high tide-only swimming. ⊠*Queens Rd., Km 80, Coral Coast* ☎*650–0044* ⊕*www.outrigger.com* ⌁*207 rooms, 47 bures* ⚐*In-room:*

safe. In-hotel: 4 restaurants, room service, 4 bars, tennis courts, pool, gym, spa, beachfront, diving, water sports, children's programs (ages 3–12), laundry service, public Internet ☐AE, D, DC, MC, V ⑩EP.

★ Fodor'sChoice ☆**Warwick Fiji Resort & Spa.** Epitomized by its
$$$ two pools, one a serene "infinity," the other hosting kids' activities and a swim-up bar, Warwick caters beautifully to all markets. A renovation slowly working its way through the hotel has left much of the "Suva" wing with superior bathrooms (Oceanviews 85–97 are closest to the water, with good side on views). This wing is also by the quieter pool. Couples may find the adults-only Warwick Club area worth the splurge during school holidays. It includes Continental breakfast, afternoon snacks, and predinner local drinks. Stone steps over water lead to the beautiful spa with its sauna and hot and cold pools. The resort's lagoon setting allows for all-day swimming off the mainland's largest beach. Children under 16 stay free with parents; children under 13 eat free from the Kids Menu. The restaurants, ranging from Italian to Japanese, are excellent; Wicked Walu (reviewed above) is among the Coral Coast's best. **Pros:** Fantastic beach; range of quality dining options; great staff. **Cons:** Outdated "Nadi" wing. ☒*Queens Rd., Km 98, Coral Coast* ☎*653–0555* ⊕*www.warwickfiji.com* ☞*240 rooms, 10 suites* ⌂*In-room: safe, refrigerator, VCR (some). In-hotel: 5 restaurants, room service, bars, tennis courts, 2 pools, gym, spa, beachfront, diving, water sports, children's programs (ages 3–12), laundry service, executive floor, public Internet* ☐*AE, DC, MC, V* ⑩*EP, CP, FAP.*

$$ ☆**Wellesley Resort.** A boutique hotel fashioned after a New Zealand good ol' boys club, Wellesley has style, luxury, and its crest imprinted on items from bathrobes to the lavish bedspreads. The European-style villas are spacious and comfortable with king-size beds; Premiums are a bit larger, with TVs and a two-seat table in the living area. When you aren't lounging by the pool, on the beach, or choosing a meal from the eclectic, reasonably priced menu, you might horseback-ride or go on a Pacific Harbour–based tour. **Pros:** Luxurious rooms; personal service. **Cons:** Set back from the beach; could be a tropical resort anywhere. ☒*Off Namaquaqua Rd., Queens Rd., Km 108, Coral Coast* ☎*650–8000* ⊕*www.wellesleyresort.com* ☞*14 suites* ⌂*In-room: no TV (some), Wi-Fi. In-hotel: restaurant, room service, bar, pool, spa, beachfront, waters ports, no elevator, airport shuttle* ☐*AE, DC, MC, V* ⑩*EP, FAP.*

PACIFIC HARBOUR

241 km (150 mi) southwest of Nadi

The "Adventure Capital" of Fiji is a collection of resorts on both sides of Beqa Lagoon. Its 144 km (190 mi) of coral reef formed around an extinct volcano crater comprise one of the largest barrier reefs in the world. Diving opportunities include renowned shark-diving and more than 20 sites, including shipwrecks. Meanwhile, Pacific Harbour is also base camp for many of the country's most exciting activities, including white-water rafting through a breathtaking gorge, world-class surfing, and idyllic waterfall tours.

Picture-perfect Beqa, Royal Davui, and Vatulele Islands, among others, contribute lush patches of rain forest and white-sand beaches to the crystal clear lagoon. These islands are home to excellent, upscale resorts, with one equally recommendable, rustic but cozy exception. Mainland Pacific Harbour has a range of accommodation options as well.

Arts Village. Fiji's largest-scale cultural attraction includes performances, restaurants, and a shopping center. You can take a guided boat tour aboard a traditional drua (double-hulled canoe), a temple tour, or walking tour of a "magical island," each of which introduces you to aspects of traditional Fijian life including craft-making, cuisine, and these experiences include some theatrics of their own. You can also just settle into the outdoor grandstand for a performance. The Firewalking show (Monday–Saturday at 11 AM) is excellent and includes a *meke* (traditional song and dance), a mock war reenactment, and the famous Beqa Firewalkers traversing hot coals. There are more than 50 shops, including a Handicraft Marketplace where crafts are made on-site, and more than 10 restaurants. One-hour Island Boat Tours and Island Temple Tours leave every half-hour 9–4. ✉ *Cultural Center, Queens Rd. at Km 144, next to Tsulu Backpacker, Pacific Harbour* ☎ *345–0065* ⊕ *www. artsvillage.com* 🖭 *$15, $40 per family* ⊙ *Closed Sun.*

WHERE TO STAY & EAT

$$ 🖭 **Beqa Lagoon Resort.** Private, luxuriously appointed bures
★ set on magnificent grounds and a reputation for excellent diving make this boutique resort a favorite among divers. All bures carry a tropical, open-plan motif, and six of the garden bures are set around a large koi pond and connected by bridges. Beachfront bures have fenced-in yards

Legend of the Beqa Firewalkers

On the island of Beqa, there lived a famous storyteller who often entertained his tribe, the Sawau. It was customary for the people of the village to bring him gifts in exchange for his eloquent tales. Once, upon being asked what he would like, he requested that each member of the audience bring him the first thing they found while hunting the next day.

One of the Beqa warriors went fishing for eels. The first thing he caught felt like an eel but when pulled from the mud, revealed itself to be a spirit god. The warrior set off to present his find to the storyteller but the spirit god pleaded for his freedom, offering all kinds of gifts in exchange. He was ignored until he offered power over fire, which piqued the warrior's interest.

In order to prove the spirit god's promise, a pit was dug and lined with stones. A huge fire burned in the pit until the stones became white with heat. The spirit god leapt upon the stones and told the warrior to follow. He hesitated but finally did and, to his surprise, felt no pain from the heat. He was then told that he could be buried alive for four days in a cannibal oven without being hurt. The warrior neglected to test this but, ever since then, members of the Sawau tribes are able to walk on white-hot stones.

including large decks and private plunge pools; there are also four two-bedroom bures. In addition to its diving, led by highly experienced local divemasters, the resort emphasizes cultural experiences with firewalking and kava ceremonies, traditional dances, local village visits and lovo cooking demonstrations. The 14-day rotational menu (meal plan $60 per day; $50 for children, with a separate menu) includes two hot dishes as part of a buffet breakfast, two choices for lunch, and two choices of entrée within a three-course dinner, which might include fresh wahoo with a Provençal sauce and saffron risotto. Children ages 2–11 stay free. **Pros:** Great diving; cultural offerings; beautiful "infinity pool." **Cons:** Tidal beach; beachfront bures set close together. ⊠*Beqa Island* ☎*330–4042, 800/542–3454 in U.S.* ⊕*www.beqalagoonresort.com* ⤳*25 suites* ⟠*In-room: no phone, safe, refrigerator (some), no TV. In-hotel: restaurant, bar, pool, spa, beachfront, diving, water sports, laundry service, public Internet, airport shuttle* ▤*AE, MC, V* ⎢⊙⎢*FAP.*

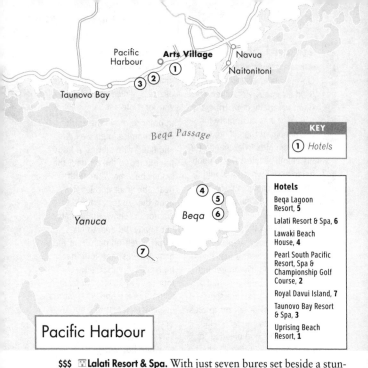

Pacific Harbour

KEY

① *Hotels*

Hotels

Beqa Lagoon Resort, **5**

Lalati Resort & Spa, **6**

Lawaki Beach House, **4**

Pearl South Pacific Resort, Spa & Championship Golf Course, **2**

Royal Davui Island, **7**

Taunovo Bay Resort & Spa, **3**

Uprising Beach Resort, **1**

$$$ ⊞ **Lalati Resort & Spa.** With just seven bures set beside a stun-
★ ning bay, this intimate all-inclusive is popular with hon-
eymooners. Minnesotan owners Clint and Jayne Carlson
describe it as a "place to switch off and relax," and most
do just that in addition to scuba diving, half-day picnic
trips to a smaller island, and village tours. Bures are large,
two-room affairs with walk-in showers, high ceilings, and
generous porches facing out to sea. The honeymoon bure
is spectacular, with a granite bathroom counter, double
showerheads, and a private outdoor courtyard with another
shower, small waterfall, and a hot tub; it also has a TV and
DVD player. The menu features mostly American dishes
such as lasagna and rack of lamb—while it doesn't offer
choices, the chef will work with you. Meals are communal,
but you can choose to dine on your porch or out on the
resort's pier. **Pros:** Well-spaced bures; plenty of activities;
good spa. **Cons:** Tidal beach; no selection at meals. ⊠*Beqa
Island* ☎*347–2033* ⊕*www.lalati-fiji.com* ➫*7 bures* ⌂*In-
room: no a/c, no phone, refrigerator, DVD (some), no
TV (some). In-hotel: restaurant, room service, bar, pool,
gym, spa, beachfront, diving, water sports, no elevator,*

laundry service, public Internet, no kids under 14 ⊟*AE, MC, V* ⊚|*FAP.*

$ ⊤**Lawaki Beach House.** Only rain forest and constellations encroach upon guests at this basic escape run by couple Christine and Sam Tawake (she Swiss, he Fijian) out of their home. Each of the two bures has two single beds that can be pushed together and a basic en suite bathroom with hand-held showerheads. The six-bed dorm is screened-in but also has mosquito coils. There's plenty of room to camp amid the grass volleyball court and Ping-Pong table on the soft, even lawn. Snorkeling here is excellent, with a beautiful reef just off the front. There's a TV and Internet accesss in the main house. Breakfast is Continental and dinner might include a delicious curry platter, pasta Bolognese, or coconut-lemon chicken and dessert. **Pros:** Complete escape; warm owners. **Cons:** Bures close together; no selection at meals. ⊠*Beqa Island* ☎*368–4088* ⊕*www.lawakibeachhouse.com* ⇱*2 bures, 6-bed dorm* ⚇*In-room: no a/c, no phone, no TV. In-hotel: restaurant, bar, beachfront, water sports, laundry service, public Internet* ⊟*No credit cards* ⊚|*FAP.*

$$ ⊤**Pearl South Pacific Resort, Spa & Championship Golf Course.** The lobby, with water cascading down the mirror behind its bar, wouldn't be out-of-place in Los Angeles and neither would much of the clientele at this Mediterranean-style resort geared to couples and businesspeople. Corporate conferences bring suits from the capital to the Pearl's 18-hole golf course while the drop-dead gorgeous pool lures Aussies and Americans in search of a tropical getaway. Newly refurbished rooms are in step with the stylish, if pricey, eclectic restaurants. Each themed penthouse has a cozy living area and stand-alone tub in its bathroom. **Pros:** Friendly, professional staff; central Pacific Harbour location. **Cons:** Smallish rooms; could be anywhere. ⊠*Queens Rd., Km 145, Pacific Harbour* ☎*345–0022* ⊕*www.thepearlsouthpacific.com* ⇱*72 rooms, 6 suites* ⚇*In-room: ethernet. In-hotel: 3 restaurants, room service, bar, golf course, tennis, pool, gym, spa, beachfront, water sports, laundry service, public Internet, airport shuttle* ⊟*AE, MC, V* ⊚|*EP.*

★ **Fodor's**Choice ⊤**Royal Davui Island.** Between four types of pillows, three private beaches, a personal plunge Jacuzzi pool, $$$$ and the communal pool, there's no downside to the choices at this all-inclusive boutique resort. Set on a private 8-acre island, each of the resort's modern beach house–style villas juts out from a central hill to offer cruise ship-esque ocean views. Each features a king-size bed, a hot tub below electric roof shutters, double sinks, walk-in shower, full living room, and a plunge pool on one of two decks. Premium suites are simply larger than Deluxes, and the "Davui Suite" has a full pool. You can have spa treatments in your room and furnished picnic lunches on the beach. Excellent scuba-diving is available right off the beach. A typical dinner menu includes two appetizers, three entrées such as seared swordfish with lobster potatoes, bok choy, salmon roe, and sauce vierge, and two desserts. **Pros:** Total privacy; incredible views; great snorkeling and diving. **Cons:** Tidal beaches. ⊠*Royal Davui Island* ☎*336–1623* ⊕*www. royaldavui.com* ⤳*16 villas* ♿*In-room: safe, refrigerator, no TV. In-hotel: restaurant, room service, bar, pool, spa, beachfront, diving, water sports, no elevator, laundry service, public Wi-Fi, airport shuttle, no kids under 17* ☰*AE, MC, V* ⦿*FAP.*

WORD OF MOUTH. "The snorkeling was fantastic, the [Royal Davui Island] staff treated us like family and the bures—well—I can't say enough about them." –bdavis

$$$$ ⌗**Taunovo Bay Resort & Spa.** If you want to have your tropical vacation and all the creature comforts, too, you'll enjoy the opulent four-bedroom villas at this boutique resort opened in early 2008. Designed by Martin Grounds of Four Seasons Bali fame, each identical villa features Fijian-style thatched roofing and can be divided a number of ways. Suites include a private "infinity pool" and lavish bathrooms with dual bowl sinks, bath, outdoor hot tub, and indoor and outdoor showers. Beachfront villas, in one- to four-bedroom configurations, have better views to the sand, larger private "infinity pools," living rooms, theater rooms with full entertainment systems and full kitchens including dual ovens and ranges, and a stainless-steel fridge. Guests can have the fridge stocked prior to their arrival and/or hire a personal chef by the meal. Although the beachfront isn't jaw-dropping, the 3-acre island 25 minutes away leased by the resort is. There's an upscale restaurant, sushi and tapas bars, a beach café, cocktail lounge, and a full spa. Children under 12 stay free. **Pros:** Total privacy; state-of-the-art amenities; central Pacific Harbour location. **Cons:** The pristine beach is a boat ride rather than steps away. ⊠*Queens Rd., Km 144, Pacific Harbour* ☎*999–2227* ⊕*www.taunovobay.com* ⤳*10 villas* ♿*In-room: kitchen (some), refrigerator (some), DVD, Wi-Fi. In-hotel: 3 restaurants, room service, bars, pool, gym, spa, beachfront,*

water sports, no elevator, laundry service, concierge, airport shuttle ☐AE, MC, V ⧓EP.

★ **Fodor'sChoice** ⬚**Uprising Beach Resort.** Roomy, smartly designed $ bures and its proximity to Viti Levu's famed diving and rafting opportunities set Uprising apart from other bure-and-dorm combinations. Bures sleep up to four and include outdoor showers and a pleasing amount of closet and shelf space. Beachfronts are 60 ft. (18 meters) from the surf; a family bure sleeps seven. A stay in the 24-bed dorm-bure includes a towel and good, modern bathroom facilities. The restaurant serves hearty portions from an eclectic menu. A two-course Continental breakfast and free Internet are big pluses. **Pros:** Spacious bures; friendly staff; central location. **Cons:** Can be extremely buggy in the open-air restaurant. ☒*Queens Rd., Km 146, Pacific Harbour* ☎*345–2200* ⊕*www.uprisingbeachresort.com* ⤴*12 bures, 1 dorm* ⚲*In-room: no a/c, no phone, refrigerator, no TV. In-hotel: restaurant, 2 bars, pool, beachfront, water sports, no elevator, laundry services, public Internet, public Wi-Fi, airport shuttle* ☐MC, V ⧓CP.

SPORTS & THE OUTDOORS

ADVENTURE TOURS

★ **Fodor'sChoice** **Rivers Fiji** (☒*Pearl South Pacific Resort, Queens Rd., Km 145, Pacific Harbour* ☎*345–0147*) offers three fantastic day trips. The minimum age for all trips is 8 and children 8–11 are half-price (one per adult). The Luva trip includes a traditional kava ceremony, kayaking through Class II rapids, hiking, and a boat ride through Navua Canyon. Snacks are provided but do have a substantial breakfast. It costs $205 and runs Tuesday, Thursday, Saturday.

The upper Navua rafting trip takes you through the magnificent "Grand Canyon of Fiji," famed for its many waterfalls and 130-foot (40 meters) high black volcanic rock walls. The more popular of the two trips, it costs $275 and runs Monday, Wednesday, Friday, and Saturday.

The Deuba Coastal sea-kayaking trip takes you on two-person, sit-on-top sea kayaks down the lower Navua River, through mangrove forests, and along the Pacific Harbour coastline. It includes a picnic lunch on a beach and snorkeling. Timing is subject to the tides and the cost is $95.

☺ Day tours with **Discover Fiji** (☒*Navua* ☎*345–0180* ⊕*www.* ★ *discoverfijitours.com*) combine elements, including canoeing up the Navua River, visiting the river's largest waterfall, riding a bamboo bilibili (native raft), and taking a village tour complete with a traditional yaqona (or "kava") ceremony. Discover Fiji's overnight tours vary in length from one to six nights and include village stays and camping. Prices range from $115 to $199, depending on your picked up.

BOATING & FISHING

Xtasea Charters (⊠*Pacific Harbour* ☎*345–0280* ⊕*www. xtaseacharters.com*) offers full- and half-day big-game and reef fishing charters aboard a fully equipped 40-foot luxury fly-fish cruiser. Live-aboard charters are also available.

GOLF

Pearl Championship Golf Course & Country Club (⊠*Opposite Pearl South Pacific Resort, Queens Rd., Km 145* ☎*345– 0923*), a par-72, 6,908-yard course designed by Robert Trent Jones Jr, includes 66 bunkers and multiple water hazards on 12 of the 18 holes. The facility has a driving range, pro shop, and a restaurant serving café-style fare. The clubhouse is open 8–7. Green fees are $30 for hotel guests and $40 for nonguests for 18 holes; $15 and $20 respectively for 9 holes. Golf carts and lessons are available.

JET SKIING

Jetski-Safari (⊠*Pacific Harbour* ☎*345–0933* ⊕*www.jetski-safari.com*) operates guided tours of Beqa Lagoon. The four-hour trips include snorkeling and lunch on a small uninhabited island.

SCUBA DIVING

Among Fiji's most renowned experiences is shark-diving in Beqa Lagoon, a roughly 40-mi-wide extinct volcanic crater home to one of the world's largest barrier reefs. Silvertips, gray reef, whitetip reef, blacktip reef, sicklefin lemons, and tawny nurse sharks as well as large bull and occasional tiger sharks come to feed on the fish bait provided at a depth of 82–98 ft. (25–30 meters) on the reef ledge while divers observe. Because of the depth, all divers must be certified.

There's also excellent wreck-diving at four purpose-sunk Taiwanese trawlers, each roughly 110 feet (33 meters) long. The first was sunk in the late-1990s. The wrecks are home to schools of barracuda, pipefish, a giant camouflaging frogfish, stonefish, lionfish, leaf scorpion fish, and moray eels.

Soft coral dives take place at more than 20 sites around Pacific Harbour. Highlights here include large pinnacle clusters, which give divers the impression of walking between buildings, and the rare blue ribbon eel.

IS IT SAFE? **Sharks don't want to eat people. When they do attack it's because the person is silhouetted on the surface and mistaken for something else, or (much rarer) invading their territory. With Fiji's shark-feeding trips, you'll be at the sharks' eye-level and easily recognized as not being among their natural prey and, essentially, ignored in favor of the free meal provided by your outfitter. There are no territorial issues because the sharks have entered people's territory, not the other way around.**

Aquatrek Beqa (✉*Pearl South Pacific Resort, Queens Rd., Km 145, Pacific Harbor* ☎*888–0286* ⊕*www.aquatrak. com*) is one of Fiji's major operators, with a second base in Taveuni. Aquatrek's shark dive positions divers around the perimeter of the dive site before a bin of fish is brought down for the sharks to feed on.

Beqa Adventure Divers (✉*Lagoon Resort, Queens Rd., Km 144, Pacific Harbour* ☎*345–0911* ⊕*www.fiji-sharks.com*) or "BAD" has a two-part shark dive that includes 17 minutes observing the shark-feeding at a depth of 98 ft. (30 meters), where the bull sharks are most common, before heading up among the smaller species.

Nai'a (✉*Pacific Harbour* ☎*345–0382, 888/510–1593 in the U.S.* ⊕*www.naia.com.fj*) offers chartered live-aboard scuba diving for up to 18 guests in nine staterooms aboard its 120-foot motorsailer yacht. The 10-crew yacht was last refitted in 2000 and includes a dedicated dry camera and video room. Nitrox diving is available. Prices start at US$2,940 double-occupancy for seven days including all meals, tanks, weights, unlimited air refills and round-trip transfer from the Nadi-area.

SURFING

Twelve miles off-shore, **Frigates Passage** is a world-class left-hander break over a coral reef. Waves here are often big barrels and rides can go for 330 ft. (100 meters) or more. It's best March–November and good at all tides. Beqa Lagoon Resort, Batiluva, and Yanuca Island Resort access the break from Pacific Harbour while Matanivusi Surf Resort (*see above*) and Waidroka Bay Resort run trips from the Coral Coast. You can also charter Xtasea's boat (*see Fishing, above*).

SUVA

49 km (30 mi) northeast of Pacific Harbour.

The cosmopolitan capital of the South Pacific is set on a hilly peninsula at the southeastern end of Viti Levu. Its residents are a mix of Fijians, Indo-Fijians, and expats from Australia, New Zealand, and Asia who are drawn to the capital by government jobs, business opportunities, and institutions such as the Fiji Institute of Technology and the largest branch of the University of the South Pacific. The constant influx of jovial tourists and imposing cargo ships gives the capital a sense of motion and self-involvement not found elsewhere in Fiji. Suva is a great place to formally discover the local culture through its museum and government buildings, and to alternately experience and escape urban Fijian life through its many restaurants, stores, calm waterfront, and verdant rainforest park.

EXPLORING SUVA

Numbers in the margin correspond to points of interest on the Suva map.

Suva may look like a big city to visitors fresh out of Nadi or the pockets of development along Queens Road, but its peninsular setting makes it easy to get oriented. Victoria Parade is the main drag, lined on the left by shops, then many of the city's restaurants, bars, and clubs, and by lastly government buildings as you head south. Locals enjoy their lunches and the harbor views along Stinson Parade, which is a great place for a stroll.

Despite Suva being Fiji's largest city, the people here are extremely friendly. Don't be surprised if, upon asking directions on a crowded bus, three people conference as to the best way you should go. But beware of people who approach you and quickly ask your name: A popular scam involves quickly carving your name into a simple wooden sword they have with them and insisting that you buy it. It's best to take taxis when traveling at night outside of the busy section of Victoria Parade.

❶ **Colo-I-Suva Forest Park.** Just 15 minutes north of the bustling city center is this oasis of flora and birdlife, crisscrossed by streams and rivers. You can walk a quarter-mile (half-kilometer) nature trail or hike the longer trails totaling more than 6.5 km (over 4 mi). There are three swimming pools including a Main Pool with a rope swing and nearby pic-

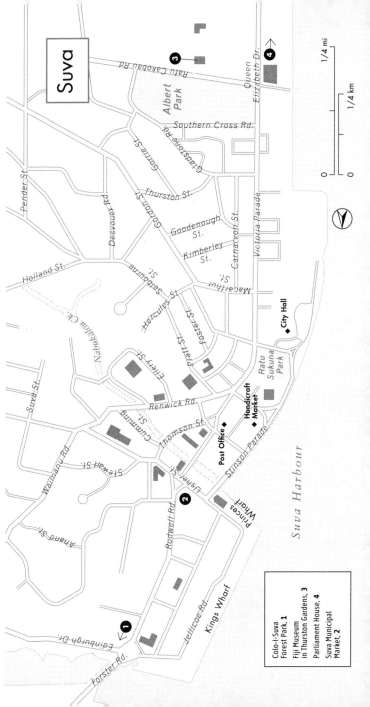

Suva

Colo-I-Suva
Forest Park, **1**

Fiji Museum
in Thurston Gardens, **3**

Parliament House, **4**

Suva Municipal
Market, **2**

Albert Park

Ratu Sukuna Park

◆ City Hall

◆ Post Office

◆ Handicraft Market

Suva Harbour

Princes Wharf

Kings Wharf

Rau Cakobau Rd.
Southern Cross Rd.
Thurston St.
Goodenough St.
Kimberley St.
MacArthur St.
Renwick Rd.
Thomson St.
Holland St.
Pender St.
Gorrie St.
Gladstone Rd.
Desvouex Rd.
Gordon St.
Selbourne St.
Carnarvon St.
Victoria Parade
Queen Elizabeth Dr.
Hercules St.
Foster St.
Pratt St.
Ellery St.
Cumming St.
Usher St.
Stewart St.
Suva St.
Anand St.
Rodwell Rd.
Waimanu Rd.
Nabukalou Ck.
Stinson Parade
Jetticoat Rd.
Forster Rd.
Edinburgh Dr.

1/4 mi
1/4 km
0

nic tables, and two Upper Pools preserved in their natural states. Both areas have toilet facilities. Be on the look-out for the Ant-Plant (Hydnophytum species), recognizable by its swollen trunk base and nourished by the food brought by its resident insects. You can hire a guide for $25.

In the early morning bird-watchers might spot the Fiji Goshawk and Blue-Crested Broadbill, which are found only in Fiji. The park is also home to Sulphur-Breasted Musk Parrots, barking Pigeons, Golden whistler, Slaty Flycatchers, Golden Doves, and Spotted Fantails among other species. One minute up the road from the entrance is the Raintree Lodge restaurant (*see below*), a nice setting for a post-exploration meal. You can take the Sawani bus from the city. The visitor center is in the modest group of buildings just after a big bend on the left. ⊠*Princes Rd., Colo-I-Suva, 10 km (6 mi) northeast of central Suva* ☎*332–0211* ☐*$5* ⊘*Daily 8–4.*

❸ Fiji Museum in Thurston Gardens. It's hard to imagine Fiji's warrior past given the warmth and hospitality of its people but visit the national museum and you'll begin to understand. The centerpiece of the first room is a drua or double-hulled canoe used for seafaring and transporting warriors. It's so large that it required five men using oars each up to 12 feet (3.6 meters) long and hewn from a single tree simply to keep it on course. A grueling variety of war clubs, details of a sometimes fatal method of target practice, various artifacts, and an informative model of a Fijian home are also on display. Detailed exhibits trace the history of Euro-Fijian relations, including the mutiny aboard the HMS *Bounty* and cannibalism. You can see a cannibal fork and the boiled sole of an eaten missionary's shoe. Upstairs, Indo-Fijian exhibits of exquisite dresses, agricultural innovations, and Hindi displays provide insight into the experience of the other half of Fiji's population. The gift shop sells books, handicrafts, spa products, and artwork. The museum is just outside of the city center in the picturesque Thurston Gardens. ⊠*Cakobau Rd., at Queen Elizabeth Parade* ☎*331–5944* ⊕*www.fijimuseum.org.fj* ☐*$7* ⊘*Mon.–Thurs. 8–4:30, Fri. 8–4, Sat. 9:30–4:30.*

❹ Parliament House. Completed in 1992 the Parliament grounds are designed like a Fijian village. The largest building, a massive, thatched-roof bure considered the "chief's house" is built on the site's highest point, on a traditional high yavu (earth mound) and is the meeting chamber of Parliament.

The 71 members of the House of Representatives and 32 senators convene here beneath traditional masi tapestries representing the three traditional confederacies that make up the Fiji Islands. Each house of Parliament uses a ceremonial mace to close sessions and Parliament cannot sit without the presence of both. If democracy has been restored to Fiji prior to your visit, you should be able to sit in on a session of Parliament. ⊠*Visitor entrance on Battery Rd., Nasese* ⊕*www.parliament.gov.fj* ⊞*Free.*

OFF THE BEATEN PATH. A colossal $20-million building was nearing completion in Nasese, on the tip of the peninsula, to house the Great Council of Chiefs (GCC), whose members act as an electoral college in choosing the president and vice-president as well as a number of Senate members. It's uncertain whether tours will be offered in the controversial building, which some consider an extravagant use of taxpayers' dollars. ⊠*Nasova.*

❷ **Suva Municipal Market.** The largest municipal market in the South Pacific is a fantastic place to take in the local atmosphere. Row after row of stalls are laden with produce, clothes, shoes, and handicrafts. Brightly colored bins of spices dot many tables and, outside, women sit on blankets under tarps to stay cool amid their goods. The roots and weighing scales upstairs comprise the widest selection of kava in all of Fiji. As with most municipal markets in the country, it's beside the bus station and the majority of goods come, along with their owners, fresh from the countryside daily. Throughout the market, the Fijian and Indo-Fijian sellers are generally patient and happy to chat. ⊠*Corner of Usher St. and Rodwell Rd.* ⊞*Free* ⊗*Mon.–Sat. 8–5.*

NEED A BREAK? Excellent coffee imported from Melbourne and refreshing smoothies make the centrally located kiosk Kahawa (⊠*Suva Central Bldg., 2nd fl., corner of Renwick Rd. and Pratt St.* ☎*330–9671*) a great place to recharge. If you like the brew, consider visiting the full-size location in Ra Marama House on Gordon Street (just south of the Tanoa Plaza Hotel) for its free wireless Internet (but no power outlets), serene atmosphere, and wider food selection.

Making Amends

One of the last persons to be eaten in Fiji, as the many tribes bowed to pressure from Christianity, was the British missionary Reverend Thomas Baker in 1867. Some say the chief borrowed a comb from the missionary while others say it was a hat. The missionary tried to remove the object and touched the chief's head, which is forbidden. Baker and eight Fijian followers were promptly clubbed to death and eaten. The cooked but uneaten sole of the missionary's shoe appears in the Fiji Museum in Suva.

In 2003 descendants of the chief invited descendants of Thomas Baker to their remote village of Nabutautau on Viti Levu to take part in a complex ceremony designed to lift a curse locals felt had been placed on the impoverished village when they ate the missionary. Among the 600 attendees were the Fijian prime minister, the chief's great-grandson, and 11 of the missionary's descendants, including Baker's great-great-grandson. Offerings reportedly included a cow, specially woven mats, and 30 sacred carved sperm-whale teeth or *tabua*.

WHERE TO EAT

AMERICAN

$$ ✕**Bad Dog Café.** For the tepid of palate or homesick, this multifaceted expat magnet has all the comfort foods. The American-style menu featuring everything from pizzas and pastas to burgers and steaks is served in three areas. There's a T.G.I.F.-style seating area that permits smoking and has a full bar, a café section with a coffee bar and sweets on display, and a surprisingly intimate, candlelight dining room. Drinks are half-off 5–6 PM daily and the polished bar keeps the margaritas, sangria, shots, and cocktails flowing until 11. Sports memorabilia and state license plates are mercifully omitted, but they do sell branded clothing. ⊠ *218 Victoria Parade* ☎ *331–2884* ▭ *AE, MC, V.*

CHINESE

$$ ✕**Fong Lee Seafood Restaurant.** The combination of plastic flower tablecloths, red carpet, and small chandeliers of glass balls is just kitschy enough to state the emphasis is not on the decor but the food at this authentic Chinese place on the main strip. For more than 16 years, locals and expats have been coming for seafood specialties such as steamed fish, deep fried squid, and lobster served in generous, family-style

portions; meat dishes are also offered. Service is good and continues to be so after 6:30 when the restaurant begins to fill up for dinner. ✉*293 Victoria Parade* ☎*330–4233* ▭*No credit cards* ☉*Closed Sun.*

ECLECTIC

$$ ✕**Fiji Malthouse Brewery & Restaurant.** Above its own brewery ★ 15 minutes from the city center, "Malt" serves delectable wood-oven pizzas, high-quality meat and seafood dishes, and delicious home-brewed beer in a laid-back atmosphere. If you can't decide between the gourmet pizzas, which include combos such as chicken in tandoori spice with onion, roasted pumpkin, and banana, they'll make one half-and-half. Dishes such as braised lamb shank with vegetables panache, baked potato, and mint gravy, and herb-crusted or tempura-battered fish with chips, aioli, pesto, and salad garnish are also on the menu, but many guests are here simply for the five types of beer. Each 100% malt, they include lagers, a wheat beer, and a light and dark ale. ✉*88 Jerusalem Rd.* ☎*337–1517* ▭*AE, DC, MC,V.*

$$$ ✕**The Point After.** Over-water deck seating and flavorful seafood are the trademarks of this spot a short taxi ride south of the city center. The menu or "Captain's Log" is presented on a wooden paddle while water laps at the side of the restaurant. There are steaks and curries, but local dishes such as tuna steak marinated in a Hawaiian teriyaki sauce, then grilled or basted with olive oil and dredged with a Fiji Cajun spice blend fully engage the senses in the seafaring atmosphere. A two-man cover band completes the cruise ship atmosphere Friday nights and the views are best savored at sunset. ✉*Queen Elizabeth Dr., Nasese* ☎*330–2476* ▭*AE, MC, V.*

INDIAN

$ ✕**Hare Krishna Vegetarian Restaurant.** Of the many branches of ★ this Suva staple, this one's upstairs seating—open 11–3—is the most relaxing place to enjoy one of the chain's 17 kinds of vegetarian curries. The corner real estate offers a fantastic view of the impressive Sacred Heart Cathedral from comfortable, cushioned wicker chairs. The air-conditioning doesn't hurt, but there are also plenty of cream and milk shake flavors to cool you down. Curries are served cafeteria-style by friendly, hair-netted staff, and there's a large array of toffees downstairs as well as all-day, un-air-conditioned seating. ✉*16 Pratt St.* ☎*331–4154* ▭*No credit cards* ☉*Upstairs open 11–3 only.*

QUIET & THE COUP

Parliament House is an eerily quiet place in the democracy-less days leading up to new elections, which self-appointed Prime Minister Frank Bainimarama has promised will be held by March 2009. On the last day the building was open, December 6, 2006, it was surrounded by Commodore Bainimarama's troops, who interrupted senators as they debated a motion condemning the bloodless coup of a day earlier.

In the wake of the coup, business carried on virtually as usual in the western half of the country, although the tourism industry suffered severely under the sanctions imposed by a number of countries and has yet to fully recover. In Suva many locals were disappointed that there was not a curfew as there had been after the coup in 2000, which had reduced the city's crime rate to virtually nothing.

★ **Fodor's**Choice ✕**Old Mill Cottage Café.** You get far more than $ you pay for at this Suva institution hidden behind shrubbery, one block east of the main drag. The menu is on a blackboard and the food is served cafeteria-style but don't be deterred: It's prepared fresh and tastes accordingly. Traditional Indian fare sits alongside local fish and vegetable dishes, all classically prepared. The staff will mix-and-match to your preference before you retreat to a booth or table and savor the city's finest. Authentic sweet dishes and cakes are served in the second room down the porch. It's a shame they're not open for dinner. ⊠*49 Carnavon St.* ☎*331–2134* ▭*No credit cards* ⊘*Mon.–Sat. 7–11* AM, *11:30* AM–*5* PM. *Closed Sun.*

$ ✕**Singh's Curry House.** A favorite among 9–5'ers for its spicy, cafeteria-style south Indian fare, some luck may be required to find a seat here at lunch hour. Spices from Singapore and India give the curries a more authentic flavor than much of the competition. Food is served cafeteria-style and the intense reds of the booths and yellows of the walls are in line with the hotter dishes. The patrons' sink, complete with liquid soap and paper towel dispensers, is beside a booth in the dining room, but it's all part of the fun—at least for you, who doesn't have to be back at work in 45 minutes. There's a second location in the Morris Hedstrom mall. ⊠*Corner of Gordon Str. and Victoria Parade* ☎*330–6600* ▭*No credit cards.*

2

ITALIAN

$$$$ ✕ **L'Opera.** When a director of the Asian Development Bank
★ relocated to Suva, her Italian-born husband did what he
knew best and opened a restaurant. A dramatic, dimly
lighted passage leads seemingly out of Fiji and into a mul-
tiroom, theatrical dining area, abundant in oil paintings,
finely laid tables, and overall ballroom-like decor. Thus the
stage is set for Tuscan fare, including Tasmanian salmon
and prawns sautéed in spumante wine and lemon sauce,
and homemade ravioli stuffed with seafood in a smoked
salmon sauce. There are also locations in Manila, if you
happen to be in the area. ⊠*59 Gordon St.* ☎*331–8602*
═AE, MC, V ☉*Closed Sun. No lunch Sat.*

JAPANESE

$$$ ✕ **Daikoku.** Smaller than the Nadi location, this is an equally
traditional setting for the chain's signature dynamically
prepared cuisine. Families in particular thrill to the sight
of locally caught tuna, Australian beef, and New Zealand
salmon expertly sliced, diced, and cooked before their eyes.
Punctual service and a decent wine list round out the cel-
ebratory atmosphere. ⊠*Dolphin Arcade, Victoria Parade*
☎*330–8968* *═AE, DC, MC, V* ☉*Closed Sun.*

SEAFOOD

★ Fodor'sChoice ✕ **Tiko's Floating Restaurant.** What more appropri-
$$$–$$$$ ate setting for fantastic seafood than a 35-year-old original
Blue Lagoon cruise ship? The fresh catch is written up on
the blackboard menu at either end of the dining room.
More often than not this includes lobster, sea prawns, and
fish such as Nuqa, masterfully prepared. There are smoking
and no-smoking areas as well as a private dining room in
the former captain's quarters with 270-degree views. Some
diners come later to hear the guitarist accompanied by a
slice of sticky date pudding or chocolate mud cake, but it's
worth arriving in time for sunset drinks. The restaurant
is engine-less and attached to the dock, so don't worry
about missing the boat. ⊠*Anchored off Stinson Parade*
☎*331–3626* ⚲*Reservations essential* *═AE, DC, MC, V*
☉*Closed Sun. No lunch Sat.*

STEAK

$$$ ✕ **JJ's on the Park.** The best place for steak in Suva, JJ's is on
the park and across the street from the harbor. Fan-folded
napkins (even if they are paper) and a few ol' boys' club–
style booths set the tone for succulent cuts, a classic Beef
Wellington, and a renowned burger. The $54.50 lobster is

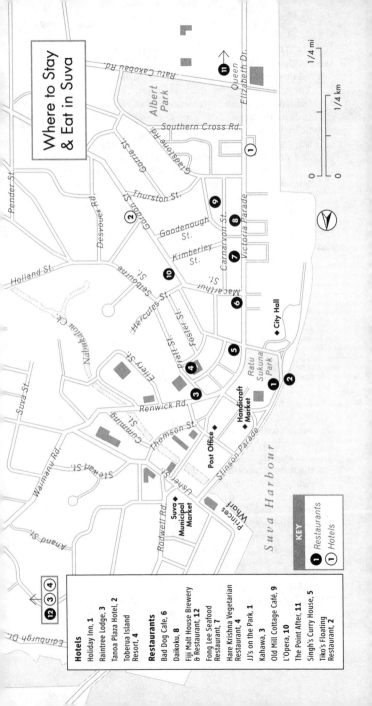

Where to Stay & Eat in Suva

Hotels
Holiday Inn, **1**
Raintree Lodge, **3**
Tanoa Plaza Hotel, **2**
Toberua Island Resort, **4**

Restaurants
Bad Dog Cafe, **6**
Daikoku, **8**
Fiji Malt House Brewery & Restaurant, **12**
Fong Lee Seafood Restaurant, **7**
Hare Krishna Vegetarian Restaurant, **4**
JJ's on the Park, **1**
Kahawa, **3**
Old Mill Cottage Café, **9**
L'Opera, **10**
The Point After, **11**
Singh's Curry House, **5**
Tiko's Floating Restaurant, **2**

KEY
1 Restaurants
① Hotels

On the Horizon

Democracy may not be present in the nation's capital but investors and developers have confidence enough in Fiji's future. The city's first Western-style malls were completed in 2007 and 2008 and the outdated Raffles Tradewinds Hotel & Convention Centre has been sold and is likely to see a refurbishment.

Elsewhere in the country, 79 upscale villas are expected to be constructed on Nananu-I-Ra Island by the company that built Hilton's Fiji Beach Resort & Spa. A short boat trip north of the mainland, Nananu-I-Ra has traditionally been a stronghold of rustic all-inclusives and private homes. There's no end of construction in sight just outside the gate of Denarau Island, where plots of marshland have been divided up stretching almost to the airport and tens of hotels planned. Some anticipate Viti Levu's development into another Hawaii. However, projects around the country have been known to stall, leaving most in the business community skeptical. Self-appointed Prime Minister Bainimarama had promised to allow competition among energy and phone service providers by October 2008. This would encourage development and lighten the overhead costs that, following the coup, weighed heavily on those in the tourism business.

also popular as is the aptly named Death by Chocolate, the smaller size of which will satiate two. The service is professional—the way expats like it—and the restaurant's setting conveys a luxurious sense of space. ⊠*JJ's on the Park hotel, Ratu Sukuna Park, Stinson Parade* ☎*330–5005* ⊟*AE, DC, MC, V.*

WHERE TO STAY

$$ 🖥**Holiday Inn.** This incarnation of the worldwide chain
★ delivers, with spacious rooms, pretty pools among manicured grounds, and highly professional staff. Superior rooms differ from standard in that each has a chair and ottoman and carpeting in place of a couch-bed and tile floor. Poolside rooms have great views across the water to the rest of the mainland. Only ground-floor rooms have bathtubs. There's a cozy cocktail area by the bar, which tends to fill during sports games. The restaurant offers breakfast and lunch buffets and a large eclectic dinner menu including the traditional dish kokoda. The hotel is on the water, a 10-minute walk directly south of the

city center. **Pros:** Pretty harbor views; lobby buzz; eclectic restaurant. **Cons:** Generic rooms. ✉ *501 Victoria Parade* ☎ *330–1600* ⊕ *www.holidayinn.com* ⬎ *130 rooms, 1 suite* ♿ *In-room: refrigerator, Wi-Fi. In-hotel: restaurant, room service, bar, 2 pools, laundry facilities, laundry service, executive floor, public Internet, no-smoking rooms* ▭ *AE, DC, MC, V* ⊠ *EP.*

$ ⊡ **Raintree Lodge.** Guests of all kinds are drawn to the pris-
★ tine rain-forest-and-lake setting of this ecofriendly resort. Tour groups and backpackers are happy with the clean, comfortable dorms and single bedrooms, couples content with the small double-bed rooms with a shared porch over-looking one of the lakes, and families enjoy the privacy of well-spaced, split-level bures with equal or better views. The larger lake was created when a 110-foot deep gravel quarry hit water during a storm one night and flooded, leav-ing a bulldozer and two 10-ton trucks submerged. Locals swim here (no, you can't scuba dive) but guests generally stick to the pool, with its bar, TV, occasional on-stage meke (traditional performance) Tuesday and Sunday nights, and BBQ buffet lunch with a live band on Sunday. Locals frequent the eclectic restaurant overlooking the lake for its Cajun chicken salad, and breakfast here is great value. A 15-minute taxi or bus ride from the city center, it's a minute's walk from Colo-I-Suva Forest Park. **Pros:** Serene location; friendly staff; privacy. **Cons:** Extreme humidity; small double rooms. ✉ *Princes Rd., Colo-I-Suva, 10 km northeast of central Suva* ☎ *332–0562* ⊕ *www.raintree lodge.com* ⬎ *10 rooms, 4 suites, 6 dorms* ♿ *In-room: no a/c, no phone, kitchen (some), refrigerator (some), no TV (some). In-hotel: restaurant, room service, bar, pool, laun-dry service, public Internet* ▭ *AE, MC, V* ⊠ *EP.*

$$ ⊡ **Tanoa Plaza Hotel.** This striking nine-story hotel with a compact marble lobby caters to the business traveler, from its brisk service to snappy same-day laundry and 24-hour room services. While on the small side and lacking in decor, rooms are neat and comfortable with queen-size beds. Deluxe rooms include free Fiji water and are on the eighth floor; you can command much the same fantastic view over Suva if you can snag a standard room on the seventh. The restaurant's eclectic menu changes monthly to appeal to long-stay corporate guests. **Pros:** Efficient staff; expansive views. **Cons:** Impersonal feel. ✉ *Corner of Gordon and Malcolm Sts.* ☎ *331–2300* ⊕ *www.tanoahotels.com* ⬎ *56 rooms, 4 suites* ♿ *In-room: ethernet. In-hotel: restaurant,*

room service, bar, pool, laundry services, public Internet ⊟*AE, DC, MC, V* ⊠*EP.*

★ **Fodor'sChoice** ⚏**Toberua Island Resort.** Personalized service, a
$$$–$$$$ tranquil ambience, and the food ensure repeat guests at this
private island hideaway, a 27-minute boat ride from the
mainland. Some staff members have been here more than
30 years and now their children work here, too. Menus
determined mere hours in advance include three-course
lunches and four-course dinners with such fare as lemon
grass-battered snapper and grilled lobster roulade salad
prepared by the resort's chef of more than 15 years. All
bures have private patios and 27-foot-high ceilings and
fringe the 4-acre island, each no more than a few steps
from the water, if you can make it past the hand-woven
hammock. A Standard Bure might adjoin the fence sepa-
rating the staff quarters while Premiums are closer to the
water. A refurbishment of the beautiful bar and restaurant
as well as the rooms in mid-2008 should make the latter
an even finer compliment to the spacious bathrooms with
outdoor showers. Activities include picnic trips to a tiny
uninhabited cay, great snorkeling, and 9-hole golf when
the island expands to 20 acres at low-tide. **Pros:** World-
class cuisine; personal service; privacy. **Cons:** Tidal beach.
⊠*Toberua Island* ☎*347–2777* ⊕*www.toberua.com* ⇆*15
suites* ⚏*In-room: no a/c, no phone, safe, refrigerator, no
TV. In-hotel: restaurant, room service, bar, golf course,
pool, spa, beachfront, diving, water sports, public Internet,
airport shuttle* ⊟*AE, MC, V* ⊠*EP, FAP.*

NIGHTLIFE & THE ARTS

Suva's assortment of nightclubs and bars is just large
enough to warrant the word "assortment," ensuring that
most visiting (and many local) night owls end up at two or
three spots. Venues are packed into and just off the strip of
Victoria Parade between Loftus and MacArthur streets, and
only a couple of these are truly safe for tourists.

A colonial-style front room is just the start of the cavernous
five-room **Traps Bar** (⊠*305 Victoria Parade* ☎*331–2922*).
Locals and a younger tourist crowd mingle and dance to
rap and R&B. One room has a projection TV and pool
table, another has a dance floor and a stage for the acous-
tic band playing old-school on Thursday and sometimes
Tuesday nights. Upstairs, older patrons hang out in the
better-lighted, low-key lounge. It starts getting crowded
around 11.

Locals and foreigners of all ages crowd into **O'Reilly's & Wolfhound** (⌂5 MacArthur St. ☎331–2322) to dance and attempt to chat while reggae, rap, and other Top 40 hits are played at a clublike decibel. The bench-seating and Guinness make more sense during the quieter happy hours 5–8, and when rugby games are broadcast. The younger set will often commute between here and Trap's in search of the best atmosphere. It's under the same ownership as, and attached to, Bad Dog Café.

Aside from O'Reilly's, the closest thing you'll find to a sports bar in Suva is the cozy bar-lounge area of the **Holiday Inn** (⌂501 Victoria Parade ☎330–1600), where expat locals gather to watch televised games. You can perch on stools or recline in the small lounge with a cocktail or something from the bar menu. If the match goes into overtime, you can probably have food from the restaurant menu delivered to the TV room.

Enjoy the finer points of a captain's lifestyle aboard **Tiko's Floating Restaurant** (⌂Anchored off Stinson Parade ☎331–3626). Attached by a walkway to the waterfront, the retired old ferry and upscale seafood restaurant has a full bar at one end of its alfresco dining room, and live music. The natural light show begins at sunset.

CELEBRATE! First celebrated in 1957, the annual Hibiscus Festival (⊕www.hibiscusfiji.com) in August includes a weeklong program of cultural performances accompanied by a fairground and food stalls, a "Queen's" beauty contest, and a carnival parade along Victoria Parade. It's primarily a fund-raising event.

SPORTS & THE OUTDOORS

DAY SPA

At this tranquil spa on the outskirts of the capital, every treatment begins with a warm foot soak in a fragrant coconut-milk bath. **Pure Fiji's** (⌂52 Karsanji St., Vatuwaqa ☎338–3611 ✎spa@purefiji.com) full spa menu includes an exfoliation treatment using coconut and sugarcane, body wraps, massages, and new treatments such as a warm sea-shell massage and a milk and honey wrap. The standard treatment time is 50 minutes and most cost between $70 and $85.

RUGBY

Fiji has one of the highest player-population ratios of any rugby-playing nation, and it's common to see kids and adults charging in lines and passing on fields across the country. Photos of its bullnecked and tree-trunk thighed superstars color the newspaper daily. The rivalry between Fiji and New Zealand, both top contenders for the Rugby World Cup Sevens title each year, is palpable. **Post Fiji Stadium** (⊠*Laucala Bay, Suva* ☎*330–2787* ⊕*www.fijirugby.com*), the official stadium of the national pastime, has a capacity of 18,000. The major tournaments of the Sevens season (a version of the game with 7 players rather than 15, at which Fiji excels) are held from late-November to June, but events are held at Post Fiji Stadium nearly year-round.

SHOPPING

The bulk of Suva's stores are squeezed into a section of narrow, angling streets south of the river and heading east from Scott Street. These include an urban array of clothing and jewelry stores, shoe shops, and cafés. The brand-new Morris Hedstrom City Complex is the country's first full-scale mall and likely an indication of things to come. The homey Curio & Handicraft Market and lively Suva Municipal Market remain Fiji institutions.

Across the street from scenic Suva Harbour, everything at the **Curio & Handicraft Market** (⊠*Stintson Parade* ☎*331–1532*) is made in the Lau Group of islands, making this one of the mainland's most authentic and least-expensive places to souvenir-shop. It's just a shame that the alleylike section of stalls is caged in. It's just as well, because the eager sellers want your full attention on the selection of handicrafts, carvings, and jewelry at each of the 71 stalls.

Fiji's first western-style mall (completed mid-2007), **Mid City Mall** (⊠*Corner of Cummings St. and Waimanu Rd.*), is one of the South Pacific's most modern buildings, complete with escalator and chic hair salon. Among the 36 office spaces and retails shops are Gloria Jeans Coffees and a branch of the popular chain Chicken Express.

The three-story **Morris Hedstrom City Complex** (⊠*Thomson St.*) mall opened in late-2007 and includes a food court, supermarket, bookstore, furniture store, and handicraft store. A planned second phase of construction will add 15 stories of office space and will make this the tallest building in Fiji.

VITI LEVU ESSENTIALS

TRANSPORTATION

BY AIR

Nadi International Airport, the entry point into the country for the vast majority of travelers to Fiji, is a 10-minute drive north of the town center and accessible by local buses headed to and from Lautoka. Suva's Nausori Airport is a 23-km (14 mi) 30-minute drive northeast of the city. Buses run between the Suva and Nausori Town, a short taxi ride from the airport. Air Pacific flies between Nadi and Suva six times a day. Air Fiji flies this route five times daily. There are also a limited number of international flights to Suva.

See By Air, in Fiji Essentials for information on international flights to Nadi, as well as airport and airline information.

BY BUS

Three bus companies run between the Nadi area and Suva daily, a journey of around 4½ hours for the nearly 200-km trip. Local buses will stop upon request while express buses stop at towns and the biggest resorts, but these will often stop on request, as well. Timetables are available at each town's bus station. Bus stations are invariably located beside the open-air municipal market in or near the center of town: Nadi's is five blocks west of Main Street along Hospital Road; Lautoka's is in the heart of the city at 7 Yasawa Street; in Pacific Harbour, the buses stop along Queens Road and in the small town of Navua south of the bridge along the water; Suva's is a short walk north of the city center on Rodwell Road. Coral Sun makes pickups by arrangement and does not stop at bus stations.

Coral Sun's single daily round-trip bus (with air-conditioning) departs Suva at 7:30 AM and arrives at Nadi Airport at noon. It departs Nadi Airport at 12:45 and arrives back in Suva at 5:15 PM. Fares range $7–$30.

Sunbeam operates crisscrossing express and local services on standard school buses 10 times daily between Suva and Lautoka. The first buses leave Suva at 3:45 AM and Lautoka at 3:15 AM. The last depart both Suva and Lautoka at 3:15 PM. There is one bus to and from Ba (a town approximately two hours north of Nadi) daily. Fares range $2.80–$15.45.

Pacific Transport runs "express" (local) and "stage" (express) service on standard school buses 11 times between Suva and Lautoka Monday–Thursday, more often on Friday and Saturday, and none on Sunday. The first departs Suva at 6:45 AM and Lautoka at 6:30 AM. The last departs both Suva and Lautoka at 6 PM. There's one bus to and from Ba daily. Fares range from $2.25 to $14.35.

2

See By Bus, in Fiji Essentials for bus contact information.

BY CAR

Viti Levu's road configuration makes it an extremely easy island to navigate. Queens Road is the sole throughway across the southern coast and, consequently, nearly all major resorts and attractions are either visible from it or have signs posted leading the way. Kings Road, a bit rougher in parts, serves the same purpose on the northern coast. Old Queens Road is rough and runs along the coast in the southwestern corner of the island. Be aware of cars moving into the path of oncoming traffic in order to overtake others on these two-lane highways. Parking is available in the towns and at virtually all resorts.

See Rental Cars, in By Car, in Fiji Essentials for rental car agency contact information.

BY MINIVAN

Minivans are a less-expensive option than taxis. They are often stationed in the middle of a town, where they wait until each seat is filled before leaving for a predetermined destination. It's a set fare and stops are made as requested. Sometimes other passengers are picked up along the way. Minivan drivers have a reputation for driving very fast and a few fatal accidents have turned many locals against this mode of travel.

BY TAXI

Taxis are abundant throughout Viti Levu and most are independently operated: if you can't hail one on the street, any hotel and most restaurants will be happy to call one for you. They are only metered in Suva. Elsewhere, ask a local what rate you should expect to pay and negotiate the fare before accepting a ride, as drivers are known to boost the fare for foreigners. In many places, taxis offer 50-cent "return fares" to passengers they pick up on their way back to a town center.

CONTACTS & RESOURCES

TOURS

Discover Fiji offers guided day-tours of the island's southern coast. The guide discusses the history of everything from the sugarcane and pine forest/mahogany industries to culture and education. You'll visit Parliament House and other government buildings and have an opportunity to shop. Pickup is anytime between 7 AM (if staying by Nadi Airport) and 10:15 AM (if in Pacific Harbour) and costs $45–$60 accordingly. One-way trips are half-price, as are children under 15.

Feejee Experience offers coach-based multiday tours, which allow you to complete their itineraries at your own pace, up to six months from your first day of travel. The Hula Loop is an active four-day itinerary, which includes such activities as sandboarding the Sigatoka Sand Dunes, trekking through the Namosi Highlands, and making village visits. The tour costs $396 and does not include accommodation. A version including mid-range accommodation costs $710 twin-share and $1,013 for single-occupancy rooms. A six-day Lei Low tour includes an added night on Beachcomber Island in the Mamanucas. It costs $558 and includes only the fifth night's accommodation.

See Sports & the Outdoors, in Nadi for more tour options.

Tour Companies **Discover Fiji** (☎*345–0180* ⊕*www.discoverfiji tours.com*). **Feejee Experience** (☎*672–5950* ⊕*www.feejee experience.com*).

VISITOR INFORMATION

The head office of the visitor bureau is in Nadi Airport. The Suva branch is housed in a small Victorian building in an open space between Scott Street and Edward Street in the city center. Both have walls of brochures and the friendly and knowledgeable staff will be happy to discuss options with you. There's also an office in Los Angeles.

Contacts **Fiji Islands Visitors Bureau Head Office** (⊕*www. bulafijinow.com* ⊙*Weekdays 9–4* ✉*Suite 107, Colonial Plaza, Namaka, Nadi* ☎*672–2433*). **Fiji Islands Visitors Bureau Suva** (✉*Thomson St., Suva* ☎*330–2433*).

Mamanuca &
Yasawa Groups

WORD OF MOUTH

"If you like to do a bit of everything—including some diving—but want better weather and beaches, choose somewhere in the Yasawas or Mamanucas."
                                    —Ahw

Written by Robert Brenner

ONE OF THE FIRST QUESTIONS TAXI DRIVERS ASK upon picking tourists up from Fiji's gateway airport in Nadi is, "Which island are you going to?" They're referring to those that make up the two groups to the west and, to be sure, the assumption that you're traveling farther is an easy one. A short ferry ride from Nadi, the Mamanuca and Yasawa islands seem to be in a world of their own. While Viti Levu's main concern is cutting and processing sugarcane, here it's all about the weather and the catch of the day. Translucent, warm surf and glittering white shores allow these islands to fulfill the glossy brochures' promise and satisfy the snow-plowed commuters' dreams.

The movie *Castaway* starring Tom Hanks was filmed on the small uninhabited island of Monuriki, but there are more hospitable places to stay in the Mamanuca Islands. These offer the greatest balance of accommodations of any one region in Fiji, with resorts catering to singles, couples, families, the cousins your spouse wanted to invite, and a few that will please all four. The more remote, volcanically formed Yasawas are traditionally a stronghold of all-inclusive hostels, but seaplanes now crisscross the group conveying guests to ultraluxury resorts. Happily, the mid-range is now making a showing here as well. The Yasawas are home to the Blue Lagoon, used in the eponymous film starring Brook Shields and noted as one of the most pristine among many breathtaking coral-crowned pools.

You'll find all the trademarks of the world's pristine tropical escapes—fantastic snorkeling, parasailing, waterskiing, and good scuba diving—here. Divers can have their pulses checked with a shark-dive at "Supermarket," one of many sites on the Mamanucas' Malolo Barrier Reef, or by mingling with pelagics in the swim-throughs up north.

EXPLORING THE MAMANUCA & YASAWA GROUPS

Like a string of iridescent pearls, the islands of these two groups stretch in a subtle arc from just off the coast of Nadi to a point north of the mainland. The first islands of the Mamanuca Group are 30 minutes by ferry from Denarau Marina; those of the Yasawas are between a two- and five-hour scenic ride away. Seaplanes, helicopters, boat-taxis, and a couple of domestic carriers are more creative and generally more costly ways to get around.

There aren't particular "sights to see" and the island resorts here are careful to offer at least a week's worth of activities

MAMANUCA & YASAWA'S TOP 5

Hit the Beach. Blindingly white, caressingly soft, and stretching for miles, there's quintessential beachfront at every price range.

Dive the Supermarket. Grey Reef, White Tip Reef, and Black Tip Reef sharks patrol this site, encouraged by the meals occasionally provided by dive operators (fish, not the customers).

Party. Sand, surf, and cheap room-and-board are enough to keep young travelers toasting with Fiji Bitter late into the night.

Water sports. What better backdrop for parasailing, waterskiing, sailing, or a spin in a kayak?

Fresh Fish. At the smaller resorts, if it came from the sea, chances are it was caught today…probably right over there…

3

within their shores. If you're looking for a bit of adventure, head to the more rugged, volcanically formed Yasawas for good hiking, particularly on Waya and Tavewa, and excursions to the caves on the coast of Tavewa. The Yasawas are also home to more traditional villages, most notably on Yasawa Island at the northern end of the chain. In the Mamanucas, you can get out and about through water sports, boat tours of "*Castaway* Island," and afternoon island-hopping tours.

ABOUT THE HOTELS & RESTAURANTS

Singles, honeymooners, older couples, and families are all catered to in the Mamanucas. Young children have all they can handle in the activity-packed larger resorts where parents have their pick among many room categories. Older families can have the courts of play and water sports with a little more room for peace and quiet at the nicer mid-size resorts. Both in the Mamanucas and Yasawas, top-end boutiques and mid-size getaways pamper with fresh daily flowers, outdoor showers, and secluded dinners to fulfill newlyweds' dreams. The majority of all-inclusive budget resorts are in the Yasawas, where young singles and couples don't mind buffet lines because the appetite they're most concerned with is only satiated by the beach.

Come meal time, your palate may be crossed by familiar warm-weather vacation fare such as lobster, swordfish, and tuna, but you may find it prepared traditional-style in coconut milk and accompanied by tasty local vegetables.

GREAT ITINERARIES

Although it's certainly possible to get a lot out of these islands in three days, once you find the resort best suited to your needs, you won't want to lift a suitcase again for at least seven, and probably longer. Many resorts operate with seven-day minimum stays as the norm, and menus and activity schedules are created accordingly.

IF YOU HAVE 3 DAYS

It's best to choose a resort you won't spend half a day getting to, so head to the Mamanucas. You can be checked-in and then check-out in a bathing suit by about noon, give or take a "welcome" drink. If you're interested in seeing more islands you'll find many of the resorts here offer island-hopping trips using their own small craft. Conversely, you can tackle these pristine beaches by day and retire to Denarau Island's international-standard comfort at night by taking a South Sea Cruises day trip that leaves daily from Viti Levu. See *Mamanucas & Yasawas Islands in a Day, in Nadi in Chapter 2.*

If you must visit the Yasawas for this short a time, a Captain Cook cruise departing from Denarau Marina is your best option.

IF YOU HAVE 5 DAYS

Awesome Adventures has a five-day trip through the Yasawas, but it's still a better idea to unwind in one place. With this much time you can appreciate the versatility of a rotating menu and take a scuba diving course—the abundance of beginner dive sites and excellent visibility make these two groups fantastic places to learn. From the Mamanucas, consider a boat tour to Monuriki Island—the setting of *Castaway*—or a South Seas day cruise out to the Yasawas. From the Yasawas, organize a romantic day on a private beach complete with picnic lunch—perhaps to the Blue Lagoon, an adventurous swim in the ancient Sawa-I-Lau caves, or an invigorating hike through one of the island's lush, volcanic terrains. Whichever group you choose to reside in, there will be time for a village tour and perhaps to see a meke.

IF YOU HAVE 7 DAYS

Seven days is the usual minimum amount of time guests spend in these parts. This gives you time to either fully unwind or take advantage of the many activities that a resort offers. Fidgety travelers might consider island-hopping with an Awesome Adventures "Bula Pass" and trying numerous budget or mid-range resorts.

IF YOU LIKE

BEACHES

These are undisputedly Fiji's finest beaches. Mana Island has a particularly beautiful stretch, with its island-tip location allowing it to divide the sand into more kid-friendly and quieter sections. Then, of course, there's the Yasawas' magnificent Blue Lagoon with intriguing coves worth exploring. Nearly every resort in the two groups can claim a stretch of sand worth envying.

SNORKELING

A relative lack of weather compared to the rest of the country makes the coral visibility exceptional and it's often just a short swim from the beach. Navini, owing to its establishment of a marine reserve, and Matamanoa have particularly great sea life.

BUDGET RESORTS

The Yasawas, and increasingly the Mamanucas, are famous for their cheap all-inclusives. The true beach bum can have a pristine setting, a place to lay his or her head and three hearty square ones for less than $100 per day.

WHAT IT COSTS IN FIJI DOLLARS (F$)			
$	$$	$$$	$$$$
RESTAURANTS			
under F$10	F$10–F$20	F$20–F$30	over F$30
HOTELS*			
under F$200	F$200–F$400	F$400–F$700	over F$700
HOTELS**			
under F$300	F$300–F$500	F$500–F$800	over F$800

*EP, BP, CP **AI, FAP, MAP; Restaurant prices are per person for a main course at dinner. Hotel prices are per night for a double room in high season and may not include a 12.5% Value-Added Tax (V.A.T.) or a 5% hotel turnover tax. Hotel prices are in U.S. dollars where noted.

MAMANUCA ISLANDS

The 20 islands of the group reside in a large lagoon formed by the 16-km (10-mi) long Malolo Barrier Reef and Viti Levu. The group stretches 35 km (22 mi) roughly in a north–south diagonal from Nadi. Small Fijian villages are spread throughout the islands.

EXPLORING THE MAMANUCA ISLANDS

Of the two groups, the Mamanucas offer superior diving. Its best-known sites, Supermarket and Gotham City, are near the middle of the group and nearly every resort has a dive operator that frequents them. You'll also find larger resorts here than in its sister group to the north, and a corresponding number of facilities: more restaurants featuring more eclectic menus, and more swimming pools. While some of the properties are relatively close together—guests at a number of resorts will disembark to smaller boats at a single ferry stop—each has its own, freewheeling ambience and is not easily seen from the others. If you want to snoop around, most resorts offer island-hopping trips, which convey guests by water taxi to three or four different islands (and their resorts) over the course of an afternoon.

WHERE TO STAY & EAT

★ Fodor'sChoice 🖼**Beachcomber Island Resort.** Every day's spring

$$–$$$ break and every morning's a challenge for most guests at this iconic Fiji party resort. The island is ruled by young travelers looking to tan by day and drink by night, but laid-back families and older travelers occasionally come for its excellent beach, overall value, and range of activities including fishing, jet-skiing, windsurfing, and parasailing. The buffet-style meals are surprisingly good, and traditional Fijian performances and a weekly lovo contribute a refreshingly cultural element. In truth, you can come for the value and take things low-key, but most people will be kicking up sand at the beach bar every night. Premium Bures have private decks and, while nothing on the small island is far from the water, a "beach wing" has six bures right on the sand. **Pros:** Fiji's biggest party; great beach; friendly staff. **Cons:** A single, huge dorm; bar-centric social life. ✉*Beachcomber Island* ☎*666–1500* ⊕*www.beach comberfiji.com* ⇌*16 rooms, 22 bures, 1 dorm* ⚐*In-room: no a/c, no phone, no TV. In-hotel: restaurant, bar, pool,*

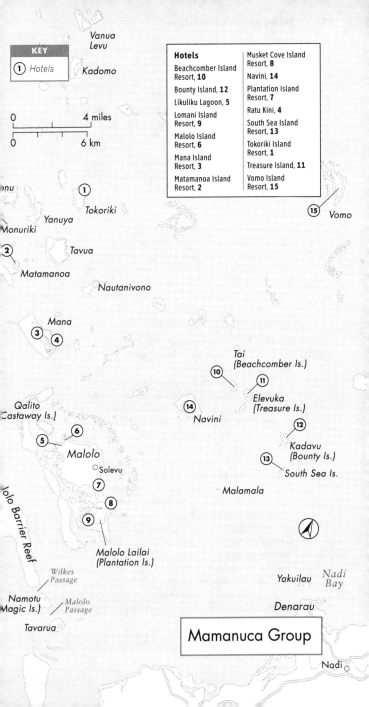

KEY

(1) *Hotels*

0 ——— 4 miles
0 ——— 6 km

Hotels

Beachcomber Island Resort, **10**

Bounty Island, **12**

Likuliku Lagoon, **5**

Lomani Island Resort, **9**

Malolo Island Resort, **6**

Mana Island Resort, **3**

Matamanoa Island Resort, **2**

Musket Cove Island Resort, **8**

Navini, **14**

Plantation Island Resort, **7**

Ratu Kini, **4**

South Sea Island Resort, **13**

Tokoriki Island Resort, **1**

Treasure Island, **11**

Vomo Island Resort, **15**

Vanua Levu

Kadomo

nu

(1)
Tokoriki

Yanuya

Monuriki

(2)
Tavua

Matamanoa

Nautanivono

Mana
(3) (4)

Tai
(Beachcomber Is.)

(10)
(11)
Elevuka
(Treasure Is.)

(14)
Navini

(12)
Kadavu
(Bounty Is.)

(13)
South Sea Is.

Qalito
Castaway Is.)

(6)
(5)
Malolo

○*Solevu*

(7)

(8)

(9)

Malamala

Malolo Lailai
(Plantation Is.)

lolo Barrier Reef

Wilkes
Passage

Namotu
Magic Is.)

Malolo
Passage

Tavarua

(15)
Vomo

Yakuilau

Nadi
Bay

Denarau

Nadi ○

Mamanuca Group

beachfront, diving, water sports, public Internet, airport shuttle ☰*AE, DC, MC, V* ⊚❘*FAP.*

$ ☲**Bounty Island.** "Uncomplicated, unspoilt, unbelievable" is this budget resort's slogan and although the no-frills food and accommodations are quite believable, they get everything else right. A sandy path leads between the resort's small bures—although their size is practically irrelevant given the hammocks and lounge chairs just outside their doors. Dorms, the larger of which are air-conditioned, have bunk beds, no views of the beach, and extremely basic, old bathrooms but, for this island setting, the price is right. The blinding white beach leads right up to a small pool; an activities bure where you can borrow snorkels, Hobie Cats, canoes, and book motorized water sports; and a bar room with a projection screen and pool table. The buffet-style meal plan is $53 per day and includes BBQs, roasts, lovos, and curry nights. ⊠*Bounty Island* ☎*666–6999* ⊕*www.fiji-bounty.com* ⤳*22 bures, 7 dorms* ♿*In-room: no phone, refrigerator (some), no TV. In-hotel: restaurant, bar, pool, spa, beachfront, diving, water sports, laundry service, public Internet* ☰*AE, MC, V* ⊚❘*FAP.*

★ **Fodor's**Choice ☲**Likuliku Lagoon.** Bures that perch entirely over
$$$$ the water, reached by a boardwalk, and superlative cuisine make it clear that this newcomer has raised the bar for Fijian island getaways. It gets the details right, with "welcome" written in flowers and freshly laid pajamas greeting guests, his and her bath products, and in-room stereos with iPod connections. A guest lounge has a TV, DVD, and CD libraries and showers for unwinding upon arrival or throughout one's stay, and a dead-sexy "infinity pool" is shaped with little peninsulas for pairs of lounge chairs. All bures feature cozy living areas, dual bowl sinks, daybeds, stereos, and sleek polished-wood interiors; all but over-water bures have outdoor showers. Deluxe Beachfronts are steps from the water, roomier, and have private plunge pools. Over-water bures have large bed-and-living areas and a generous deck with a ladder leading down into the water, and receive a daily Chef's Canape Plate. The restaurant's masterfully prepared Asian-inspired Pacific Rim cuisine includes three-course lunches and four-course dinners, the latter with *amuse bouche* (small bite) and three choices each of appetizer, entrée, and dessert. **Pros:** Superb cuisine; excellent service; lavish rooms. **Cons:** Poor beach. ⊠*Malolo Island* ☎*672–0978, 888/946–5458 U.S.* ⊕*www.likulikulagoon.com* ⤳*45 villas* ♿*In-room: safe,*

Wi-Fi (some). In-hotel: restaurant, bars, pool, gym, spa, beachfront, diving, water sports, laundry service, public Internet, public Wi-Fi, airport shuttle, no kids under 17 ⊟*AE, MC, V* |○|*FAP.*

$$$ ⊡**Lomani Island Resort.** There's plenty of room for romance in the 12, adults-only open-plan suites, around the 35-meter pool (it's big), and along the generous beachfront. The main area of this expanded former holiday house includes reception and an outdoor restaurant overlooking the beach and pool. Complimentary activities include snorkeling, handline fishing, kayaking, and bicycling. Suites are concrete with tile floors and are done almost exclusively in white. Each features a large couch in its living room and a king-size, four-poster bamboo bed. Hibiscus suites have views from both their living and bedrooms and outdoor showers; numbers 11 and 12 are slightly closer to the sand while larger ones are set farther back on the grounds. Deluxe have larger, more stylish bathrooms but only their living rooms have ocean views. Although a stand-alone suite will be added by 2009 with four more possibly to follow, the only things there aren't room for are kids under 16. There's an à la carte restaurant specializing in seafood, and three other restaurants are within walking distance. **Pros:** Intimate setting; friendly staff. **Cons:** Can be extremely buggy at dinner; must walk to neighboring resort for landline Internet. ✉*Malolo Lailai* ☎*666–8212* ⊕*www.lomaniisland.com* �’*12 suites* ⌂*In-room: safe, refrigerator, DVD. In-hotel: restaurant, room service, bar, pool, gym, spa, beachfront, water sports, bicycles, laundry service, public Wi-Fi, no kids under 16* ⊟*AE, DC, MC, V* |○|*BP, FAP.*

WORD OF MOUTH. "The best word I can think of [for the Malolo Island Resort] is 'magical.' We had the best welcome, the best stay, and the best farewell anyone could ask for." —MarsBars

★ **Fodor's**Choice ⊡**Malolo Island Resort.** Spacious bures leading
$$$ out to a fantastic beach, three restaurants, and friendly staff make this among the Mamanucas' best. With 49 bures fanned out across a path from the beach (Ocean Views are studios; Deluxes have separate bedrooms), you can have your own space along the sand or stroll to the central beach bar or the two pretty pools for people-watching. Activities such as crab races, village trips, and dolphin safaris are announced daily on a newsletter delivered to the rooms. Keep active with banana boat rides, waterskiing, kneeboarding, and island-hopping, or unwind in the small,

serene spa in the rain forest. One restaurant combines à la carte nights with theme buffets, including a made-to-order pasta bar, while the fancier Tree Tops features Mediterranean-influenced cuisine on a rotating seven-day menu. Dietary needs are especially well-catered. **Pros:** Great beach; plenty of dining options; warm staff. **Cons:** Adult and kids' pools are next to each other. ⊠*Malolo Island* ☎*666–9192* ⊕*www.maloloisland.com* ⌨*49 bures* ⌂*In-room: no phone, refrigerator, no TV. In-hotel: 3 restaurants, bars, 2 pools, spa, beachfront, diving, water sports, children's programs (ages 4–12), laundry service, public Internet, airport shuttle* ⊟*AE, MC, V* ⃝*EP, FAP.*

$$–$$$ ⊡**Mana Island Resort.** One of the Mamanucas' more upscale family resorts, Mana has a fabulous beach, well-appointed bures, and stylish pools. The resort's location on the tip of the island allows it to create two separate atmospheres: South Beach has motorized water sports, a restaurant, and ferry dock while quieter North Beach has a Jacuzzi spilling into an adults' "infinity pool" overlooking more tranquil beachfront. Six distinct room categories range from Island Bures with king-size beds, outdoor stonewall showers, and garden views, to large studio-style Beachfront Bures with separate Jacuzzi rooms leading out to a deck overlooking the beach. One restaurant features none-too-creative á la carte fare while the other offers three three-course Continental–Pacific Rim–fusion menus. **Pros:** Superb beach; lots of space and facilities. **Cons:** Mediocre food. ⊠*Mana Island* ☎*665–0423* ⊕*www.manafiji.com* ⌨*150 rooms* ⌂*In-room: safe, refrigerator, no TV. In-hotel: 2 restaurants, bars, tennis courts, 2 pools, spa, beachfront, diving, water sports, children's programs (ages 3–12)* ⊟*AE, DC, MC, V* ⃝*BP, FAP.*

$$–$$$ ⊡**Matamanoa Island Resort.** Its boutique size, stunning "infinity pool," and included full breakfast and optional three-course "table d'hote" menu make this one of the Mamanucas' classiest mid-range operations. The full range of motorized and nonmotorized water sports are available, as is diving with an in-house branch of Viti Watersports. Bures fringe a fantastic white-sand beach, each with king-size beds, bathrooms with granite counters and dual sinks, and patios. The far less–expensive Gardenview Hotel Rooms sleep two and have a queen-size bed, single sink, and are without patios or personal safes. **Pros:** Size is intimate but allows room to blend in; gorgeous beach; reasonably priced and diverse à la carte menus. **Cons:**

Gardenview hotel rooms somewhat bland. ⊠*Matamanoa Island* ☎*672–3620* ⊕*www.matamanoa.com* ⇆*13 rooms, 20 bures* ⌂*In-room: no phone, safe (some), refrigerator, no TV. In-hotel: 1 restaurant, bars, pool, spa, beachfront, diving, water sports, laundry service, public Internet, no kids under 12* ⊟*AE, MC, V* ⍩*BP, MAP, FAP.*

$$$ 🏨**Musket Cove Island Resort.** This expansive, laid-back resort is best understood as a resort town—literally. Many guests rent bicycles and a general store sells groceries, including meats to cook at barbecues around the property. A variety of water sports such as windsurfing, diving, snorkeling, and kayaking are on offer, and the Australian owners' love of sailing is evident in the day-cruise, yacht-chartering, game-fishing, and Hobie Cat–sailing options. The five room categories all feature king-size beds and range from duplex Garden Bures to newly renovated Beachfront Bures to the 10 Armstrong Island Villas. The villas share a separate pool and BBQ and have their own decks on the water surrounding their circular private island, a bridge apart from the resort. The restaurant menu is upscale Continental with a seafood bent. **Pros:** Exceptional sense of space and leisure; great boating and fishing options; chance to self-cater. **Cons:** Sprawling property can seem disconnected. ⊠*Malolo Lailai Island* ☎*664–0805* ⊕*www.musketcove fiji.com* ⇆*6 rooms, 32 bures, 16 villas* ⌂*In-room: no a/c (some), no phone (some), safe, kitchen (some), refrigerator, DVD (some), no TV (some). In-hotel: 2 restaurants, bars, pools, spa, beachfront, diving, water sports, bicycles, laundry facilities, public Internet, airport shuttle, no kids under 10* ⊟*AE, DC, MC, V* ⍩*EP.*

WORD OF MOUTH. "[Navini is] a very relaxing place to visit…Fantastic reef just off the beach, brilliant staff, great weather. What more could you ask for." –Gtnzo7

$$$ 🏨**Navini.** An owner-managed 6-acre private island resort, ★ Navini offers fantastic snorkeling in its protected marine sanctuary, a multitude of dining options as a nod to those on extended stays, and beachfront digs for its guests. There are also complimentary fishing, snorkeling, and village trips. Diving can be arranged through Subsurface Fiji, and boat charters for cruising or big-game fishing are also available. All bures are tropically appointed with queen-size beds and verandas. Premiers sleep up to three, two-room bures sleep up to five, and Deluxe/Honeymoon bures are for couples; the latter two have hot tubs. You choose either

a two- or three-meal plan for $88–$98 (less for children). Three-course lunches include a choice of sandwich or hot dish and four-course dinners include a choice between three meats and a fish entrée from a truly eclectic menu. **Pros:** Lavish staff-guest ratio; personalized experience; outstanding snorkeling. **Cons:** Bure decor could use an upgrade; meal plan not included in rate. ⊠*Navini Island* ☎*666–2188, 877/301–8772 in U.S.* ⊕*www.navinifiji.com. fj* ⟋*10 bures* ⚹*In room: no a/c, no phone, refrigerator, no TV. In-hotel: restaurant, room service, bar, beachfront, diving, water sports, public Internet, airport transfers* ▭*AE, MC, V* ⏏*MAP, FAP.*

$$–$$$ 🖭**Plantation Island Resort.** A water sports–packed sheltered ⟳ lagoon nudging 7 km (4 mi) of white-sand beach, loads of activities, and a kids' pool with waterslide keep young families returning to this 23-acre tropical playground. Waterskiing, sailing, banana boat rides, kayaking, snorkeling, and island-hopping keep the waterfront abuzz with bathing-suit clad guests, who can munch on something light from the snack bar or get a caffeine-charge at the sandy-floored Cocohut. With three pools (including one quieter "infinity pool" for the grown-ups), minigolf, 9-hole, tennis, and three places to eat, Mom and Dad will want to pack walkie-talkies along with the suntan lotion. The five room categories are sufficient if not particularly stylish, although the top-end Beachfront Bures are on the gorgeous beach. Deluxe Garden Terraces, while newer and equipped with small living areas, are much farther from the beach than the less-expensive Studio Garden Bures, some of which face the sand while others view it side-on. Two kids under 16 stay free with two parents. **Pros:** Something for everyone; large menus and $30 lunch specials; great beach. **Cons:** Old Copra Shed restaurant can be loud and feel crowded; must pay for snorkel gear. ⊠*Malolo Lailai* ☎*666–9333* ⊕*www.plantationisland.com* ⟋*192 rooms* ⚹*In-room: safe, refrigerator, no TV. In-hotel: 2 restaurants, bars, golf course, tennis courts, 3 pools, spa, beachfront, diving, water sports, no elevator, children's programs (ages 4 and up), laundry facilities, public Internet, airport shuttle* ▭*AE, DC, MC, V* ⏏*EP.*

$ 🖭**Ratu Kini.** The best in a tight string of hostels sharing the gorgeous beaches of Mana Island is Ratukini, the first one to the right as you come off the pier. Young budget-oriented travelers snorkel, dive, fish, play volleyball, and laze in the sand between hearty buffet-style meals in the open-air dining room overlooking the water. Every Thursday there's a *lovo* (traditional feast cooked in an underground oven) and traditional performance. You can sleep in basic bunk-bed dorms, twin rooms with shared facilities, double rooms, or a family bure, or you can camp. Staying here is a cheap way for social creatures to enjoy one of the Mamanucas' best beaches. Bring enough cash unless you don't mind paying a fee for credit cards. **Pros:** Great beach; friendly atmosphere. **Cons:** Basic meals and accommodations. ⊠*Mana Island* ☎*672–1959* ⊕*www.ratukini.com* ⤳*10 rooms, 3 dorms, camping* ⚬*In-room: no a/c, no phone, no TV. In-hotel: restaurant, bar, beachfront, diving, water sports* ⊟*MC, V* ⏍*FAP.*

3

$ 🚻**South Sea Island Resort.** This is about as close as you can get to enjoying a private tropical island for less than $100 a night. Owned by South Sea Cruises, the 4-acre island hostel has a single indoor guest space for the bar and "office," and a covered outdoor picnic dining area. Above these is a 32-bed dorm, including a couple of semi-private six-bed enclaves and two bathrooms. Most visitors arrive for a couple of nights as part of an 11-night Awesome Adventures package or as one of up to 300 day-trippers who scuba dive, sail, kayak, dip in the small pool, or lay out on the pretty beach. When the sand settles at night, those remaining enjoy a hearty two-course buffet-style dinner of curry, stir-fry chicken, steamed fish or the like, wager on which crab will race out of the circle first, and play simple games conducive to drinking and flirting. **Pros:** Easy to meet people; tiny island feel; beautiful beach. **Cons:** High guest turnover; can get boring after a couple of nights; no privacy. ⊠*South Sea Island* ☎*675–0500* ⊕*www.ssc.com. fj* ⤳*1 dorm* ⚬*In-room: no a/c, no phone, no TV. In-hotel: restaurant, bar, pool, spa, beachfront, diving, water sports* ⊟*AE, MC, V* ⏍*FAP.*

★ Fodor'sChoice   🚻**Tokoriki Island Resort.** Honeymooners and
$$$$ couples swoon over the privacy, beautiful grounds, and excellent service at this lavish special-occasion resort. No cell-phone reception and no clocks in the rooms (let alone TVs or Internet) make it all the easier for guests to focus on the gorgeous environs and each other. Diving, snorkeling, island picnic trips, sunset cruises, and sand volleyball keep you entranced in daylight, and a tennis court can also be lighted for night play. Come dinnertime, it's hard to imagine a more exquisite setting than one of the well-spaced, white-linen-dressed tables bordering the gorgeous "infinity

pool," with views past Tiki lamps reflected in the water to palm trees silhouetted against the sea. The excellent Continental fare, including a choice of six entrées at dinner, is accompanied by the sound of crashing waves. Deluxe bures are polished dark-wood affairs with spacious bathrooms featuring both walk-in indoor showers and beautiful outdoor ones. Double doors open onto small decks and the sand. Sunset Pool Villas are larger with outdoor daybeds next to private "infinity pools" and total privacy up to a shared short lawn sloping away to the beach. **Pros:** Lavish accommodations; great staff; plenty of selection at meals. **Cons:** Mediocre beach; Deluxe bures may be too dark for some tastes; $1/minute Internet. ✉ *Tokoriki Island* ☎ *672–5926, 818/731–6106 in U.S.* ⊕ *www.tokoriki.com* ⌂ *34 bures* ⌂ *In-room: no phone, safe, refrigerator, no TV. In-hotel: restaurant, room service, bar, tennis court, 2 pools, spa, beachfront, diving, water sports, laundry service, public Internet, no kids under 12* ☰ *AE, DC, MC, V* ⧉ *EP, FAP.*

$$$ ⊠ **Treasure Island.** It's easy to understand why this Fiji icon ☺ has been a family-favorite for more than three decades. The 66 bures practically ring the 14.5-acre island, each with a beeline right to the marvelous beach. Nightly entertainment such as fire dancing, a "Fancy Hat competition," and karaoke foster the family friendliness while 12-hole minigolf and a freshwater pool are classic child-pleasers. From deep-sea fishing to Hobie Cat-sailing, there's also a full water sports arsenal on hand. Bures, reminiscent of international hotel rooms, are comfortable, each with a queen and single bed and a porch; duplexes are also available. Dining options include a full à la carte menu, with fare such as linguine de mare and aged sirloin beef with béarnaise sauce, in-between three theme nights. A second restaurant specializes in flambé. You can also dine in a "Sunset" bure or by the pool, and banquets are held on the beach. **Pros:** Exceptional beach; reasonable international menu; colorful activities. **Cons:** Hotel room–esque bures. ✉ *Treasure Island* ☎ *666–6999* ⊕ *www.fiji-treasure. com* ⌂ *66 bures* ⌂ *In-room: no phone, refrigerator, no TV. In-hotel: 2 restaurants, bars, tennis court, pool, gym, spa, beachfront, diving, water sports, children's programs (ages 3 and up), laundry facilities, laundry service, public Internet* ☰ *AE, DC, MC, V* ⧉ *EP, FAP, MAP.*

$$$$ ⊠ **Vomo Island Resort.** This private island resort is everything its price tag would imply—a lavish all-inclusive, a setting

for haute cuisine, a photo shoot waiting to happen—and one thing it wouldn't: it's child-friendly. For $70.50 a night, kids—ages 4–14—can kayak to a local cay, windsurf, sail, kayak, and snorkel; children under 4 are free. Regardless of whether the little athlete comes along, the grown ones will be satiated by 9-hole pitch-and-putt golf course, tennis, volleyball, badminton, and croquet. Lounge chairs line the pool, the meal-time setting for those foregoing the opportunity to eat on a beachside platform or their personal deck. The all-inclusive menu presents such globe-spanning dishes as potato gnocchi, Thai green curry, and New Zealand beef striploin, all lavishly accompanied. Hillside Villas are 640-square-feet (60 square meters) with separate living areas and bedrooms and Jacuzzis. Beachfront Villas have the same plus outdoor dining areas and are steps from the sand. There's also a two-bedroom villa. **Pros:** Fantastic views throughout; lavish accommodations; excellent cuisine. **Cons:** Resort could almost be on any tropical island. ✉*Vomo Island* ☎666–7955 ⊕*www.vomofiji.com* ➪29 *villas* ⌂*In-room: refrigerator, no TV (some), ethernet. In-hotel: restaurant, room service, bars, golf course, tennis court, pool, spa, beachfront, water sports, laundry service, airport shuttle* ▤*AE, DC, MC, V* ⋈*FAP.*

SPORTS & THE OUTDOORS

DAY CRUISES

Seaspray Day Cruise (☎675–0500 ⊕*www.ssc.com.fj*) sails guests on an 83-foot twin-mast schooner to Monuriki, as well as to a village on quiet Yanuya Island for a kava ceremony and a BBQ lunch. Unlimited drinks on board, snorkeling gear, and transfers from Nadi and Coral Coast hotels are provided. The ship departs Denarau Marina at 9 and returns at 6. It costs $175 for adults and $95 for children from Denarau; it's cheaper if you're picked up from an island in the Mamanucas farther out.

FISHING

Subsurface Fiji (☎666–6738 ⊕*www.subsurfacefiji.com*). A morning of game-fishing or two to three hours of sportfishing for up to four people costs $160 per hour.

MOTORIZED WATER SPORTS

Chances are, **Subsurface Fiji** (☎666–6738 ⊕*www.subsurface-fiji.com*) runs the motorized water sports at your resort. Water-skiing, wake-boarding, and knee-boarding are $60–$80, banana boat rides are $20 per person and require at least three people, and Jet Ski rentals are $80 for 15 minutes, $140 for 30 minutes, and $240 for an hour.

SCUBA DIVING

The Mamanucas' most famous sites include Supermarket, where divers encounter Grey reef, White tip reef, and Black tip reef sharks. At Gotham City, a large array of fish and brilliant soft corals reside among three pinnacles. You can also see parts of a crashed B26 Bomber and the swim-throughs and Clown fish garden of Plantation Pinnacle, patrolled by Grey reef sharks and occasional barracuda. There are sites for every level of experience and the fantastic visibility here (up to 50 meters) makes this a great place to learn. Nearly all Mamanuca Islands resorts have in-house operations or nearby companies they work with.

The Mamanucas' most popular dive company is **Subsurface Fiji** (☎666–6738 ⊕*www.subsurfacefiji.com*), a PADI-certified company that runs the operations at 17 resorts, including a few on Viti Levu. The company offers the full range of courses and nitrox is available. It visits 44 sites on the Malolo Barrier and outer barrier reefs. The diverse sites offer wreck dives, coral walls, swim-throughs, and a variety of coral, small and pelagic fish, and sharks. Prices range from $120 for one dive to $690 for a four-dive open-water course including equipment.

Reef Safari (⊕*www.reefsafari.com.fj*) has bases at South Sea Island and Amunuca Island Resort on Tokoriki. A one-tank dive costs $95, a two-tank dive costs $180, and night dives cost $115. You can take an open-water course, including six dives, at South Sea Island for $545.

SURFING

From Malolo Lailai (Plantation Island, Lomani Island, and Musket Cove resorts), a local nicknamed **Small John** takes surfers out to Namotu Island to surf Wilkes Passage. It's $40 per person or $30 per person for a group of 5–8. On Saturday, he's sometimes able to ferry surfers to the renowned Cloudbreak, featured in the movie *The Endless Summer 2,* which is closed to all but guests of Tavarua Island Resort the rest of the week.

YASAWA ISLANDS

4 hours by ferry from Nadi to Yaqeta in the group's middle

The nearest Yasawa Island is about 40 km (25 mi) and a two-hour South Sea ferry ride from Nadi, and the group embraces its remoteness over the length of its 80 km (50 mi). The 20 islands are generally more rugged, the villages more traditional, and the resorts smaller and more intimate than those of the Mamanucas. Most resorts are toward the northern end of the group on Tavewa, Nanuya Lailai, and Nacula. Set amid this cluster is the famed Blue Lagoon, film location for the 1980 remake of the eponymous movie. Its crystal clear waters, fringing reefs, and sea life, including angelfish, butterfly fish, octopi, and green and hawksbill turtles have earned the northern end the reputation of being one of the most idyllic parts of the group often likened to "paradise." The islands here are generally larger than those in the Mamanucas and more luscious, as their soaring volcanic peaks attract rain. On some of the islands, dense rain forests inhabited by skittish land crabs encroach upon tidal stretches of sand, with sporadic volcanic rock partitions. Dive sites here include canyons and swim-throughs amid a range of hard and soft coral.

EXPLORING THE YASAWA ISLANDS

Depending on where you stay and what excursions you make, you might see the famed Blue Lagoon through your bedroom window or on a trip that might even entail swimming in the dramatic Sawa-I-Lau caves featured in the film. A few of the budget properties on Tavewa and Nacula are visible across a channel from each other but island-hopping is uncommon, with the majority of resorts existing in largely self-sufficient, eco-friendly worlds of their own. You'll enjoy a high degree of privacy out here.

WHERE TO STAY & EAT

$$ **Nanuya Island Resort.** A rare mid-range option in the Yasawas, Nanuya offers 12 spacious, comfortable accommodations, good food, and wonderfully personable staff. There are good snorkeling off the beach, and highly personalized diving, fishing, kayaking, and cave-swimming a 45-minute ride north. Yes, you're sharing the "Blue Lagoon" with the lavish Turtle Island resort for approximately 1/35th of the price. The 180-square-foot Deluxe Villas each have

Yasawa Group

SOUTH PACIFIC
OCEAN

KEY

① *Hotels*

Yawini
Yasawairara ○

Yasawa ①
✈

Vawa ○
○ Bukama

○ Nabukeru
Sawa-i-lau
○ Navotua

Tamusua Passage

Nacula

Nacula ○

Sawa-I-Lau Caves
Tavewa ◆ ○ Nasisili

Blue Lagoon
② *Nanuya Laila*
Matacawa Levu
③ *Turtle Island (Nanuya Levu)*
Vuake ○

Matayalevu ④
Yaqeta

Naivalavala Passage

Bligh Water

Gunu ○ ○ Somosomo

Sono ○ *Naviti*

Ethel Reefs

0 ———————— 20 mi
0 ———————— 20 km

Naukacuvu
Drawaga
Nanuya Balavu
Narara
Nacilau Point
Koromasoli Point
⑤ Wayalevu ○
Likuliku Bay *Waya*
Yalobi ○ ○ Natawa
○ Namara
Wawasewa

Hotels
Nanuya Island Resort, **2**
Navutu Stars Resort, **4**
Octopus Resort, **5**
Turtle Island Resort, **3**
Yasawa Island Resort, **1**

a queen- and two single beds and pretty stone-wall semi-outdoor showers. The cheaper Traditional Tree Houses are set into the hills and sleep two in a double or two single beds. Continental breakfast is included; there's an all-day dining menu and the numerous à la carte dinner options might include grilled-beef fillet with salad, fries, and hollandaise sauce or pan-seared hapuku on sun-dried tomatoes, bok choy, and green tea noodles. **Pros:** Fantastic staff; intimate "Blue Lagoon" setting; a menu to satiate meat eaters and vegetarians. **Cons:** No accommodations right on the beach. ⊠*Nanuya Lailai* ☎*666–7633, 666–6322* ⊕*www.nanuyafiji.com* ⇆*12 bures* ⚏*In-room: no a/c, no phone, refrigerator, no TV. In-hotel: restaurant, bar, spa, beachfront, diving, water sports, laundry service, public Internet* ⊟*AE, DC, MC, V* ⚏⦿*CP.*

★ **Fodors**Choice ⊺ **Navutu Stars Resort.** A cosmopolitan Italian
$$$–$$$$ couple built this resort as an escape for the "stressed" and, with just nine romantically appointed bures fringing a quintessential Yasawa shore, couples are certain to recover the love lost during the daily grind. When guests aren't relaxing on their daybeds, lounge chairs, or hammocks (Beachfront bures have all three), they can take guided snorkeling tours, island-hop, dive with a local operator, visit a village, fish, take guided walks, kayak, or hike to hilltops. All bures have 26-foot ceilings, king-size beds, dual stone sinks, and outdoor daybeds. Beachfronts are well-spaced with high bamboo borders; each has a wall of French doors opening onto a thatch-covered deck just shy of the sand and the lagoon. The larger Grand Bures are built on rocky outcrops on a separate bay, have large tubs in their living rooms, and steps leading down to the beach. Á la carte menus feature reasonably priced Mediterranean fare and a meal plan is also available. **Pros:** Privacy; personalized experience; plenty of selection at meals. **Cons:** Little local cuisine. ⊠*Yaqeta Island* ☎*664–0553* ⊕*www. navutustarsfiji.com* ⇆*9 bures* ⚏*In-room: no a/c, no phone, no TV. In-hotel: restaurant, room service, bars, pool, spa, beachfront, water sports, laundry service, public Internet, airport shuttle, no kids under 12* ⊟*MC, V* ⚏⦿*CP, FAP.*

★ **Fodors**Choice ⊺ **Octopus Resort.** The best budget resort west
$ of the mainland is seated on dreamy Likuliku Bay in the southern Yasawas, and doesn't act its price. The cheapest bures have queen-size beds and balconies and even dormers get bath and beach towels. Hiking, hand-line fishing, village visits, and island-hopping are offered each week and evening activities include mekes, crab races, beachside party

games, and a weekly film-showing. Five great-value accommodation options range from a well-maintained nonbunked
13-bed dorm (rare for Fiji) to two beachfront rooms with
open-air bathrooms on the sand, to an air-conditioned room
in a three-bedroom lodge. A mandatory $33 per day meal
plan entails three-course dinners emphasizing seafood in
traditional dishes served with local vegetables; lunch usually includes sandwiches and pizzas. There are also a kids'
menu, youngster activities, and babysitters on-call. **Pros:**
Gorgeous setting; warm and engaging staff; activity-packed.
Cons: Vegetarians won't find the greatest range of dinner.
✉ *Waya Island* ☎*666–6337* ⊕*www.octopusresort.com*
🛏*20 bures, 1 lodge, 2 rooms, 5 bungalows, 1dorm* ♿*In-
room: no a/c (some), no phone, no TV. In-hotel: restaurant,
bar, beachfront, diving, water sports, laundry service, public
Internet, airport shuttle* ▤*MC, V* ⊧⊙⊧*FAP.*

$$$$ 🏝**Turtle Island Resort.** Take a look at Fiji's original ultraluxury resort by the numbers: 100 staff for a maximum
of 14 guests, 14 beaches, 1,000-square-foot bures and 1
personal "Bure Mama" per couple, who tends to all needs
and uses a digital camera, with guests' permission, to craft
a photo album for them to take home. Everything from
scuba diving to champagne-and-lobster picnics on reserved
beaches is included, with the exception of spa treatments.
The expansive bures feature 21-foot high ceilings, dual
showerheads, floor-to-ceiling windows, four-poster king-
size beds and private verandas with daybed and fish ponds
leading out to the famed Blue Lagoon. Grand bures have jet-
ted hot tubs, and the elevated Vonu Point cottage has even
greater privacy and the ultimate view. Á la carte breakfasts
are served on the sand, chef's choice three-course lunches
are taken around the island (if not ordered from a special
picnic lunch menu), and communal dinners are also chef's
choice, although guests can make requests or dine alone.
There's a six-night minimum stay. **Pros:** Ultimate pamper-
ing; 14 beaches to yourself; menus designed by Jacques
Reymond. **Cons:** Little selection at meals. ✉*Turtle/Nanuya
Levu Island* ☎*800/255–4347 in the US*⊕*www.turtlefiji.
com* 🛏*14 bures* ♿*In-room: no a/c, no phone, refrigerator
(some), no TV. In-hotel: restaurant, bar, spa, beachfront,
diving, water sports, bicycles, laundry service, public Internet, airport shuttle, no kids* ▤*AE, MC, V* ⊧⊙⊧*AI.*

WORD OF MOUTH. "For snorkeling, you can't beat Fiji. We spent a
week at Yasawa Island Resort, and found the swimming, beach,
and snorkeling outstanding." —Angler973

★ **Fodor'sChoice** 🏨 **Yasawa Island Resort.** Picnic excursions to one
$$$$ of 11 deserted beaches and excellent in-house diving and
high-tech game fishing are among the first-rate options
at this boutique resort. The remote region's resistance to
modernism means guests can visit especially traditional villages and see a particularly meaningful *meke* (traditional
dances). A world-class Baravi spa commands magnificent
ocean views from beneath a thatched roof at the water's
edge. All the open-plan bures are airy, modern twists on
the Fijian style set on the beach. Each has indoor and outdoor showers and dual sinks. Deluxes are split-level with
larger lounge areas and more covered deck space including
two daybeds and a hammock. There are also a two-bedroom bure and a Honeymoon bure with an outdoor dining
area and private pool. Owner Garth Downey's wine cellar
compliments superb contemporary international cuisine
served at two-course lunches and three-course dinners.
Pros: Fantastic spa; excellent and varied selection at meals;
privacy. **Cons:** Long ferry ride to get here. ⊠ *Yasawa Island*
☎*672–2266* ⊕*www.yasawa.com* ⌁*18 bures* ⌂*In-room:
no TV. In-hotel: restaurant, room service, bars, tennis, spa,
beachfront, diving, water sports, laundry service, public
Internet, airport shuttle, no kids under 13 except in Dec.,
Jan., and June 15–July 15* ☰*AE, DC, MC, V* ⎕*FAP.*

SPORTS & THE OUTDOORS

Although it's possible to arrange a trip to a secluded beach
from the Mamanucas' most romantic resorts, isolated
patches of sand and surf lie rampant—okay, laze lethar-
gically—throughout the northern islands. Whether you
go for a full day or a few hours of picnic lunching, many
resorts here will whisk you to your own private stretch
of paradise.

CRUISES

Captain Cook Cruises (☎*670–1823* ⊕*www.captaincook.com.
au*) offers Yasawa Island cruises aboard its 120-passenger
MV *Reef Escape* with prices including accommodation,
meals, snorkeling equipment, and some activities. You can
opt for four-bunk cabins or staterooms with floor-to-ceiling
windows opening onto the outside deck. Breakfast includes
a hot and cold buffet; some lunches are à la carte, some are
buffet; dinners are mostly three-course à la carte menus.

The "3 Night Southern Yasawa Islands" cruise and the
"4 Night Northern Yasawa Islands" cruise visit beautiful

white-sand beaches, a village for a traditional ceremony, and snorkeling and diving sites. The "7 Night Northern Fiji Dateline Tour" sets sail from Nadi and stops at an island in the Yasawas, two islands on Viti Levu's northern coast, the old capital of Levuka in the Lomaiviti Group, Savusavu on Vanua Levu, the waterfalls in Taveuni's Bouma National Heritage Park, the international dateline and a third island off Viti Levu. The company also offers three- and four-day "Sailing Safaris" through the Yasawas aboard a 108-foot schooner. Itineraries include snorkeling with manta rays, fishing, and village visits. Other options include day cruises and lunch and dinner cruises, all leaving from Denarau Marina on Viti Levu.

Awesome Adventures (✉*Denarau Marina* ☎*675–0499* ⊕*www.awesomefiji.com*) offers all-inclusive packages in collaboration with budget resorts throughout the two island chains. Popular with young budget travelers, these range from 5 days/4 nights spent on two islands to a 12 day/11 night tour encapsulating five islands and a live-aboard cruise. A "Full-Monty" option throws in excursions to caves, sailing day trips, introductory scuba dives, etc. Each package departs daily, so you'll be sharing a ferry and buffet lines for the next 5–12 days with the same people. Most people who opt for these itineraries are social, with some traveling solo: for the best chance to bond with fellow travelers, ask your booking agent for a popular start date. Conversely, although you cannot know how many people will already be on the islands you'll be visiting or arriving on the second day, you can grant yourself more privacy by requesting a less-popular start date. The closer to the date you book, the better an idea they should have.

HIKING

Waya Island in the southern Yasawas has some of the group's best trails, offering dramatic ridge-line views amid knee-high grass. Nearby Wayasewa ("Little Waya") also has great walking trails as does Nacula, the group's third-largest island. Most of the resorts offer good hiking. At many, you can also visit a local village.

SCUBA DIVING

In keeping with the group's sense of adventure are the Yasawas' dive sites, characterized by swim-throughs and canyons and a population of sharks and rays. Sites include a steam ship wreck from the early 1900s with resident eels, a winding canyon at "Whiskeys Reef," and "Turtle Rock," home to stingrays, sharks, and one of the best places in the country to spot turtles. Unusual for the "soft coral capital of the world," as Fiji is known, are a couple of sites dominated by intricate hard coral features, which make for exciting navigating. Nearly all Yasawa Islands resorts have in-house operations or nearby companies they work with.

Offering free transfers to and from Turtle Island as well as many of the Yasawas' budget resorts, **West Side Water Sports** (⊕*www.yasawa-dive.com*) visits 20 sites within a 10-mi radius of Nanua Lailai using two custom-built, 30-foot and 37-foot boats. A one-tank dive costs $110, a two-tank dive $165, and a PADI Open Water Course $625.

Reef Safari (⊕*www.reefsafari.com.fj*) has a base at Manta-ray Island Resort. A one-tank dive costs $95, a two-tank dive costs $180, and night dives cost $115. You can take an open-water course including six dives at Manta Ray for $545 or at Nananu Lodge for $465.

MAMANUCAS & YASAWAS ESSENTIALS

TRANSPORTATION

BY AIR

Coral Air's seaplane, based out of Nadi Airport, can be chartered for sightseeing tours and will likely do island transfers as well. PacificSun flies between Nadi and Malolo Lailai Island, where there's an airstrip between Plantation Island and Musket Cove resorts, four times a day. Turtle Airways offers seaplane charters between Nadi and Turtle Island Resort for US $888 per couple. Arrangements can be made to charter a flight to another resort.

Island Hoppers runs helicopter charters to the Mamanucas from Nadi Airport, Denarau Island, and a few Coral Coast resorts. A minimum of two people is required and only 33 lbs (15 kg) of baggage are allowed per person.

Pacific Island Seaplanes offers chartered seaplane flights between Nadi and anywhere in Fiji and will land right in front of the resort.

See Air Travel, in Essentials in Viti Levu for information on international flights to Nadi.

Air Contacts Coral Air (☎672–4490 ⊕ www.coralair.com). **Island Hoppers** (☎672–0410 ⊕ www.helicopters.com.fj). **Pacific Island Seaplanes** (☎672–5644 ⊕ www.fijiseaplanes.com). **Pacific Sun** (☎672–0888, 310/568–8676 in U.S. ⊕ www.pacificsun.com.fj). **Turtle Airways** (☎672–1888, 360/256–8116 in U.S. ⊕ www. turtleairways.com).

BY BOAT

The vast majority of people heading for the Yasawas do so aboard Awesome Adventures' large yellow luxury cata-maran. Prices range $90–$110 each way from Denarau off Viti Levu to the various islands. Add $20–$35 for a seat in the Captains Lounge including unlimited beer, wine, and soda. A "Bula Pass" grants one round-trip ferry transfer to the Yasawas and unlimited trips between the islands over the allotted number of days. However, the ferry only makes one round-trip out to the islands per day. A 7-day pass is $269 and a 21-day is $419. Trips booked in advance include coach transfers from some Nadi hotels.

Guests of Plantation Island, Lomani, and Musket Cove as well as day-trippers can take the luxury catamaran Malolo Cat to the island Malolo Lailai. Adult fares are $55 round-trip, including transfers from Nadi Airport or area hotels.

Anyone heading to the Mamanucas will more than likely board one of South Seas Cruises' two large luxury cata-marans. The staff on-board handle passengers' luggage, and one catamaran has TVs showing movies. South Seas runs seven routes daily through the island group, and most resorts advise guests as to which to take and the pricing. For $20 extra, the Captains Lounge has more comfortable seating and unlimited beer, wine, and soft drinks.

Boat Contacts Awesome Adventures (✉ Denarau Marina ☎675–0499 ⊕ www.awesomefiji.com) **Malolo Cat** (✉ Denarau Marina ☎672–2444 Plantation Island, 672–2488 Musket Cove). **South Seas Cruises** (✉ Denarau Marina ☎675–0500 ⊕ www.ssc.com.fj).

CONTACTS & RESOURCES

VISITOR INFORMATION

Neither island group has a tourist office. *See Visitor infor-mation, in Fiji Essentials for information on Fiji's tour-ism offices.*

Lomaiviti
Group

4

Written
by Robert
Brenner

A 15-MINUTE FLIGHT OR SHORT BOAT RIDE EAST OF Suva, the Lomaiviti Group is a world away. The group is comprised of nine rugged main islands and a few smaller ones dotting the Pacific Ocean and the Koro Sea. Most of the islands are home to pre-European villages. A 200-meter cliff called "Chieftain's Leap" on Wakaya Island was the jumping point for a chief and many of his followers who faced capture by advancing enemies in 1848. The island is now owned by Fiji Water mogul David Gilmour and is the site of one of the country's most exclusive resorts. On Leleuvia, guests can walk from the small rustic resort to a large metal "Kannibal Pot" in the middle of the island.

It's a long, bumpy ride from the Bureta airstrip to the town of Levuka on Ovalau, the group's largest island, and every small jolt seems to knock back the hands of time. The group's only town was the British colony's capital 1874–82 and appears stuck in a time warp, with only the motorized pulse of Fiji's largest fish cannery to disturb its paint-chip wood-frame houses and affable, easygoing residents from their late-19th-century sleep. History buffs will marvel at the breathing colonial relic that is Beach Street. The culturally curious will be rapt with a day tour into the heart of Ovalau or the angelic a cappella voices of the natives at a church service on any island.

Certified divers get the chance to see Scalloped Hammerheads, Blue Ribbon eels, and many other large and small species amid little human traffic in the Lomaiviti's depths. All will appreciate the white sand and cobalt waters of the off-shore islands. Your budget and taste may lead you to a mid-range family resort, an ultraluxury hideaway frequented by celebrities, a century-old hotel, or a rustic resort with communal meals and shared bathrooms. Nowhere in Fiji will seem farther away from home than the latter two, replete with the charm and simplicity of these time-forgotten islands.

EXPLORING THE LOMAIVITI GROUP

The heart of the group is Levuka, a small commercial center anchored by a "Main Street" (in this case, Beach Street) with general stores, a few quirky but welcoming places to stay, and residents apparently free of any pressing engagements. A 20-minute to hour-and-a-half boat ride in various directions brings you to either a huge, aloof estate popular with the rich and famous or to no-frills places, the greatest strength of which is their setting and staff, or an establishment between the extremes. All offer day trips to Levuka.

ABOUT THE HOTELS & RESTAURANTS

The Lomaiviti Islands have representation at both extremes of amenities, with two properties offering bare-bones rooms and shared bathrooms and one counting international celebrities among its clientele. The mid-range is decidedly lacking; most of the quirky but welcoming Ovalau properties offer modest accommodations at prices that are reasonable if not down-right cheap.

Ovalau's four restaurants are all in Levuka and a few of the hotels there serve breakfast. Many of the private island resorts frequent Levuka's general stores in order to buy the provisions they cannot catch or grow themselves.

WHAT IT COSTS			
$	**$$**	**$$$**	**$$$$**
RESTAURANTS			
under F$10	F$10– F$20	F$20– F$30	over F$30
HOTELS*			
under F$200	F$200–F$400	F$400–F$700	over F$700
HOTELS**			
under F$300	F$300–F$500	F$500–F$800	over F$800

*EP, BP, CP **AI, FAP, MAP; Restaurant prices are per person for a main course at dinner. Hotel prices are per night for a double room in high season and may not include a 12.5% Value-Added Tax (V.A.T.) or a 5% hotel turnover tax. Hotel prices are in U.S. dollars where noted.

OVALAU

In its heyday in the mid-1800s, the island's only remaining population center was the bustling capital of Fiji. The Tui Viti or King of Fiji himself, British and American envoys, and ambitious traders traded in Fiji's assets while conmen, fugitives, and drunks milled about its wharf and filled its more than 50 bars. When the British relocated the seat of government to Suva in 1882, most everything else soon followed.

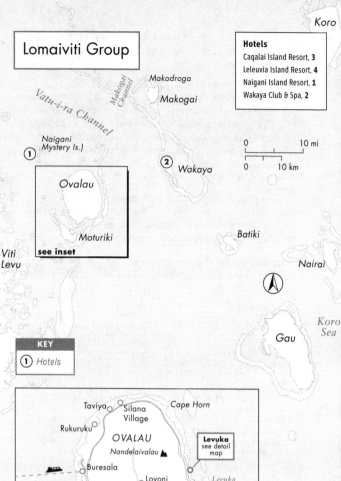

Lomaiviti Group

Hotels
Caqalai Island Resort, **3**
Leleuvia Island Resort, **4**
Naigani Island Resort, **1**
Wakaya Club & Spa, **2**

Koro

Makodroga

Makogai

Makogai Channel

Vatu-i-ra Channel

Naigani Mystery Is.)

①

② *Wakaya*

Ovalau

Moturiki

see inset

Viti Levu

Batiki

Nairai

Koro Sea

Gau

0   10 mi
0   10 km

KEY
① *Hotels*

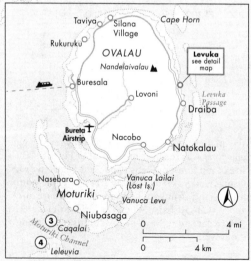

Taviya   *Silana Village*   *Cape Horn*

Rukuruku

OVALAU

Nandelaivalau ▲

Levuka see detail map

Buresala

Lovoni

Levuka Passage

Draiba

Bureta Airstrip

Nacobo

Natokalau

Nasebara

Vanuca Lailai (Lost Is.)

Moturiki

Vanuca Levu

Niubasaga

③ *Caqalai*

④ *Leleuvia*

Moturiki Channel

0   4 mi
0   4 km

LOMAIVITI'S TOP 4

Stroll along Beach Street. Few places in the world have preserved history, both physically and in spirit, the way Levuka's main street has.

Dine at the Whale's Tale. Its international cuisine belongs in Suva while its prices and cordial service are right at home.

Dive Wakaya Passage. Hammerheads, barracudas, and manta rays are regulars at the 1,000-meter drop-off here.

Visit a Village. Whether on Ovalau or one of the islands shared by a resort, the people of the Lomaiviti group are welcoming and proud of their traditions.

4

What remain today are a street of simple colonial wood-frame buildings that haven't changed in more than a century, a small, friendly population, and a rich history you can almost hear whispered in the wind. Around the island, there are scenic highland trekking and a welcoming village; off-shore are dive sites frequented by some of Fiji's largest fish species, dolphins, and whales.

EXPLORING OVALAU

The center of island life is Levuka. The attraction here is more in the almost surreal colonial atmosphere than in any one feature. A stately war memorial to locals who died in the world wars, a clock tower, and the 150-year-old Royal Hotel (Fiji's oldest) are among the sights coloring a pleasant waterfront stroll. The Fiji Museum is part of the Levuka Community Centre, which has a library and recreational facilities. Next door at Ovalau Watersports, German expat Andrea is a good person to introduce yourself to and ask any logistical questions, as she is the agent for most tour and accommodation bookings throughout the island group.

The fish cannery of the Pacific Fishing Company (PAFCO) isn't much to look at with its wharf-side containers and hulking frame, but it's the island's major employer. The town is dead on Sunday until late afternoon, which makes for a unique spectacle in and of itself, and can give visitors the impression of being on an empty movie set.

Numbers in the margin correspond to points of interest on the Levuka map.

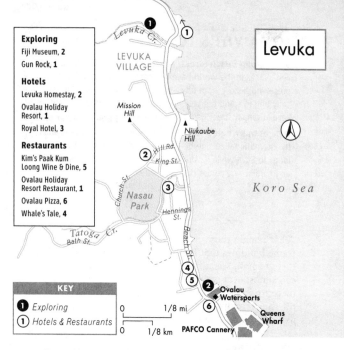

Levuka

Koro Sea

LEVUKA VILLAGE

Mission Hill

Niukaube Hill

Hill Rd.
King St.

Church St.

Nasau Park

Hennings St.

Tatoga Cr.
Bath St.

Beach St.

Ovalau Watersports

Queens Wharf

PAFCO Cannery

KEY
1 Exploring
(1) Hotels & Restaurants

0   1/8 mi
0   1/8 km

2 **Fiji Museum.** This modest branch of the Suva-based museum contains old photos of Levuka, which confirm that little of the townscape has changed since it served as Fiji's capital nearly 150 years ago. Also on display are cannibal forks and war clubs. ⊠*Levuka Community Centre, Beach St., Levuka* ☉ *Weekdays 8–1 and 2–4:30, Sat. 9–1.*

1 **Gun Rock.** This peak visible in the hills behind Beach Street bears the scars of cannonballs fired by the HMS *Havannah* in 1849. The gesture was meant to intimidate King Ratu Cakobau into treating Fiji's resident Europeans more favorably. The rock was again fired upon by a naval captain in 1874 in order to entertain a group of chiefs. You may climb the rock (it offers great harbor views) but you should first ask the Tui Levuka (local chief) or a member of his family for permission as a sign of respect. Inquire in town about the family's whereabouts. ⊹ *About 1.5 km (1 mi) north of Levuka.*

GREAT ITINERARIES

If you can't relax here, you can't relax anywhere. As one proprietor puts it, "A nap is a perfectly legitimate activity." For those with limited time, however, there are a few rewarding activities to get you moving, albeit at a "Fiji Time" pace.

IF YOU HAVE 3 DAYS

Spend your first day in Levuka. Stroll down Beach Street, talk with a few locals and take in the atmosphere. Browse through the branch of the **Fiji Museum ❷**, pop into Ovalau Watersports next door and book an island day trip, Epi's Midland Tour, or scuba diving for the following day. Dine at Whale's Tale for lunch or din-

ner…or both. On Day 2, enjoy your all-day excursion and try a new restaurant for dinner. On the third day, take another day trip if so inclined or relax at your accommodation. Head back to your favorite Levuka restaurant (or the Ovalau Holiday Resort restaurant, if you haven't tried it) for dinner.

IF YOU HAVE 5 OR 7 DAYS

Head out to one of the island resorts. At some point during your stay, make an excursion to Levuka. If you find yourself smitten, consider returning a second time to do Epi's Midland Tour. While at your resort, visit the nearest village, scuba dive, or snorkel and put the time in for a tan.

WHERE TO EAT

CHINESE

$ ✕**Kim's Paak Kum Loong Wine & Dine.** Great views over Levuka harbor from its second-floor porch seating and decent Cantonese food make a visit to this restaurant worthwhile as part of a longer stay in the area. The owners are Cantonese, their menu a classic combination of proteins, including fish and prawns, available in a range of sauces, as well as curries and vegetarian options. The five-spice chicken is a standout, if the owner's there to make it. Stately black-and-white portraits of Fijian chiefs on one wall are juxtaposed with equally grave portraits of Fijian rugby stars on another, and American country music plays in the background. ⊠*Beach St.* ☎*344–0069* ▭*No credit cards* ⊙*Mon.–Sat. 7–2 and 6–9, Sun. 6–9.*

ECLECTIC

★ **Fodor's**Choice ✕**Whale's Tale.** Levuka's best restaurant has a
$ sense of humor—its kitchen is in a thatched roof "bure" within the restaurant. Seashells daintily line the shelves on

one wall, a small collection of books rests on another and perhaps serves more than just decor as visitors spend a lot of time here once they've tasted the dishes. The menu is inexplicably international—Walu steak, pasta with capers, olives, and tomato sauce, and banana with rum crepes—and the prices, at $5 for filling lunch specials, are as outdated as the colonial-style building itself. It's too bad they aren't open for breakfast. ⊠*Beach St.* ☎*344–0235* ▭*No credit cards* ⊙*Mon.–Sat. 10–3 and 6–10.*

INDIAN

$$ ✕**Ovalau Holiday Resort Restaurant.** A soothing breeze, bamboo ceilings, and fresh frangipani and hibiscus create a cozy, tropical setting for excellent curries across the road from the beach. The blackboard menu changes every four days depending on what's in town but you can always be best on the curries. Prawn and crab are the chef's picks and all are served with roti, rice, chips, or local root vegetables. Traditional Fijian dishes will be cooked on request, sandwiches are offered at lunchtime, and everything is made-to-order. There's a full bar and, at night, the lights are turned low, the R&B up. The restaurant is about a 20-minute drive out of town. ⊠ *Ovalau Holiday Resort, Beach St., Levuka* ☎*344–0329* ▭*No credit cards* ⊙*Mon.–Sat. 6–9* AM, *noon–2, 6–9* PM, *Sun. 6–9* PM.

PIZZA

$ ✕**Ovalau Pizza.** Worthy of the island title, the pizzas here are crispy and a bit greasy—just as they were meant to be. Between classic combinations such as Hawaiian (ham and pineapple) and Fijian-styles such as Pizza of the Sea (cheese, fish, onion, and tomato), you can't go wrong. On long holiday weekends, the staff fires up the BBQ in the large side yard and grill up chicken, fish, and sausages. Their bacon and egg pizza is a popular breakfast. Cordial manager Kata Vueti plays field hockey for the women's national team, and it's clear she applies her work ethic to the kitchen. ⊠*Beach St.* ☎*344–0429* ▭*No credit cards* ⊙*Mon.–Sat. 7–2 and 6–9, Sun. 6–9.*

WHERE TO STAY

$ ▦**Levuka Homestay.** Set into a hill at the edge of Levuka are the old capital's nicest accommodations. Rooms are well-appointed and loaded with towels. They're set in a row up the hill, with the lowest commanding harbor views and three of the four equipped with air-conditioning. The included breakfast with your hosts is a major affair, during which Australia natives John and Marilyn Milesi enthusiastically share their encyclopedic knowledge of the island (just be aware that they smoke). There's no pool but there are stunning views over Levuka from one of their two comfortable living areas, a considerable book library, and a TV and DVD player for good measure. **Pros:** Close to restaurants; home-feel; hosts' knowledge. **Cons:** Home-feel; dependence on town restaurants for lunch and dinner. ✉*Levuka* ☎*344–0777* ⊕*www.levukahomestay.com* ⌕*4 rooms* ⌂*In-room: no a/c (some), no phone, refrigerator, no TV. In-hotel: laundry service, public Internet, airport shuttle* ☰*MC, V* ⭘*BAP.*

$ ☵**Ovalau Holiday Resort.** Those looking for independence and a somewhat rustic experience head to the self-contained units here, a bumpy 20-minute ride from Levuka's main drag. Coral bone paths lead to the two-bedroom bungalows spread out on a wide lawn. Each can be divided into separate units with a double and single bed or a double bed, separate kitchens (a portable gas stove is available on request) and a shared bathroom. The tidal beach across the street offers good snorkeling a little way out and tours can be arranged through Ovalau Watersports, such as a seven-hour around the island tour. You can also camp here. The resort is particularly popular with middle-age couples, although singles looking to escape come here, too. Children under 12 stay free. There's a good restaurant on-site (*see above*). **Pros:** Independence; tidal beach across the street. **Cons:** Basic furnishings; must drive into town. ✉*Beach St., Levuka* ☎*344–0329* ⊕*www.owlfiji.com/resort.htm* ⌕*14 units* ⌂*In-room: no a/c, no phone, kitchen, refrigerator. In-hotel: restaurant, bar, pool, water sports, laundry service, public Internet, airport shuttle* ☰*No credit cards* ⭘*EP.*

$ ☵**Royal Hotel.** This Fiji institution opened in 1852 and little
★ has changed since. It's the country's oldest operating hotel and is today run by the same family that founded it. The first floor has a large, comfortable parlor room, a dining room, and a dedicated billiards room where you almost expect to see ghosts chalking their cues. The bedrooms are very basic and befit the turn of the 20th century with wooden shutters on the windows, antique dressers and beds, and simple en suites. Seaside rooms, for the same price, have great waterfront views and the corner double has a large outdoor seating area. A small restaurant serves all-day breakfast and a movie is shown nightly. In the front

IF YOU LIKE

COLONIAL HISTORY

From cannon ball–scarred Gun Rock to Fiji's oldest working hotel, Levuka is teeming with remnants of the past and people who, if they can't tell you the story themselves, know someone who will.

RUSTIC ESCAPES

Two of the resorts here are overflowing with what's lovingly called "character." Regardless of whether you stay in the dorms or the bures, communal meals, exceedingly friendly staff and shared facilities ensure nothing comes between you and the island's natural wealth.

SMALL-TOWN ATMOSPHERE

Levuka's architecture isn't the only carryover from the past. The genuine friendliness of local store owners, restaurant managers, and most residents will take you back a hundred years as surely as the wood-frame houses. It would be difficult not to greet familiar faces on your second full-day in town.

and side garden, six cottages of various configurations surround a small pool but unless you really have to cook, we recommend not passing on the chance to check into a piece of history. **Pros:** The charm of history. **Cons:** Not a modern, up-to-date facility. ⊠*Beach St., Levuka* ☎*344–0024* ⊕*www.royallevuka.com* ⇌*15 rooms, 9 suites* ⌂*In-room: no a/c, no phone, no TV. In-hotel: bar, pool, gym, laundry service, public Internet, airport shuttle* ▤*MC, V* ⍥*EP.*

SPORTS & THE OUTDOORS

DAY TRIPS

★ All the below day trips are organized through **Ovalau Watersports** (⊠*Beach St.* ☎*344–0166* ⊕*www.owlfiji.com*). The German couple that runs the company has more than 35 years of diving instructing experience between them and their passion for the area has inspired them to lead its promotion. They handle bookings for many of the smaller island resorts and offer a number of dive-and-accommodation packages. Highlights of diving in the Lomaivitis include schools of barracudas, rare Ghost pipefish, and hard-to-spot and notoriously poisonous stonefish. In deeper water you'll see Pilot whales, Spinner dolphins, and humpback whales. A two-dive day costs $140. You can do 10 dives in five days for $580 and an all-inclusive PADI open-water course costs $590. Wharf dives are $55/$77 with gear rental and night dives from shore are $88/$121 with gear rental. Half-day snorkeling trips cost $44.

★ **Fodor's**Choice Seat of the first capital of Fiji and site of epic battles, Ovalau is steeped in history. **Epi's Midland Tour** (✉ lovoni@owlfiji.com) brings all of it to light over the course of this day tour into the heart of the island. The tour begins with a trek through rain forest and a discussion of native medicines and foods. Upon arriving at the village of Lovoni, you present a sevusevu (a ceremonial gift) to the chief and have a traditional meal prepared by Epi's family. He then reveals the history of Fiji in detail with emphasis on Ovalau and Lovoni before showing you around the village. The tour costs $150 for 1–3 guests, $40 per person for a group of four, and includes round-trip transportation.

The pretty surrounds and friendly hosts of **Silana Village** (✉ silana@owlfiji.com) make it a versatile day trip destination. A small village tour with a picnic costs $15 (minimum 2 guests) and a tour with a welcome ceremony and meke performances is $35 (minimum 10 people). You can hike to an ancestral village in the hills, swim and snorkel, fish, and horseback ride, or you can use your entrée to the village to explore Ovalau's cultural side through mingling with the locals. It's about a 30-minute drive from Levuka; once you've booked, you can go independently. To book truck travel it's $3 one-way; a taxi is $20 one-way.

For a day in the island life, the sole resort on the beautiful, 72-acre **Lost Island** (✉ info@owlfiji.com) offers day-trippers its modest beach, good snorkeling, fishing, and trekking in its rain forest. It's a 20-minute boat ride from Levuka Wharf. It costs $65 per person (minimum 2 guests) including lunch; transfers cost $20 each way.

SCUBA DIVING

Although its diving is often overshadowed by the country's larger reefs, Lomaiviti has deep-water sites where divers can spot some of Fiji's largest ocean-dwellers.

Wakaya Passage has a 3,280-ft. (1,000-meter) drop-off known for its scalloped hammerhead sharks, barracuda, and manta rays. **The Goldfish Block** is a shallow dive that often gets divers a glimpse of Blue Ribbon eels, Garden eels, anemonefish, and anthias, among other particularly colorful sea life. **The Cathedrals** is a particularly adventurous dive past blue coral-lined walls into a maze of swim-throughs and caves. **Levuka Passage,** two minutes from Levuka Wharf, is home to reef sharks, morays, whip corals, and pelagics. **The Pipeline** takes experienced divers down to a depth where they can see giant grouper, eagle rays, schools of batfish, and several species of shark.

OTHER ISLANDS

As an archipelago, Lomaiviti has many other islands in its province than just Ovalau. If you're looking for the ultimate "get-away-from-it-all," check out the resorts on Wakaya Island, Naigani Island, Caqalai Island, and Leleuvia Island—all private islands.

WHERE TO STAY

$ ☒ **Caqalai Island Resort.** This is among the most rustic resorts in Fiji, which also makes it one of the most memorable if you want personal time with excellent sand, surf, and sun in a minimally impacted setting. ■TIP→ If you can't handle outhouse toilets and water-tanks-with-faucets in place of sinks, this isn't for you. Activities include excellent snorkeling and diving, boat trips to nearby Moturiki island for trekking, and village tours on Sunday in time for the 10 AM church service, which invariably features remarkable a cappella singing. The 10 small bures include double beds, one with a single bed, and one with two doubles, and 10-bed dorm gets its sheets adorned with fresh hibiscus flowers. The included three meals a day are usually good as well as hearty (although vegetarians cannot be picky) and dinner is accompanied by pleasant acoustic guitars and song. **Pros:** Warm staff; natural feel; rarely more than 10 guests at a time. **Cons:** Power turned off by 10; shared bathrooms; cold-water only. ✉*Caqalai Island* ☎*343–0366* ✐*caqalairesort@yahoo.com* ⇋*10 rooms, 1 dorm* ♿*In-room: no a/c, no phone, no TV. In-hotel: restaurant, beachfront, water sports, laundry service* ⦿*FAP.*

$ ☒ **Leleuvia Island Resort.** You may think you're intruding
★ on a village when you see the traditional bures and sand paths upon your boat's approach, but that's before the shiny new bar and volleyball court catch your eye. Accommodations here include traditional Fijian bures furnished only with double beds, Duplexes with a double and single bed, Family Lodges, which sleep five, and three dorms. Guests don't mind the small, rustic accommodations as they spend their time in the pristine water or on the fine white sand. Communal meals include Continental breakfasts,

Settling a Score

On July 4, 1849, the American consul John Brown Williams's home caught on fire following a cannon explosion during his celebration of America's Independence Day. Seeing the house aflame, locals ran over and looted it, and afterward felt no moral obligation to return the consul's things. Brown held Ratu Cakobau, the self-appointed Tui Viti (King of Fiji), responsible for $5,000 in property (some believe he greatly inflated the value). Cakobau faced a dilemma: He could accept responsibility for the debt and simultaneously affirm his purported rule over the Fijian people or he could turn over both the debt and leadership. He decided to accept responsibility and ignore the debt, hoping it would go away.

American gunboats called at Levuka in 1851 and 1855 to encourage Cakobau to pay the debt, which had by this point been inflated to $45,000. In 1867 a U.S. battleship entered the harbor and threatened to bombard the town. The following year Cakobau granted the Australia-based Polynesia Company almost 200,000 acres in exchange for payment of his debts; the company wanted to produce cotton in Fiji as world prices soared because of the American Civil War.

With that problem solved, Cakobau was still unable to unite the tribes of Fiji, which had always denied his claims to rulership over the island group, and defended their autonomy in battle with varying degrees of success. A confederacy of chiefs with three regional governments had broken up in 1867 after just two years. On October 10, 1874, he ceded rule over the Fiji Islands to Queen Victoria, signing the deed of cession in Levuka. The capital was relocated to Suva in 1881 because of Levuka's exposed harbor and the surrounding mountains' limitation of its growth.

4

---

sandwiches for lunch, and theme dinners (Chinese, Indian, lovo, and eclectic) on a seven-day rotation. The experience here is a rustic one, but where else can you watch two species of turtle lay eggs outside your bure? The resort also has a "barefoot" conference facility for corporate events. **Pros:** Pristine island setting; natural feel; warm staff. **Cons:** Shared bathrooms; cold-water only; power turned off by 11. ⊠*Leleuvia Island* ☎*354–0021* ⊕*www.leleuvia.com* ⇱*14 bures, 3 dorms* &*In-room: no a/c, no phone, no TV. In-hotel: restaurant, bar, beachfront, water sports, laundry service* ▤*MC, V* ⏉*FAP.*

$$ ⊞**Naigani Island Resort.** Popular with expat families and
☾ couples alike, Naigani has a winning combination of activi-
ties and classic escape credentials. Suva-based families like
its proximity to the capital and its giant waterslide, while
couples enjoy the intimacy it affords when school is in ses-
sion. Play options include a "barefoot" par-27 golf course
with three greens, beachfront swimming pool with swim-
up bar, fishing, windsurfing, and other water sports. The
island has beautiful white-sand beaches leading into excel-
lent snorkeling and its sole village welcomes guests. The
Plantation Villas and two-bedroom villas are roomy and
tropically furnished; the latter have kitchens and balconies.
The restaurant's one-course lunches and four-course dinners
are a combination of local and international cuisine. Din-
ner offers more choices and, might include crepes di mare
followed by a cream of pumpkin soup and coconut lamb
satay or beef casserole. **Pros:** Stunning beaches; friendly
staff; good selection at meals. **Cons:** Seclusion; no-romance
zone at school holidays. ⊠*Naigani Island* ☎*603–0613*
⊕*www.naiganiisland.com* ⇋*5 rooms, 11 villas* ⌂*In-room:
no a/c (some), no phone, refrigerator, no TV. In-hotel:
restaurant, room service, bar, pool, golf, beachfront, div-
ing, water sports, laundry service, public Internet, airport
shuttle* ⊟*AE, DC, MC, V* ⎱⎰*EP, MAP, FAP.*

$$$$ ⊞**Wakaya Club & Spa.** An ultraluxury hideaway popular
with celebrities, Wakaya guests are met with a chilled bottle
of Taittinger champagne upon arrival and an organic fruit
basket is replenished throughout their stay. Bathrooms in
the 1,650-square-foot Garden and Ocean bures have dual
basin sinks, bathtubs, bidets, and lead to outdoor lava rock
showers. The king-size four-poster beds are dressed in Fili
D'oro sheets. Garden bures are set back from the beach
while all others are steps from it. Three larger bures range
from one to three bedrooms and from 2,400-square-feet
to a separately staffed 16-acre hilltop estate. From every
bure, reception is an intercom button away. All rates include
early-morning check-in and late-afternoon check-out, and
two one-tank dives daily. Four chefs and two pastry chefs
produce Japanese-influenced Pacific Rim cuisine (Nobu
Matsuhisa is a frequent guest), served whenever and almost
wherever guests please. **Pros:** Privacy; personalized ser-
vice; world-class cuisine. **Cons:** Seclusion; included sun-
tan lotion is only SPF 15. ⊠*Wakaya Island* ☎*344–8406,
800/828–3454 U.S.* ⊕*www.wakaya.com* ⇋*10 suites* ⌂*In-
room: safe, no phone, DVD (some), no TV (some), WiFi.*

In-hotel: restaurant, room service, bar, golf course, tennis court, pool, gym, spa, beachfront, laundry service, diving, water sports, public Internet ⊟AE, MC, V ℮IAI.

LOMAIVITI ESSENTIALS

TRANSPORTATION

BY AIR

Air Fiji operates two flights to and from Suva to Bureta Airstrip on Ovalau Monday–Saturday. The first departs Suva at 7:15 AM and arrives at 7:30 AM. The second departs Suva at 5 PM and arrives at 5:15 PM. The return legs of these flights depart Bureta Airstrip at 7:40 AM and 5:30 PM. On Sunday, only the afternoon flights go.

Be sure to catch the Air Fiji shuttle to and from Bureta Airstrip. It meets each days' flights and costs around $10 while the rocky 45-minute-long journey might cost $40 by taxi. The day before you leave, arrange to be picked up by the shuttle at the Air Fiji office on Beach Street. The office closes early on Saturday and is closed on Sunday.

Contacts **Air Fiji** (☎ *344–0139* ⊕ *www.airfiji.com.fj*).

BY FERRY

Patterson Brothers Shipping operates a combination bus-ferry service between Suva and Levuka daily. One-way, it involves a 1.5-hour bus ride from Suva to Natovi Landing, a one-hour ferry to Buresala on Ovalau, and a one-hour bus ride to Levuka. Call to confirm times and pricing.

Contacts **Patterson Brothers Shipping Company** (✉ *Beach St., Levuka* ☎ *331–5644 in Suva, 344–0125 in Levuka*).

BY TAXI

Taxis are readily available on Ovalau and are cheaper than they are on the mainland.

CONTACTS & RESOURCES

BANKS & EXCHANGE SERVICES

The shops and restaurants on Ovalau only accept cash. The two banks in the Lomaiviti Group, Colonial and Westpac, are on Beach Street in Levuka and are open weekdays 9:30–3:30. Both accept and exchange traveler's checks, foreign currency, and most major credit cards. The Westpac Bank has the Lomaiviti Group's only ATM.

Vanua Levu

WORD OF MOUTH

"The best diving sites are in the Somo-somo Strait, between Vanua Levu and Taveuni."

—ALF

Written
by Robert
Brenner

THE HEART OF THE "FRIENDLY NORTH" IS FIJI'S second-largest island (8,992-square km [3,472-square mi]), home to roughly a fifth of the country's population. Characterized by a lack of development relative to other parts of the country, hilly Vanua Levu comprises mainly dense rain forest, small coastal villages, and two disparate coastal towns on its north and south sides. Labasa is a major sugar producer set amid sugarcane fields, while Savusavu is a modest hub of tourism and foreign investment on the coast. Between the two lies one of Fiji's most diverse rain-forest reserves, Waisali. From Savusavu, the fantastically scenic (and jolting) Hibiscus Highway rolls east past resorts and then quiet but welcoming villages.

The only part of the island geared to tourism is the small port town of Savusavu. The town has become one of the major yachting centers in the region and, thanks to local land laws, has become favored for property investment. Regardless of where you stay around Savusavu, you'll have access to an untouched rain-forest reserve, an equally undisturbed barrier reef and a small, friendly town set contentedly amid it all. If the barrier between feeling like a tourist and being accepted as a neighbor can truly be overcome in one part of Fiji, it's on Vanua Levu or "Great Land."

5

ABOUT THE HOTELS & RESTAURANTS

The boutique resorts of Vanua Levu carry colossal reputations. Jean-Michel Cousteau Resort caters to families with its excellent, engaging children's program, comfortable setting, and superlative cuisine. Namale combines one of the region's most lavish spas with all the sports facilities you could wish for on an active holiday. Not far from the sugar town of Labasa is a seven-bure hideaway meshing colonial charm with an idyllic private island setting.

While Savusavu offers world-class resorts at the top-end, its mid-range is decidedly lacking. Koro Sun offers a good if slightly jumbled product but otherwise, the best value for the money is in a holiday cottage or house. In contrast to Taveuni's rental offerings (*See Chapter* 6), some of Savusavu's have excellent beachfronts, and self-caterers will appreciate the wider selection of goods in town.

There are few good dining options in Savusavu and even less elsewhere on the island. Fortunately, those that are worthwhile offer great value. You'll find the usual bemusing international menu at some of the restaurants: Let the day's specials guide you.

WHAT IT COSTS IN FIJI DOLLARS ($F)			
$	$$	$$$	$$$$
RESTAURANTS			
under $F10	$F10–$F20	$F20–$F30	over $F30
HOTELS*			
under $F200	$F200–$F400	$F400–$F700	over $F700
HOTELS**			
under $F300	$F300–$F500	$F500–$F800	over $F800

*EP, BP, CP **AI, FAP, MAP; Restaurant prices are per person for a main course at dinner. Hotel prices are per night for a double room in high season and may not include a 12.5% Value-Added Tax (V.A.T.) or a 5% hotel turnover tax. Hotel prices are in U.S. dollars where noted.

SAVUSAVU

7 km (4 mi) northwest of Taveuni. Savusavu Airport is 8 km (5 mi) from the center of town.

Savusavu is flanked by a huge bay teeming with fish and striking mountain ranges, clad in ancient jungle greenery. Rich in sandalwood, *beche-de-mer* (the sea slugs—or sea cucumbers—on the bottom of lagoons), and copra, Savusavu was a popular port in the sailing ship days of the 19th century. Copra, which is the roasted shells of cut coconuts (from which coconut oil is pressed) remained the region's main revenue crop throughout much of the 20th century. A number of foreign- and locally owned properties are available to rent, ranging from small cottages to large, hillside luxury retreats. Most are a short way from the town, which has a modest but sufficient number of grocery stores, shops, and restaurants.

EXPLORING SAVUSAVU

The area's major sights are spread wide, from scuba diving excursions departing out of Savusavu Bay to villages along the Hibiscus Highway to the east and the rain forest reserve off Savusavu Road in the north. Taxis are readily available and, although they now have set fares for certain destinations, you may be able to negotiate a deal for a return trip or in making transit arrangements for a couple of days.

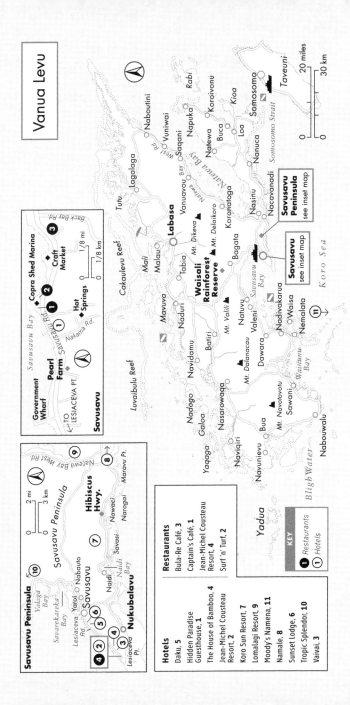

Vanua Levu

Savusavu

Government Wharf
Pearl Farm
1
Hot Springs
Nakama Rd.
Savusavu Rd.
1 Copra Shed Marina
2
Craft Market
3
Back Bay Rd.
Savusavu Bay
TO LESIACEVA PT.
LESIACEVA PT.
0   1/8 km
0   1/8 mi

Savusavu Peninsula
Savurekareka Bay
Valaga Bay
10
Savusavu Peninsula
Natewa Bay West Rd.
9
Hibiscus Hwy.
7
Nawaci
Narogai Maravu Pt.
8
Nabouto
Nasasobo
Yaroi
5
6
Savusavu
Naidi
Nukubalavu
Lesiaceva Rd.
Naidi Sovasi
Savasi Bay
Lesiaceva Pt.
4
2
3
4
0   3 km
0   2 mi

KEY
1 Restaurants
① Hotels

Restaurants
Bula-Re Café, **3**
Captain's Café, **1**
Jean-Michel Cousteau Resort, **4**
Surf 'n' Turf, **2**

Hotels
Daku, **5**
Hidden Paradise Guesthouse, **1**
The House of Bamboo, **4**
Jean-Michel Cousteau Resort, **2**
Koro Sun Resort, **7**
Lomalagi Resort, **9**
Moody's Namena, **11**
Namale, **8**
Sunset Lodge, **6**
Tropic Splendor, **10**
Vaivai, **3**

Naboutini
Naboutini
Vuniwai
Rabi
West Rd.
Napuka
Koroivonu
Kioa
Lagalaga
Saqani
Natewa
Buca
Loa
Nanuca
Somosomo
Taveuni
Somosomo Strait
Tutu
Natewa Bay
Koronatoga
Nasinu
Nacavanadi
Savusavu Peninsula
see inset map
0   20 miles
0   30 km
Mt. Dikeva ▲
Mt. Delaikoro ▲▲
Bagata
Savusavu
see inset map
Savusavu Bay
Koro Sea
Mali
Labasa
Malau
Tabia
Naduri
Navidamu
Batiri
Mt. Valili ▲
Natuvu
Valeni
Dawara
Mt. Dalanacau ▲
Nadivakarua
Waisa
Nemalata
11
Waisau Bay
Mt. Novotovotu ▲
Sawani
Bua
Mt. Navotovotu
Navunievu
Navigiri
Nabouwalu
Bligh Water
Yadua
Yaqaga
Galoa
Nadogo
Nasarowaqa
Vanuavou Bay
Mavuva
Cakaulevu Reef
Luvaibulu Reef
Koronatoga
Waisali Rainforest Reserve

VANUA LEVU'S TOP 3

Dive Namena. The swim-throughs and canyons inhabited by a diverse array of marine life make this pristine barrier reef an experienced diver's playground.

Road Trip. A short trip east along the Hibiscus Highway affords spectacular mountain and rain-forest vistas.

Toast the Bay. Knock back a chilled mug of Fiji Bitter (or two) at the classic Savusavu Yacht Club.

Check departure times at the bus station and you might consider taking a bus out of town and hailing a taxi back. Fortunately, the town is a central point between many of the sights, making it easy to split morning and afternoon activities with lunch on Main Street.

Hibiscus Highway. The stretch of rough road from Savusavu east and then up the eastern coast of the Natewa Peninsula passes through pristine rain forests, presenting magnificent views from mountain ridges. Because bus service along this road is infrequent and rains and occasional flooding can make driving the mostly unpaved road difficult, the best way to see it is to negotiate with a taxi for a tour. Prices vary but you can expect to pay roughly $1 per km.

Nukubalavu Village. This village of 300, about 8 km (5 mi) southwest of Savusavu, is relatively large in Fijian terms. Its chiefly title, *Tui Na Savasavu,* is one of the highest on the island. The U.S.-based Seacology organization has signed a contract to provide them with a preschool building. In return, the people have agreed to allow the preservation of a 25,600-acre marine reserve in the bay, where the villagers will not fish or exploit the waters in any way for 20 years. As in many Fijian villages, the people have conservative views and expect modesty and deference from Western visitors. The village has the best beach in the area. It is, however, tied to a recently established resort, so access can be a matter of negotiation.

Pearl Farm. Savusavu-born Justin Hunter, whose father was American, studied marine biology and worked in the U.S. before returning to start this pearl farm in 2000. Oysters are carefully implanted with mussel tissue that forms the core of the future pearl. They are then attached to ropes dangling down into Savusavu Bay where they grow and, twice a year, are harvested. A tour of the farm begins with a presentation on the history of cultured pearls at the J. Hunter Pearls office. You can take a glass-bottom boat out to see the undersea farm and possibly go for a snorkel. During harvesting months, you can see the pearl implanting and harvesting process. The tour concludes in the company's large showroom, where gold, black, and a variety of pastel-hued pearls are for sale. ⊠*Naverea Rd., Savusavu* ☎*885–0821* ⊕*www.pearlsfiji.com* ⊡*$25* ⊙*Tours weekdays 9:30* AM *and 1:30* PM.

Waisali Rainforest Reserve. One of Fiji's most diverse rain forests, this 300-acre reserve is rich in spectacular mountaintop vistas, bird species, and exquisite trees, flowers, and plants, including those used in traditional medicines. Waisali contains a population of the endangered Fiji ground frog (*Platymantis vitianus*), which was once thought to have become extinct thanks to sugarcane development during the colonial period. Happily, scientists have found them in Waisali along with other populations considered important. Most of the forest in the reserve is intact and undisturbed, although a short walking trail from the entrance culminates in a pretty waterfall. ⊹ *20 km (12 mi) north of Savusavu off Savusavu Rd.*

WHERE TO EAT

ECLECTIC

$ ×**Bula-Re Café.** This is a popular alternative to the Captains Café at the other end of the main street. An espresso machine serving cappuccinos, lattes, and the like, and a range of homemade desserts emphasize the "café" aspect but here, too, curries and seafood are the specialties. A special might be walu and prawns in a white wine sauce on yellow rice with grilled tomato and salad. The international menu is reasonably priced and the restaurant's outdoor waterfront seating affords excellent views. ⊠*Main St.* ☎*885–0377* ⊟*No credit cards* ⊙*Mon-Sat 9* AM*-10* PM.

$ ×**Captain's Café.** Across the 90-year-old Copra Shed marina from Surf 'n' Turf, this café might offer the most diverse menu in Fiji, serving breakfast, lunch, and dinner. American-style sandwiches and burgers are advertised alongside Indian and Thai curries on the board indoors, and enchila-

GREAT ITINERARIES

Friendly people, scattered attractions, and resorts keep life in and around Savusavu chugging along at a "Fiji Time" pace. Many visitors are content to pull up a chair on a restaurant deck, order the fish special, and admire the bay views. If you're in town on a Saturday, be sure to drop by the municipal market. If you're here on a Sunday, consider battling the yachties for a brunch-time table at Surf 'n' Turf.

IF YOU HAVE 3 DAYS

This is not enough time to fully appreciate one of the better resorts, but it's plenty of time in which to see the area's top sights and get a sense of the local character. On Day 1 head out to **Waisali Rainforest Reserve** early for a serene walk through orchids and 100-year-old Yaka and Yasi softwoods. Have an alfresco lunch back in town at one of the waterfront restaurants. Head to the **Pearl Farm** by 1:30 for a tour; take a snorkel if you care for a dip

with the jewels-to-be. On Day 2 go scuba diving or negotiate with a taxi for a tour up the **Hibiscus Highway**. In the afternoon take a public bus out to **Nukubalavu Village**, bringing along a *sevusevu* (gift) of kava from the local market in order to impress the chief. Bring a snorkel for possible use after being rewarded with a tour of the village. At night drop by the Savusavu Yacht Club for a nightcap. On Day 3 fish, play golf, dive, or just relax. Make a dinner reservation at Jean-Michel Cousteau if you can foot the bill.

IF YOU HAVE 5 OR 7 DAYS

Let the resort you choose guide your experience. Each of the better resorts offers excellent tours and activities incorporating the attractions above and showcasing the best of the Savusavu experience. Make an excursion into town at least once for a mid-afternoon beer at the Savusavu Yacht club or a perusal of the Saturday market.

das and fajitas are advertised on the blackboards outside. The nicely presented curries are particularly good value, served with rice, roti, or naan and a small vegetable side. The fruit salad dessert is as refreshing as the views from the rail-less deck seating, which leads you to forgive the quirky service. Oh, and they serve pizzas, too. ⊠*Copra Shed Marina* ☎*885–0511* ▭*MC, V.*

INTERNATIONAL

★ Fodor'sChoice ✕**Jean-Michel Cousteau Resort.** Diners enjoy
$$$$ the work of one of Fiji's finest kitchens in the two cozy
dark-wood open-air seating areas around the resort's bar.
All-inclusive for guests, the set-menu lunches and dinners include a choice between three appetizers, three or
four entrées, and three desserts. Satiate your appetite with
Savusavu Bay Pearl Oyster shells with seared scallops on
salad followed by Australian beef tenderloin wrapped in
bacon with roasted pumpkin, baby potato, and zucchini
and a choice of Chasseur or Figaro sauce. Dessert might
be orange cream caramel or tiramisu. Vegetarians will find
at least one tantalizing option at every course. ⊠*Lesiaceva
Point* ☎*885–0188* ⊟*AE, MC, V.*

$$–$$$ ✕**Surf 'n' Turf.** A dock overlooking beautiful Savusavu Bay is
★ the setting for Savusavu's best nonresort dining experience.
The chef, a former Cousteau Resort executive chef, visits
the local market each day in order to select the fish for that
day's specials. This might include seared ahi tuna with garlic
mash dressed with wasabi and lime cream and topped with
a cucumber relish. The *pièce de résistance*, however, is a $50
six-course menu the chef prepares before guests using stoves
on wheels. It includes lobster, steak, and prawn dishes and
must be requested in advance. Homemade ice cream hits the
spot for dessert, and there's an excellent brunch on Sunday.
⊠*Copra Shed Marina* ☎*828–3095* ⊟*MC, V.*

WHERE TO STAY

$–$$ ⌂**Daku.** Somewhere between the Cousteau Resort and
the hostels (literally and figuratively) is Daku. Its studio-
style ocean-view bures are underwhelming and, along with
the rest of the property, across the street from the ocean.
However, two brand-new self-contained ocean view villas
showed promise with air-conditioning and private plunge
pools at $295 a night. A decent pool with lounge chairs runs
alongside the restaurant, which offers curries and Fijian
fare. The resort hosts seven-day workshops ranging from
novel writing to quilting for which it will book your airfare.
Fishing, snorkeling, biking, kayaking, and village tours
are on offer, and rates include round-trip airport transfer.
Pros: Unique educational offerings; packages with flights
included. **Cons:** Tired-looking bathrooms; 25-minute walk
to town. ⊠*Lesiaceva Rd.* ☎*885–0046* ⊕*www.dakuresort.
com* ⌂*14 units* ⚐*In-room: no a/c (some), no phone, refrig-*

IF YOU LIKE

BOUTIQUE HOTEL LUXURY

Namale and Jean-Michel Cousteau are among the very best at what they do. If you're looking to be pampered in one of the South Pacific's most lavish spas or want an upscale yet comfortable, active experience for a young family, look no further than these two small resorts.

A WARM RECEPTION

What can you expect from the "friendly" region of one of the friendliest countries in the world? You'll be able to chat with almost anyone you meet and to learn a thing or two about Fiji and its people when you do.

DIGGING THE LOCAL SCENE

The many cottages and luxury houses for rent around Savusavu make it easy for visitors to sample the "Friendly North" lifestyle. Because the locals are used to yachties dropping anchor for up to months at a time, Westerners who want to blend in will go relatively unnoticed picking up provisions at the supermarket or falling into a routine at the cafés.

erator (some), no TV. In-hotel: restaurant, bar, pool, water sports, airport shuttle ⊟*MC, V* ⊚*EP.*

$ ⚈**Hidden Paradise Guesthouse.** This cheap, clean place is behind a restaurant at the more lively end of town. Bathrooms (one per gender) are shared and the shower is cold-water only, but the included breakfast goes above and beyond Continental with eggs and bacon upon request. Staff are friendly, beds comfortable, and insects happily unaccounted for. Two rooms, each with a double and a bunk-bed, have optional air-conditioning for an extra charge. There's a shared kitchen. **Pros:** In-town; friendly staff. **Cons:** Front rooms can catch noise from the kitchen; one shower. ⊠*Main St., Savusavu* ☎*885–0106* ⤶*6 rooms* ⚭*In-room: no a/c (some), no phone, no TV. In-hotel: restaurant, bar, laundry facilities* ⊟*No credit cards* ⊚*CP.*

$$ ⚈**The House of Bamboo.** This two-bedroom house is 99 steps above the same pristine white stretch of sand used by the Vaivai House. *See review below.* Its hardwood deck features a saltwater plunge pool and king-size daybed under a thatched roof to match that of the veranda, all of which overlooks the bay. Each bedroom has a king-size bed and one has a two-person tub also overlooking the water. There's a selection of music and movies to match the full enter-

tainment system in the living room, and a fully equipped kitchen. The house is a short walk along the beach from Jean-Michel Cousteau Resort and a 10-minute drive from town. **Pros:** Privacy; great beach; luxury amenities. **Cons:** Steps up to house may be difficult for some. ⊠*Lesiaceva Point* ☎*885–1002* ⊕*www.fijibeachshacks.com* ⮑*1 house* ⟁*In-house: no a/c, no phone, kitchen, refrigerator, DVD, pool, beachfront, laundry facilities, airport shuttle* ☐*AE, D, MC, V* ⊙*EP.*

★ **Fodor'sChoice** ⊠**Jean-Michel Cousteau Fiji Islands Resort.** Its scuba diving, children's program, and food have long made this one of Fiji's top resorts. Each day, kids have a choice of activities including village and market trips, rain-forest hikes, and organized snorkel trips that are often led by the resident marine biologist. A gorgeous split-level pool area has one part spilling into a second with tiled counters for bar service and luxurious canopied daybeds, making this possibly the chicest and most comfortable pool-area in Fiji. The Oceanfront bures have newer furniture and larger closets than Garden Views as well as views of the ocean, but massage bures partially block the view of two. Oceanfront Suites have the addition of a double daybed in a front corner room and actually have smaller porches. Lunch and dinner feature international menus with choices of three appetizers, three or four entrées, and three desserts prepared by senior chefs the resort has trained overseas, and vegetarians will be extremely pleased. The first two kids under 12 stay free. **Pros:** Fantastic food; renowned diving; kids won't want to leave. **Cons:** Ocean-view categories could be closer to the beach. ⊠*Lesiaceva Point* ☎*885–0188* ⊕*www.fijiresort.com* ⮑*25 bures* ⟁*In-room: no a/c, no phone (some), safe, refrigerator, no TV. In-hotel: restaurant, 2 pools, spa, beachfront, diving, water sports, children's programs (ages infant–13), laundry service, public Wi-Fi, airport shuttle* ☐*AE, MC, V* ⊙*FAP.*

$$$–$$$$ ⊠**Koro Sun Resort.** Like a man buying an expensive convertible, this classic Fiji resort has added fourth and fifth room categories to weather middle-age. The ocean-view bures are outdated-looking and lack an ocean view worth noting. For a tad more, the two-bedroom Fairway Palms bures have pleasant white tones and wood furnishings, indoor and outdoor showers, and private plunge pools, although they sit on the golf course and nearly on each other. Up in the hills are four villas ranging from one to three bedrooms. Spanking-new, two-story Edgewater bures are sleek and modern,

fully self-contained, and have plunge pools and docks. Golf, tennis, volleyball courts, and a waterslide make this a great family choice. Children under 12 stay free. **Pros:** Excellent spa; huge range of sporting activities. **Cons:** Edgewater bures and beach are across road; restaurants serve same menu. ✉*Savusavu* ☎*885–0262 Ext. 103, 877/567–6786 in U.S.* ⊕*www.korosunresort.com* ⤙*24 bures, 13 villas* ⌂*In-room: no phone (some), kitchen (some), refrigerator (some), DVD (some), no TV (some). In-hotel: 2 restaurants, room service, bars, golf course, tennis courts, 2 pools, gym, spa, beachfront, diving, water sports, bicycles, children's programs (ages 3–11), laundry service, public Internet, airport shuttle* ▭*MC, V* ⧌*FAP.*

$$$ ▥ **Lomalagi Resort.** The villas here are none too fancy, but their magnificent views over pristine Natewa Bay and their beautifully manicured grounds are. Some of the mostly middle-age couples and honeymooners who come here order room service to the wide decks of their large studio-style units, all of which have two-person tubs and large walk-in showers. Owner and Seattle-native Collin McKenny consults guests prior to their arrival and has the chef design the all-inclusive menu. Guided snorkeling, fishing, dolphin-watching, and diving (bring your own gear) are available from her small boat. A patch of sandy beach is a short downhill hike or complimentary drive away. The two slightly cheaper villas are lower on the hill and so have less-impressive views. Villa 5 has the best view, while Villa 6 is the most isolated. **Pros:** Serene private setting; fantastic sense of personal space. **Cons:** Isolated from local culture; underwhelming dining room decor. ✉*Salt Lake Rd., turn-off for which is about 24 km (15 mi) east of Savusavu, along Hibiscus Hwy.* ☎*851–0585* ⊕*www.lomalagi.com* ⤙*6 units* ⌂*In-room: no a/c, no phone, DVD, VCR. In-hotel: restaurant, room service, bar, pool, water sports, bicycles, laundry service, public Internet, airport shuttle, no kids under 12* ▭*MC, V* ⧌*EP, FAP.*

$$$$ ▥ **Moody's Namena.** A private island south of Vanua Levu, this resort offers extremely personalized service to a maximum of 12 guests. Five spacious bures are well-spread on two cliff-top ridges, a sixth sits on the beach. Each is a studio-style hexagon with a king-size canopy bed and walls that slide open in order to capture the breeze and views. Certified divers can explore Namena Barrier Reef, considered among Fiji's premiere dive areas; snorkeling is great off the beach. The 110-acre island has a fantastic

array of wildlife, including turtles that come to lay their eggs. Meals are communal although guests can dine on their porches, and the kitchen takes requests. Breakfast includes classic hot fare and a main dish; lunch is an all-you-can-eat buffet; and dinner includes a salad, entrée, and dessert. Technically in the Lomaiviti Group, the island is much closer to Vanua Levu and guests fly into Savusavu. **Pros:** Privacy; highly personalized experience; breathtaking views. **Cons:** Lacks some luxury amenities common at this price point (pool, outdoor shower, air-conditioning); no selection at dinner. ✉ *Namenalala Island* ☎ *881–3764* ⊕ *www.moodysnamenafiji.com* ⟿ *6 bures* ⚷ *In-room: no a/c, no phone, In-hotel: beachfront, water sports, airport transfer, no kids under 16* ⊟ *MC, V* ⊘ *Closed Mar. and Apr.* ⦙⊙⦙ *FAP.*

$$$$ ⬚**Namale.** Motivational speaker Tony Robbins' resort is an
★ exclusive, lush affair emphasizing both an active and relaxing holiday. Hiking through rain forest or to the resort's own blow hole, tennis, volleyball, basketball, bicycles, and even bowling encourage guests to their feet. Giving guests a perfect out is the magnificent 10,000-square-foot spa with four soaking tubs overlooking the blow hole and the Koro Sea. All bures have private decks and large walk-in showers. Honeymoon Bures feature two-person spa tubs and deck-side plunge pools with ocean view. Large air-conditioned villas and a 2,000-square-foot two-bedroom "Tatadra (Dream) House" have private pools, exceptional views, and modern entertainment systems. Motivational conferences are often held here as part of packages. Three-course lunches and dinners include a choice of two appetizers, three entrées (including a vegetarian option), and two desserts. **Pros:** Magnificent spa; extensive sports facilities. **Cons:** Tidal beach. ✛ *9 km (6 mi) east of Savusavu, on Hibiscus Hwy.* ☎ *885–0435, 800/727–3454 in U.S.* ⊕ *www. namalefiji.com* ⟿ *18 bures* ⚷ *In-room: no a/c (some), no phone, DVD (some), no TV (some), Wi-Fi (some). In-hotel: restaurant, tennis courts, pools, gym, spa, beachfront, diving, water sports, bicycles, laundry service, public Internet, airport shuttle* ⊟ *AE, MC, V* ⦙⊙⦙ *FAP, AI.*

$ ⬚**Sunset Lodge.** The new kid on the block, Sunset's draw is mid-range amenities at budget prices. Three of the rooms have cold-water en suites, TVs, and air-conditioning—a steal for a couple that doesn't mind a double bed. There are "family rooms," which lack amenities but have a double and single bed, and double rooms and single rooms, all of which share bathrooms and showers. A modest Continental breakfast is included, and the rooms' second story setting keeps them relatively bug-free. **Pros:** Good-value "master bedrooms"; 10-minute walk into town. **Cons:** Little natural light; motel atmosphere. ⊠*Lesiaceva Rd.* ☎*885–2171* ⇆*6 rooms* ⚭*In-room: no a/c (some), no phone, no TV (some)* ▭*No credit cards* ❑*CP.*

$$ 🖼**Tropic Splendor.** This cottage 20 minutes out of Savusavu offers beachfront seclusion. The 600-square-foot, self-contained unit is true-to-form with polished hardwood floors and interior. Inside is a king-size bed with romantic netting, a lounge and a full entertainment system including more than 400 DVDs. Outside is a bamboo garden shower, a large covered deck, and a two-person hammock steps from a black sand beach. A basket of fresh-picked fruit is delivered daily and twice-weekly cleaning service is included, as are kayaks. ✛ *Off Savusavu Rd., north of Savusavu* ☎*851–0152* ⊕*www.tropicsplendor.com* ⇆*1 cottage* ⚭*No a/c, no phone, kitchen, refrigerator, DVD, beachfront, water sports, laundry facilities, airport shuttle* ▭*MC, V* ❑*EP.*

$$ 🖼**Vaivai.** Near the tip of the peninsula, this 820-square-foot
★ (250-square-meter) modern house is visible from the plane as you fly in. Although not as big as its neighbor with the swimming pool (recently taken off the rental market by its owners), the house has a fantastic open-plan design with 25-foot-high (8-meter-high) ceilings and a wraparound deck showcasing expansive bay views. The master bedroom has air-conditioning and a king-size bed; there's a second bedroom and room to sleep a total of six. The beach is across a small road and down a few flights of steps; town is a 10-minute drive away; and the Jean-Michel Cousteau Resort and its excellent restaurant are a short walk's distance. Cleaning and babysitting services can be arranged. **Pros:** Privacy; great beach. **Cons:** Steps up to house may be difficult for some. ⊠*Lesiaceva Point* ☎*617/3899–0793 in Australia* ⊕*www.fijiparadise.com.fj* ⇆*1 house* ⚭*Kitchen, refrigerator, DVD, beachfront, laundry service, airport shuttle* ▭*AE, D, MC, V* ❑*EP.*

NIGHTLIFE

The yachtie hangout during boating season, the 20-year-old **Savusavu Yacht Club** (☎885–0651) in the Copra Shed on the marina has an old-school feel. The open-air bar and deck overlook the moorings. Entertainment includes a "Chicken Draw," in which patrons buy raffle tickets to win roast birds, and a Joker Draw for the accumulated pot of money. Happy hour is announced by the ringing of a bell with a seaman's rope. Sailing trophies and the names of board members immortalized on wooden plaques look down on a mixed crowd of locals and visitors as they knock back Fiji Bitter and Corona and, if they're not sailing the next day, maybe even shots.

SPORTS & THE OUTDOORS

From raising sails in the bay to drop-shots on resort tennis courts, Savusavu's small town and quiet, resort-dotted countryside offers a wide range of active endeavors, if you know where to look. The upscale resorts lay out options from scuba diving to hiking for guests and independent operators will also direct and/or guide visitors to the area's best boating, kayaking, fishing, and trekking, providing the necessary equipment. While good snorkeling is generally a given throughout Fiji, Savusavu Bay's sharp rocks make it a poor snorkeling area.

BOATING

Savusavu is home to Fiji's most popular marina and yacht club. From May through October the town sees a constant flow of sailors who bring a significant amount of business to its grocery stores, restaurant, and, of course, its yacht club. The marina is well-run, providing all the requisite services, and many yachties use its harbor as a base from which to explore the "Friendly North."

Copra Shed Marina (☎885–0457) has eight stern-to-wharf berths for boats of up to 65 feet (20 meters) and 17 moorings for vessels of various sizes. Within the yacht complex are hot showers, toilets, laundry, Internet and office services, telephones, and waste oil and garbage disposals. Maintenance and repair services can be arranged.

Before coming ashore, visitors must be cleared by officials, available 8–4:30, for a fee of $100. A quarantine fee of $33.75, payable at the local hospital, also applies. Rates at anchor are $7/day in-season, $5/day off-season; moorings are $10/day in-season, $8/day off-season; stern-to-berth (including power and water) costs $14/day in-season, $10/day off-season. Discounts are offered on longer stays.

★ **Tui Tai Cruises** (☎*885–3032, 253/777–4290 in U.S.* ⊕*www. tuitai.com*) offers five- and seven-day itineraries aboard their luxury vessel that include lots of mountain-biking and kayaking opportunities. There are chances to dive and snorkel daily at the best and most remote dive spots in the "Friendly North" as well as visits to Taveuni's Bouma National Park, villages, and hidden harbors. An onboard spa follows guests to the most scenic terra firma spots. The 142-foot (42 meters) cruiser has 12 cabins, each with same-day laundry service and 800-thread-count Egyptian sheets. Meals are either served alfresco on board or at pristine on-shore locations. Breakfast might be vegetable frittatas, lunch a complex Indian curry, and the three-course dinner might include a soup, glazed mahimahi, and sticky date pudding.

DAY TRIPS

The three major resorts—Koro Sun, Namale, and Jean-Michel Cousteau—offer nonstrenuous walks and guided Waisali Rainforest Reserve tours. The Coustea Resort offers a guided "medicine plant walk," Koro Sun has morning treks into its 90 acres of rainforest, and Namale offers a walk to a local village in addition to more challenging hikes. Anyone can embark on the short trail into the untouched Reserve, which leads to a waterfall.

Eco Divers-Tours (✉*Copra Shed Marina* ☎*885–0122* ✑eco-divers@connect.com.fj) offers full-day (9–3) waterfall hikes and full-day biking tours including lunch and snacks and a half-day (9–noon) version of each. A full-day waterfall hike or a bike tour costs $65, a half-day hike costs $25, and a half-day bike tour costs $30. Bicycles can be rented for $30 per day.

Rock'n Downunder Divers (✉*Waitui Marina* ☎*885–3447 or 932–8363* ✑ockndownunder@connect.com.fj) offers a half-day waterfall tour ($60), half- and full-day beach and bay tours ($70 and $120), and a half-day village tour ($60). The company rents out bicycles ($35) and offers half- and full-day bicycle tours ($50 and $70). Half-day tours include snacks and towels; full-day tours also include lunch.

FISHING

Expat skipper Gary of **Ika Levu Fishing Charters** (☎944–8506 ⊕*www.fishinginfiji.com*) has more than 20 years' experience. He runs two boats: 24-foot *Ika Lev* or the 41-foot *Our Way,* in search of big game. The larger boat can take up to four passengers and is available for half-day (7–12:30) and full-day (7–4:30) fishing charters at $1,012.50 and $1,687.50, respectively. Multiday customized tours including a live-aboard option are available departing from points around Fiji. The boats can also be chartered for scuba diving and surfing.

Seahawk Yacht Charters (☎885–0787 ⊕*www.seahawkfiji. com*) specializes in overnight trips. Its 53-foot classic yawl sleeps up to six in three cabins and one of its owners joins the trip as chef. Most itineraries focus on Vanua Levu, where the captain can steer guests to local dive companies, villages, fishing spots, and beaches. The charter will also sail the Mamanucas and Yasawas for an extra fee on request. The minimum charter is three days. Rates vary from $150/person per day to $250/person per day depending on season, level of service, and meal plan.

GOLF

Koro Sun (⊠*Koro Sun Resort, Savusavu* ☎885–0262) has a 9-hole, 1,840-yard, par-60 golf course that winds its way through the resort property. It includes two particularly challenging holes—the 130-meter 7th and 116-meter 16th—where golfers cannot see the green from the tee.

SEA-KAYAKING & SNORKELING

The upscale resorts have their own kayaks, snorkeling gear, and guided tours.

Rock'n Downunder Divers (⊠*Waitui Marina* ☎885-3447 or 932-8363 ✐rockndownunder@connect.com.fj) rents out kayaks (half-day $25 single, $45 double; full-day $50 single, $90 double). You can take a tailored guided tour for $5 per hour. The company also offers half- and full-day snorkel trips ($70 and $120) and half- and full-day beach and bay tours ($70 and $120). All half-day trips include snacks and towels if needed; full-day trips also include lunch.

SCUBA DIVING

The Namena Barrier Reef, 15 mi south of Vanua Levu, includes more than 30 mi of untarnished reef track. Divers are rewarded with swim-throughs, dramatic drop-offs, large and small fish, intricate hard-coral formations and, of course, magnificent soft coral. Jean-Michel Cousteau ranks the site around Namena Island as one of the 10 best in the world. KoroSun Dive also gets out to the Rainbow Reef.

The Jean-Michel Cousteau resort's renowned operation **L'Aventure** (⊠*Lesiaceva Point* ☎*885–0188, 800/246-3454 in U.S.* ⊕*www.fijiresort.com/dive_sites.shtml*) dives more than 15 sites in the Koro Sea using its 37-foot enclosed-cabin boat aptly named *L'Aventure*. The boat departs the resort with up to 12 divers each morning around 8:30, sometimes returning at 12:30 and sometimes going until 4 PM with an included picnic lunch. A one-tank dive costs US$80, a two-tank dive is US$133, and full certification costs US$525, not including equipment rental. Call in advance to reserve space.

KoroSun Dive (☎*885–2452* ⊕*www.korosundive.com*), a PADI- and SSI-certified operation, runs day trips to the Rainbow Reef in Somosomo Strait in addition to trips to Namena Barrier Reef. It uses two 33-foot purpose-built boats with freshwater showers. A one-tank dive costs US$70, a two-tank dive is US$115. Night dives and certification courses are priced on request.

For avid (though not necessarily experienced) fans of diving ages 18–35, the six-week program **Fiji Dive, Marine Conservation and Culture** (☎*970–7906* ⊕*www.diving-fiji. com*) combines cultural immersion, diving certification or advancement, and marine conservation work. Participants start with a certification or advancement course with Koro-Sun Dive. They spend a week living in a very basic village outside of town while learning how to conduct Marine Protection Area (MPA) research from the Jean-Michel Cousteau Resort's resident marine biologist. The second week or so is spent at Hidden Paradise Guesthouse while they begin research. The group then moves to a house in the area and continues its dive research. The last week or so of the trip is spent relaxing at either the Beach House or Mango Bay Resort on Viti Levu's Coral Coast. The program costs US$3,950. Six-week marine conservation internships involving a longer village stay are also available, as are one-three week luxury packages with an optional marine biology component.

SHOPPING

Savusavu's Main Street has a few supermarkets. Saturday is the biggest day at the local market in town, which sells fresh fish and produce throughout the week. Most stores and government offices close early in the afternoon on Saturday and are closed all day on Sunday.

LABASA

81 km (50 mi) from Savusavu

Vanua Levu's second airport is a half-hour drive outside of this sugar town. Like northeastern Viti Levu, the town is serviced by a narrow-track railroad transporting sugar, and the town's population grows exponentially during cane-crushing season (roughly May–December) as seasonal workers come up to harvest. This is the best point of entry in the north if you're headed for the area's superb off-shore resort, Nukubati. Unless you're coming here for the resort itself, save your exploring days for the water or rain forest.

WHERE TO STAY & EAT

CHINESE

$ ✕**Oriental Restaurant & Bar.** Here's one globe-spanning restaurant where you shouldn't settle on a curry simply by default. The Chinese dishes are good, large, and best enjoyed family-style. Second prize goes to the range of traditionally prepared seafood such as lobster, prawns, and fish cooked in *lolo* (coconut milk). The strange wood canopies with rope netting over most of the tables are even stranger in light of the honest attempt at Asian decor made by illustrated tapestries. Avoid weekend afternoons, when locals crowd the bar and many of the tables with tall bottles of Fiji Bitter. To find it, look for the big sign on a building across from the bus station. ⊠*Jaduram St.* ☎*881–7321* ⊜*No credit cards* ⊗*Daily 10–3 and 6–10.*

$-$$ ☎**Grand Eastern Hotel.** Most expats and Fijian businesspeople won't stay anywhere else in Labasa. This old-school hotel has two levels of rooms surrounding a pretty pool and professional, friendly service. Garden views have tile floors, simple bathrooms with walk-in showers, and decent closet space. Deluxe rooms are carpeted and have updated but very small bathrooms, newer furnishings, and views to the pool. Rooms of both types each have a double and single bed. The in-house restaurant, the Colonial Arms ($$), is Labasa's most upscale. The menu includes entrées such as seafood ragout and chicken breast stuffed with apricot and camembert cheese with a Frangelico sauce. The resort is at the end of a parking lot, a block past the train tracks at the eastern end of town. **Pros:** Professional staff; good in-house restaurant. **Cons:** Bland setting. ⊠ *Rosawa St.* ☎ *881–1022* ⊕ *www.hexagonfiji.com* ⇌ *22 rooms, 2 suites* ⌂ *In-room: refrigerator. In-hotel: restaurant, bar, pool, no elevator, laundry service, airport shuttle* ☰ *AE, MC, V* ⊚ *EP.*

$$$$ ⊡ **Nukubati Island Resort.** The only private island resort off
★ the northern coast of Vanua Levu makes some other "hide-aways" look like they're in traffic. The island is blessed with gorgeous white-sand beaches and its proximity to the magnificent but less-visited Great Sea Reef is a real treat for divers; snorkeling is great right off the beach. You can also fish, sail, and surf November–March. The spacious, simply furnished bures have a colonial feel. Beachfronts, a small lawn away from the sand, have queen-size beds and private rear patios. Honeymoon bures are farther apart with large porch lounges and open-plan sink areas leading out to their private patios. Meals are served whenever and wherever guests want, perhaps in the open-air dining pavilion or at a table and chairs set up on the beach. The emphasis is on fresh-caught seafood such as crab and lobster, often artfully presented in their shells. The fact that a wine cellar stocks some of the all-included alcohol accentuates the resort's sense of class. **Pros:** Entirely personalized experience; world-class seafood, remoteness. **Cons:** Remoteness. ⊠ *Nukubati Island* ☎ *881–3901, 888/692–4375 in U.S.* ⊕ *www.nukubati. com* ⇌ *7 bures* ⌂ *In-room: no a/c, no phone, refrigerator, no TV. In-hotel: restaurant, room service, bar, tennis court, spa, beachfront, diving, water sports, laundry service, airport shuttle* ☰ *AE, DC, MC, V* ⊚ *AI.*

VANUA LEVU ESSENTIALS

TRANSPORTATION

BY AIR

Air Fiji has four daily flights from Nadi to Savusavu and two daily flights back. Pacific Sun has three daily flights to and from Nadi. The flight takes 45 minutes to an hour. Both airlines have offices at the Copra Shed Marina. From Savusavu airport, it's less than 3.2 km (2 mi) into town.

A local bus passes every two hours or so and taxis are available. Nearly all Savusavu-area accommodations will arrange transport. Pacific Island Seaplanes offers chartered seaplane flights between Nadi and anywhere in Fiji and will land right in front of the resort.

Air Fiji does one daily round-trip early-morning trip between Nadi and Labasa and six daily round-trips between Suva and Labasa. Pacific Sun has one daily nonstop flight each way between Nadi and Labasa, and one or two non-stop flights from Suva-Labasa and Labasa-Suva depending on the day. The airport is amid cane fields about 10 km (6 mi) outside of town.

Airlines Air Fiji (☎885–0538 ⊕www.airfiji.com.fj). **Pacific Island Seaplanes** (☎672–5644 ⊕www.fijiseaplanes.com). **Pacific Sun** (☎885–0141 ⊕www.pacificsun.com.fj).

Airports Labasa Airport (LBS) (☎881–1035). **Savusavu Airport (SVU)** (☎885–2433).

BY BUS

In the Savusavu area, local buses run throughout the day from the station in the center of town out to villages along the Hibiscus Highway. It's roughly 1½ hours each way. Buses also run from the station down to Lesiaceva Point. Both can be extremely crowded during "rush hour," when most locals go to and from work at the resorts. Fares are reasonable.

There are inexpensive daily buses between Savusavu and Labasa, about a three-hour ride. These depart between 8:30 and 3:30 PM from the station in each town.

BY CAR

Trip n Tour rents three- and five-door Toyota RAV4s for $80–$130 per day and Yamaha scooters for $35–$45 per day, with the lower rates applying to longer rentals.

The Savusavu Hot Springs Hotel rents two-door and four-door Toyota RAV4s for $110–$130 per day with discounts on longer rentals. It also rents scooters for $45 per day.

Rental Car Agencies Trip n Tour (✉Copra Shed Marina ☎885–3154). **Savusavu Hot Springs Hotel** (✉Nakama Rd., off Lesiaceva Rd., west of Copra Shed Marina ☎885–0430).

BY FERRY

Bligh Water Shipping operates ferries transporting people and vehicles between most of Fiji's major destinations, including Savusavu, Taveuni, Lautoka, and Suva. From Lautoka, the trip takes 11.5 hours. From Natovi (north of Suva), it takes 6.5 hours. From Taveuni, the journey is about 5 hours. Prices vary widely according to passengers' age and in which class/cabin they travel, but even economy rates are not much cheaper than domestic airfares. Check the Web site for schedules.

Beachcomber Cruises traditionally operates service to Savusavu; however, at the time of research their ship was undergoing repairs and service was uncertain.

Contact **Beachcomber Cruises** (⊕ *www.beachcomberfiji.com*). **Bligh Water Shipping** (☏ *885–3192* ⊕ *www.blighwatershipping.com.fj*).

CONTACTS & RESOURCES

BANKS & EXCHANGE SERVICES

Each of Savusavu's banks has a 24-hour ATM. Westpac, ANZ, and Colonial are on the main street in town.

Taveuni

WORD OF MOUTH

"If I had 6 days, I'd spend a day checking out Nadi, then fly to Taveuni for diving and exploring. We stayed at Garden Island Resort, which is reasonably-priced, has great views, and caters to divers. There are also several great hiking destinations and a couple of small villages to visit."

—ALF

Written
by Robert
Brenner

THE "GARDEN ISLAND OF FIJI" IS 110,000 ACRES OF DENSE, virgin rain forest and high volcanic peaks. The island is rich in flora such as the red-and-white Tagimoucia flower, which only grows here and on a small part of Vanua Levu. Taveuni's fauna flourish in the absence of the mongoose, which was introduced to many Fiji islands in order to reduce the rat population and which subsequently decimated frog and lizard species. Bird-watchers are smitten with the red-breasted musk parrots, silktails, and rare orange-breasted doves among the many other species that thrive here.

In 1990 roughly a third of the island became protected as Bouma National Heritage Park with monetary aid from the government of New Zealand. The park is effectively an ecotourism project split among four villages each of which oversees and collects admission from a different part. A rich collection of waterfalls, walking trails, and magnificent reefs on and around the island is within easy reach to visitors.

Some of Fiji's best snorkeling is at remote Vuna Reef off the island's southern tip, shallow cousin to the great Rainbow Reef. Both are home to some of the world's most brilliant soft coral as well as a wondrously diverse array of large and small fish species. Many resorts have excellent, highly personal in-house dive operations.

ABOUT THE HOTELS & RESTAURANTS

When the first resorts were built on Taveuni, developers were limited in the size of the resorts they could build owing to the difficulty of procuring materials so far from the mainland. This proved a blessing in disguise as intimate boutique resorts—targeting the U.S. market in particular—are now the region's trademark. The island also has a wealth of self-contained rental cottages, the most modest of which have fantastic cliff-edge views. These, combined with the first-rate attractions of the national park, make for a rewarding independent holiday.

Honeymooners and couples seeking space and privacy as well as a highly personalized experience will find the offshore islands and Matei-area resorts have their interests at heart. The top resorts cater strongly to the U.S. market with luxury amenities, relatively prompt service, and, in most cases, prices advertised in U.S. dollars. Virtually *all* Taveuni rates do not include government taxes of 17.5%.

TAVEUNI'S TOP 4

Great White Wall. Emerge from an underwater tunnel 90 feet down to the sight of a seemingly glowing white coral wall.

Tavoro Waterfalls. Swim beneath the cascade in one of the world's most pristine environments.

Seeing Orange. Spot the elusive Orange Dove during an early-morning trek up Des Voeux Peak—and bring your camera!

The View. Nearly all Taveuni's accommodations offer spectacular cliff-edge views over Somosomo Strait and beyond.

The dining experience on Taveuni is primarily resort-based. In the Matei area the resort restaurants are all within walking distance and welcome nonguests. For self-caterers, there are supermarkets in Matei and Naqara.

6

WHAT IT COSTS IN FIJI DOLLARS ($F)			
$	$$	$$$	$$$$
RESTAURANTS			
under $F10	$F10–$F20	$F20–$F30	over $F30
HOTELS*			
under $F200	$F200–$F400	$F400–$F700	over $F700
HOTELS**			
under $F300	$F300–$F500	$F500–$F800	over $F800

*EP, BP, CP **AI, FAP, MAP; Restaurant prices are per person for a main course at dinner. Hotel prices are per night for a double room in high season and may not include a 12.5% Value-Added Tax (V.A.T.) or a 5% hotel turnover tax. Hotel prices are in U.S. dollars where noted.

EXPLORING TAVEUNI

Taveuni is unique because many of the island's top accommodations are within walking distance of Matei airport, which is on the island's northern tip. None of these is especially close to the island's star attraction, Bouma National Heritage Park. The Matei area is the closest, about a

Taveuni

Hotels

Coconut Grove, **7**
Garden Island Resort, **9**
Karin's Garden, **3**
Lomani Cottage, **8**
Maravu Plantation Resort, **1**
Matangi Private Island Resort, **13**
Matei Point, **6**
Paradise Taveuni, **10**
Qamea Resort & Spa, **12**
Taveuni Island Resort, **2**
Taveuni Palms, **5**
Todranisiga, **4**
Vatuwiri Plantation, **11**

Restaurants

Tramonto, **1**

KEY

1 *Restaurants*
① *Hotels*

GREAT ITINERARIES

Depending on where you stay, Taveuni lends itself equally well to days filled with kayaks, scuba gear, and rain-forest trails and those taken with hammocks, tropical drinks, and sand. Regardless of where you stay in Taveuni, you're going to want to hit some part of **Bouma National Heritage Park** and if you have even the slightest interest in diving, this is one of the world's top places to indulge.

IF YOU HAVE 3 DAYS

Early on your first morning, Trek to the Tavoro Waterfalls in **Bouma National Heritage Park** and take a dip in the falls. On the way back to your Matei or Waiyevo-area accommodation, have lunch at Coconut Grove Cottage if not staying somewhere with a restaurant. Snorkel and relax in the afternoon. If you plan to dive, arrange an outing for the following morn-ing. On Day 2, scuba dive or hike **Des Voeux Peak** in the morning and visit storied **Somosomo Village** in the afternoon. On Day 3, return to Bouma for the Lavena Coastal Walk, or dive/snorkel once (or twice) more.

IF YOU HAVE 5 DAYS

With this amount of time, you can take a dive course or do a package. If you're not diving, make a half-day or more snorkeling trip to **Vuna Reef** with a packed picnic lunch to enjoy on a quiet beach near the blow hole. Throw a horse-back-riding, kayaking, or bicycling trip in among your trips to **Bouma National Heritage Park** and your village visit.

IF YOU HAVE 7 DAYS

Let your choice of resort guide you. Be sure to make at least one trip to **Bouma National Heritage Park** and to go scuba diving or snorkeling on the magnificent reefs.

35-minute drive away. The farther south you go, the rougher the road gets and thus the time it takes to get to the park is compounded. The resorts will arrange tours and excursions of any kind and, if possible, dive boats will usually pick up guests right from their beachfront.

★ Fodor'sChoice **Bouma National Heritage Park.** Taveuni got the nickname "Garden Island of Fiji" for this multifaceted park covering almost 259 square km (100 square mi), or nearly a third of the island. The park's four villages offer guided walks, waterfall visits, snorkeling off traditional rafts, a hike, and bird-watching through the virgin rain forest and along the pristine coast. The **Lavena Coastal Walk** is a scenic walk past rain forest and traditional gardens

---

IF YOU LIKE

DIVING
This region has two of the South Pacific's top reefs. Both the Rainbow and Vuna are rich in soft coral, small fish, and pelagics.

BOUTIQUE RESORTS
Few resorts in the north host more than 40 guests at a time and many significantly less. Expect to have staff who know your name within the hour, personalized activities, and private beachfront dining at your fingertips.

BIRD-WATCHING
The famed Orange Dove, stunning Silktail, and Red Shining Parrot are just a few endemic species flitting about the lovingly cut trails through Taveuni's lush rain forest.

INDEPENDENCE
The abundance of fully furnished cottages with full kitchens and fantastic views makes this island an enticing option for travelers looking not only to "get away from it all" but to do so on their own comfortable slice of cliff-edge property.

---

of cassava, papaya, kava, and other crops, over a river to pristine waterfalls and a swimming hole. The trail begins at Lavena village, 6 km (3.7 mi) south of the park entrance, and passes great swimming and snorkeling spots as it traces the coast. It's a four-hour walk round-trip, but makes an enjoyable half-day or longer. Groups of four or more can also take a three-hour boat tour to seven waterfalls inaccessible on foot and walk back along the coast, if they so choose. ✛*35-minute drive southeast of Matei* ☎*920–5834* ⊕*www.bnhp.org* ✉*$8, $10 for a guide (optional), $45 for boat tour.*

The first of the **Tavoro Waterfalls,** or Bouma Falls, is a three-hour walk up the Tavoro River from its visitor center. It's one of the most spectacular waterfalls in Fiji and was featured in the movie *Return to the Blue Lagoon*. The second and third waterfalls are successively farther away and more difficult to get to, and have smaller swimming pools. ✛*30-minute drive southeast of Matei* ☎*888–0390* ⊕*www.bnhp.org* ✉*Falls walk $8.*

Bird-watchers and those looking for a more strenuous experience will enjoy the **Vidawa Rainforest Hike.** This half-day guided tour takes you through rain forest and ancient village sites and up to excellent views over the island and reefs. Birds you may see include Lady Monarchs, Blue-Crowned

Broad Bills, Silk Tails, and the storied Orange Dove, of which no known photographs exist. The tour includes lunch and refreshments. The trail begins across the road and slightly north of the Tavoro Waterfalls visitor center. ✉ *Vidawa Rainforest Hike visitor center, Vidawa village, about a 30-minute-drive southeast of Matei* ☎ *990–5833* ⊕ *www.bnhp.org* ✎ *$40.*

Des Voeux Peak. Nearly 1,219 meters (4,000 feet) up, this peak offers Taveuni's best views over Vanua Levu and the Somosomo Strait. The trip requires a 30- to 40-minute 4WD ride and then a 20-minute walk and is best done earlier in the day before clouds begin crowding in at the top. You can rent a car (*see Essentials at end of chapter*) or organize the trip through your hotel. ⊹ *South of Waiyevo, just north and inland from Wairiki Catholic Mission.*

At **Waitabu Marine Park & Campground** you can swim and snorkel over a fringing reef that has been a marine-protected area (MPA) since 1998, when the Waitabu people and other villages agreed to stop over-fishing. There are guided snorkeling tours using bilibili or traditional bamboo rafts followed by tea and music on the beach. A cheaper option does not include rafts or tea. The campground offers 12 tent sites near the water's edge, and communal cooking and bathroom facilities. It's slightly north of Vidawa village on the coast. ⊹ *Near Vidawa village, about a 30-minute-drive southeast of Matei, Bouma National Heritage Park* ☎ *888–0451* ⊕ *www.bnhp.org* ✎ *$40 with raft and tea, $20 without. Camping $10 per person per night.*

Somosomo Village. The largest village on Taveuni, it's the seat of government and home of Taveuni's high chief. The Great Council of Chiefs meeting house, a stately thatched bure, is visible from the road, and there's also a graveyard here. Tours can be organized through your accommodation. ⊹ *North of Naqara on western coast.*

Waitavala Waterslide. Not far from Garden Island Resort is this local hangout where kids slide down a natural chute of smoothed rocks into a natural pool. It has a beautiful rain forest setting but be careful: The ride can leave you with bumps and bruises. ⊹ *Near Waiyevo on western coast.*

Wairiki Catholic Mission. The Catholic Church here was built in 1907 in honor of a French missionary who successfully advised Taveuni's warriors in how to defeat invading Tongans in a major battle. It's an imposing stone structure

A Brief History of Taveuni

Unlike in much of the country, the majority of Taveuni's original settlers came from Polynesia, with traces of the Polynesian language stronger in the island's dialects than elsewhere in Fiji. Taveuni warriors were regarded within the South Pacific as being among the region's fiercest. In the 1860s, natives turned back thousands of invading Tongans just off the coast. The tide-turning victory came after the Tongans had conquered much of Fiji, and the natives celebrated by eating their enemies with breadfruit. A 350-meter-long cave formed by a lava tube was used, it's believed, to bury the island's greatest warriors, thereby hiding their bodies from the enemy. The cave, excavated in the 1950s, is now on private property.

In the mid-1800s European settlers realized the great potential in Taveuni's fertile soil and established cotton, sugar, and coconut plantations as well as farms growing pineapples, bananas, and other fruits. A plantation founded by an Englishman in 1871 at the island's southern tip is run to this day by his descendants, who use their acres of palm trees to harvest copra, the key ingredient in coconut oil.

in the Roman style with stained-glass windows and the only seating are floor mats. Fijians are known for their beautiful a cappella singing and Sunday services here are a fantastic way to experience this. Local children are often eager to show visitors around their village afterward. The international dateline or 180th meridian, which in theory splits the island but was shifted around the Fiji island group, is denoted by a sign not far from here. ✛ *South of Waiyevo on western coast.*

OFF THE BEATEN PATH. **Blow hole and Vuna Reef.** At the very southern tip of the island, this dramatic natural feature is created by water rushing in between black volcanic rocks on the edge of coral-rich Vuna Reef, fantastic for snorkeling. It's also in the vicinity of quiet beaches ideal for a picnic lunch. At low tide, you can climb over rocks to get closer to the blow-hole, but it's not recommended. ✛ *Near Vuna Village.*

WHERE TO STAY & EAT

$$-$$$ ✕**Tramonto.** On the cliff-edge at a bend in the road, this small open-air restaurant and bar has views to rival any of its resort neighbors. The furnishings are simple but with the breeze blowing in at night and your food illuminated by lantern, who needs decor? Skip the pizzas and instead order fish, which is served up a number of ways but usually also available with chips (french fries) for $10. Thursday is a grill night featuring chicken, fish, and lobster; Saturday is an all-day barbecue; and Sunday is roast night. Happy hour is 5–7 PM, shedding $1 off drinks. A 15-minute walk from the airport, this place can get crowded. ⊠*Matei* ☎*888–2224* ▤*No credit cards* ☉*Daily 10 AM–9 PM.*

$ ⌂**Coconut Grove.** With Bouma National Park and three diving companies nearby, this can be the setting for a very active holiday, but most guests choose this three-cottage resort for just the opposite reason. The cottages are a few steps from the beach (unusual for Taveuni) and each has tropical light-wood furnishings, a queen-size bed, porch, and hammock. The two pricier ones have private outdoor showers (the Mango cottage's is grander); the third has an indoor shower and shares an outdoor one with guests coming off the sand. The dining porch's modest plastic furnishings thankfully do not reflect its restaurant-style international cuisine. Choosing the US$35 all-inclusive meal plan allows you to focus that much more on relaxing. **Pros:** Privacy; personal service; nice beach. **Cons:** Dining experience lacks ambience. ⊠*Matei* ☎*888–0328* ⊕*www. coconutgrovefiji.com* ⤳*3 suites* ⌂*In-room: no a/c, no phone, refrigerator, no TV. In-hotel: restaurant, bar, beachfront, water sports, spa, beachfront, laundry service, public Internet, airport shuttle* ▤*MC, V* ☉*CP, FAP.*

$$ ⌂**Garden Island Resort.** Its proximity to the famed Rainbow ★ Reef and great-value packages make this one of Fiji's top dive resorts. Experienced divers come here again and again for the award-winning Aqua-Trek dive team, including a dive master with 16 years' experience at this resort alone, the high-quality equipment, and the value. It's a 10- to 30-minute ride out to most dive sites, all on the Rainbow Reef. The resort rents underwater cameras and has facilities for developing and viewing slides and for viewing videos. Rooms in the hotel are clean and simple with queen and single or queen and double beds; those on the ground floor lead right out onto the lawn while those above have small

6

balconies. The dorms are shared four-bed hotel rooms. A pretty oceanfront pool and full spa offerings round out the facilities. The restaurant offers hearty traditional Fijian and European dishes. Children under 15 stay free with two adults. **Pros:** Fantastic diving; friendly staff; camaraderie among guests. **Cons:** Concrete hotel setting. ⊠ *Waiyevo* ☎ *888–0286, 800/541–4334 in U.S.* ⊕ *www.aquatrek.com* ⤳ *28 rooms, 2 dorms* ⌂ *In-room: refrigerator, no TV. In-hotel: restaurant, bar, pool, spa, beachfront, diving, water sports, laundry service, public Internet, airport shuttle* ⊟ *AE, MC, V* ⦿ *CP, FAP.*

$ ▣ **Karin's Garden.** Those interested in leading the simple life can do so in the two-bedroom self-contained house at Karin's. Although its setting back from the cliff-top precludes great views, a walk across the lawn and down steps gains you beach access and it's a relatively short drive to Bouma National Park. The house's two bedrooms, one with a queen bed and one with two singles, are joined by a living area with a full kitchen and small dining area. Karin's has a small restaurant serving European cuisine with specialties such as roast pork and Hungarian goulash. A number of resort restaurants are within walking distance. **Pros:** Spacious house; choose-your-own-adventure. **Cons:** Minimal ocean view; near to the restaurant. ⊠ *Matei* ☎ *888–0511* ⊕ *karinsgardenfiji.com* ⤳ *1 suite* ⌂ *In-room: no a/c, no phone, kitchen, refrigerator, no TV. In-hotel: restaurant, bar, beachfront* ⊟ *No credit cards* ⦿ *EP.*

$$ ▣ **Lomani Cottage.** Its full entertainment system and "infinity pool" make this Taveuni's most luxuriously appointed self-contained rental. The property's caretaker meets guests on arrival and is available to recommend and book trips, excursions, and restaurants throughout the stay. A chef specializing in curries and seafood is available on 24 hours' notice and a housekeeper is on call for $5/hour. The open-plan house has a bedroom with a mosquito-netted king-size bed, a living area and a kitchen. Outside, the pool area has two daybeds on a hardwood deck overlooking Somosomo Strait. The property's lush gardens have bananas, pineapples, avocados, mangos, and other fruits. You can enter the ocean for swimming and good snorkeling from the rocky area at the bottom of the hill. The house is about 5 mi (8 km) south of the airport. **Pros:** Privacy; magnificent views; relatively close to Bouma Park. **Cons:** Poor beach; need mobile phone to make calls. ⊠ *Vatulaga* ☎ *614/0007–7007 in Australia* ⊕ *www.lomanifiji.com* ⤳ *1 cottage* ⌂ *In-house:*

no phone, DVD, kitchen, pool, bicycles, laundry facilities, airport shuttle ⊟*AE, D, MC, V* ⊚*EP*.

$$$–$$$$ ⊞**Maravu Plantation Resort.** An open-air, tropical-chic dining area with plenty of room for intimacy and live music nightly is the epicenter of this sprawling resort popular with honeymooners. The second- and third-room categories are each a big step up from the previous one: Planters and Deluxe bures are both in double units but each Deluxe has an outdoor as well as an indoor shower and a Jacuzzi tub. Honeymoon bures are separate and have small Jacuzzi pools in private river-rock courtyards. Beyond that, Honeymoon suites have Jacuzzi plunge pools and larger outdoor showers but only number 17 also has an indoor shower; numbers 14, 15, and 16 have partial Ocean views. Ocean-view villas have everything plus a hilltop view and are 630-square-feet (58-square-meters). There's also a 735-square-foot (68-square-meters) Treehouse. Dinners are a $50 three-course set menu and include choice of two appetizers, three entrées, and two desserts. An entrée might be sweet-and-sour pork with stuffed aubergine, an appetizer coconut pumpkin soup. A full breakfast is included. **Pros:** Privacy and great amenities in higher categories; great dining atmosphere. **Cons:** Beach is across the street; somewhat bland grounds. ⊠*Matei* ☎*332–4000* ⊕*www. maravu.net* ⚲*12 rooms, 4 suites, 4 villas, 1 treehouse* ⚐*In-room: no phone, no TV. In-hotel: restaurant, room service, bars, pool, gym, spa, water sports, bicycles* ⊟*AE, MC, V* ⊚*BP, MAP, FAP*.

$$$ ⊞**Matangi Private Island Resort.** Its beachfront "Treehouse"
★ bures first put this family-owned boutique resort on the map and its stylish new "infinity pool" and soaring open-air dining bure are likely to keep it there. Island bures lack air-conditioning and have outdated bathrooms; most guests stay in the spacious beachfronts, which have intricately tiled outdoor showers (as well as indoor ones) and a polished-natural feel. The split-level Treehouse bures built into pacific almond trees are another big step up (an impressive flight of them, actually), with dual basin sinks on timber-slab counters and outdoor lava rock showers. There's also a large villa. All bures are steps from the ocean and a sand-path makes footwear unnecessary. The resort guards its honeymooners' right to private picnics on the island's breathtaking Horseshoe Bay and scenic hiking, outstanding snorkeling and scuba diving are also options. Menus fuse international and Pacific Rim fare and offer

a great selection. **Pros:** Choice of three entrées at dinner; great snorkeling/diving; warm staff. **Cons:** Beachfront bure bathrooms could be bigger. ✉*Matangi Island* ☎*888–0260, 888/628–2644 in U.S.* ⊕*www.matangiisland.com* ⇨*13 suites, 1 villa* ⌂*In-room: no a/c (some), no phone, refrigerator, no TV. In-hotel: restaurant, room service, bar, pool, spa, beachfront, diving, water sports, laundry service, public Wi-Fi, airport shuttle, no kids under 12* ▭*AE, MC, V* ⍟*FAP.*

WORD OF MOUTH. "If you are considering staying near Taveuni Island in Fiji do stay at Matangi Private Island Resort. We had the most amazing stay in a tree house at the resort. The service, food, and accommodations were wonderful." —utahlover

$ 🏠**Matei Point.** Families settle into a tropical home-away-from-home experience in these four simple but spacious houses. A three-bedroom house is exactly at the northern tip of the island with views of both sunrise and sunset. Each of the three smaller houses has its own grounds and lawn along the cliff with great views. There's a one-bedroom with a king-size bed, and two two-bedrooms each have a queen and two single beds, though they can sleep up to five. Steps lead down to a small beach on the point. Chef Dan is available to prepare gourmet meals, including bread and desserts from scratch, for US$15/night (guests provide the ingredients). **Pros:** Privacy; great views. **Cons:** Small beach; simple accommodation. ✉*Matei Point* ☎*888–0422* ⊕*www.fijilodging.com* ⇨*4 houses* ⌂*In-room: no a/c, no phone, kitchen, refrigerator, DVD (some), no TV (some). In-hotel: beachfront, water sports, laundry service, public Internet, airport shuttle* ▭*AE, DC, MC, V* ⍟*EP.*

$$$ 🏠**Paradise Taveuni.** Luxury amenities and its small size attract couples and families to this boutique property opened in early 2007. Local village tours, bird-watching, snorkeling safaris, diving, kayaking, horseback riding, and trips to Bouma National Heritage Park keep most guests busy during the day; private outdoor two-person Jacuzzi tubs and showers, an indoor shower-bath, and indigenous decor surrounding a queen-size bed welcome them back at night. Bures sleep up to four with two convertible daybeds: Ocean views face onto a large lawn, which curves away toward the sea; garden views are in a second row, looking out from between the other bures. Included meals are a Continental breakfast, one-course lunch, and two-course

dinner. Dinners, taken wherever guests like, include three theme nights and four à la carte nights. **Pros:** Intimate resort size; great diving; Jacuzzis in Oceanfront bures. **Cons:** Have to upgrade meal plan for hot breakfast and more courses; all bures are set back from the view; no beach. ✉ *Vuna Rd., Southern Taveuni* ☎ *888–0125* ⊕ *www.paradiseinfiji. com* ⚑ *10 suites* ⚏ *In-room: no a/c, no phone, refrigerator, no TV. In-hotel: restaurant, room service, bar, pool, spa, beachfront, diving, water sports, laundry service, public Internet, airport shuttle* ⊟ *AE, MC, V* ⓘ *FAP, AI.*

$$$–$$$$ 🗊**Qamea Resort and Spa.** Guests rave about the staff at this
★ fun couples resort, which merges particularly suave rooms with a natural setting. Staff-guest volleyball matches and sunset crabbing are the playful side while lounge-style lighting in the dining bure and a do-not-disturb red coconut foster the honeymooner appeal. All the bures are within steps of the beach and feature an outdoor shower, daybed living area and—great touch—heated towel racks. Honeymoon bures have hot tubs and more central location while Premium bures, set apart on the ground, feature daybeds on their decks and small private pools. Snorkeling is good straight off the beach and there's excellent diving nearby. A brand-new rain-forest spa with Guinot products has beachside massage tables. Meals offer plenty of selection and the California-style (lighter) Pacific Rim and international dishes are supplemented by a complimentary sunset cocktail and hor d'oeuvres. Owing to room and beachside meal service, some honeymooners are rarely seen. Qamea is a 30-minute combination van-and-boat ride from Taveuni's airport. **Pros:** Exceptional, personable staff; great snorkeling/diving; intimate size. **Cons:** Food not consistently five-star; dimly lighted bures. ✉ *Qamea Island* ☎ *649/360–0858, 866/867–2632 in U.S.* ⊕ *www.qamea.com* ⚑ *16 suites* ⚏ *In-room: no phone, no TV. In-hotel: restaurant, room service, bar, pool, spa, beachfront, diving, water sports, laundry service, public Internet, airport shuttle, no kids under 16* ⊟ *AE, MC, V* ⓘ *FAP.*

$$$$ 🗊**Taveuni Island Resort.** Some of the sexiest bures in Fiji and dramatic cliff-top ocean views draw honeymooners and couples to this all-inclusive. All bures have dark tile-and-wood interiors, romantic beds with coconut husk frames and mood lighting, frosted glass bowl sinks, and outdoor showers. Among the Oceanview bures, "Niusawa" gets noise from the kitchen before meals. Oceanfront bures are but a small step up in price from Oceanviews and

have the front row. The Villa has its own pool, staff, and includes alcoholic beverages. You can see the ocean from every bed and steps lead through a garden down to a long strip of white-sand beach. The dining room is a sleek city-style affair but you can enjoy the Indo-Euro-Fijian cuisine at a cliff-edge bure, on the beach, or on your bure's deck. The resort offers diving at some of Fiji's premiere sites, picnic trips to smaller islands, and easy access to Taveuni's many natural attractions. **Pros:** Unique cliff-bottom beach; great diving and snorkeling; pretty spa. **Cons:** Bures seem close; some Oceanviews look between bures to the ocean. ⊠*Matei, Taveuni* ☎*888–0441, 877/828–3864 in U.S.* ⊕*www.taveuniislandresort.com* ⇆*11 suites* ⌂*In-room: safe, refrigerator, no TV. In-hotel: restaurant, room service, bar, pool, spa, beachfront, diving, water sports, laundry service, public Internet, airport shuttle, no kids under 15* ▤*MC, V* ¶*FAP, AI.*

$$$$ ▣**Taveuni Palms.** Prior to opening this two-villa resort, Kelly and Tony Acland asked the billionaires whose private yachts they worked on what they desired in a getaway. Topping the list were privacy, personalized service, and value—all three of which this resort offers to the extreme. Each two-bedroom villa is set on 1 acre and has a staff of seven including a chef who designs guests' all-inclusive menu, including five-course dinners, in consultation with them prior to their arrival. One villa has a modern feel with marble floors, its hot tub alongside the house and an elevated view. The others are solid South Pacific with hardwood floors, hot tub bure, and beachfront location. Both have super-king beds with 900-thread-count Egyptian cotton sheets and 24-hour service is an intercom button away. Each comes with a personal boat, van, and staff to match for excursions as reasonably priced as US$150 per person for a two-tank dive and picnic lunch on a smaller island or US$100 for a guided tour of Bouma National Park and a lobster lunch. **Pros:** Total privacy; ultraperson-alized experience; fantastic-value extras. **Cons:** Seclusion. ⊠*Matei, Taveuni* ☎*888–09932* ⊕*www.taveunipalms.com* ⇆*2 suites* ⌂*In-room: kitchen, refrigerator, DVD, Wi-Fi. In-hotel: restaurant, room service, pool, spa, beachfront, diving, water sports, laundry service, airport shuttle* ▤*AE, MC, V* ¶*FAP.*

$ ▣**Todranisiga.** Couples in search of privacy and plenty of space will love the cliff-edge setting of these studio-style cottages. The three are spread over a wide lawn and a trail in one part winds through foliage down to a small beach. "Audiva" has a queen-size bed with mosquito netting, a pretty marble-tiled shower, and simple toilet and sink area. It's steps from the cliff-edge and faces directly out to the ocean, with lounge chairs on a hardwood deck to soak up the view. "Todra" has a larger, more elegant bathroom and an outdoor shower open on the side facing the ocean. It's at a slight angle to the water and has a larger veranda and a small stove. A third cottage under construction at the time of research promised to have an equally grand setting. Owner May Goulding serves breakfast at the main house and prepares other meals on request. A number of restaurants are within walking distance. **Pros:** Privacy; magnificent views. **Cons:** Must bring own water sports gear. ⊠ *Matei* ☎ *925–9893* ✐ *todrafj@yahoo.com* ⬅ *2 cottages* ⚲ *In-room: no a/c, phone, kitchen (some), refrigerator, no TV. In-hotel: restaurant, bar, spa, beachfront, laundry service, airport shuttle* ⊟ *No credit cards* ⎮CP.

$ ⌸ **Vatuwiri Plantation Resort.** One of the last working planta-
☾ tions in the South Pacific, Vatuwiri has a farm's share of animals as well as exotic pet birds, excellent snorkeling and diving close by, and two well-spaced, cliff-edge cottages. Guests can horseback ride to and climb an extinct volcanic crater on the 2,000-acre property, learn about the copra production process going on around them, fish, or simply head down the stone steps from their cottage into the sea. A dive boat from a neighboring resort will pick guests up from their personal jetties. While not particularly spacious, each cottage is brightly decorated and has privacy and magnificent views from its porch, with cottage two's view slightly superior. Five generations ago, Joanna Tarte's ancestor was one of the first European settlers in Fiji. Tarte, her father, and siblings will proudly share the family history at meals, which she prepares according to what guests like using farm-grown vegetables. **Pros:** One-of-a-kind experience; great snorkeling; animal-lovers will be smitten. **Cons:** Early-morning rooster wake-ups; far from Bouma National Park; limited selection at meals. ⊠ *Vuna Point* ☎ *888–0316* ⊕ *www.vatuwirifiji.com* ⬅ *2 suites* ⚲ *In-room: no a/c, no phone, no TV. In-hotel: restaurant, bar, water sports, laundry service, public Internet* ⊟ *AE, MC, V* ⊘ *Closed Nov. and Dec.* ⎮FAP.

6

SPORTS & THE OUTDOORS

BIRD-WATCHING

If you're interested in expedited bird-watching, you'll want to venture into the 30 acres of tropical rain forest at the multifaceted preserve **Na Bogi Ono Farms** (✉*Southern Taveuni* ☎*828–3677 or 822–0505* ⊕*www.taveuniconservation.com*). A variety of rare doves among other birds and fruit bats feast on citrus fruit plants, often within easy view. Visitors can also trek into the greenery or feed fish and snorkel among lobsters, clams, and rock cod in a 3-acre marine-protected area. Half-day tours go 8–11 and 1–4. It's 40 km (25 mi) from the airport and transfers can be arranged. Call for costs.

FISHING

Taveuni Sport Fishing (☎*888–2442*) runs four boats that head out for mahimahi, yellowfin, walu, wahu, barracuda, and occasional sail fish and marlin (the latter tagged and released). Their 26- and 28-foot boats are $185/hour (minimum 2½ hours) or $670/half-day and $875/full-day. Their 34-foot and 36-foot craft are $870/half-day and $1,300/full-day. While they do share the spoils, be aware that anything caught belongs to the boat.

GOLF & TENNIS

The private residences at **Taveuni Estates Country Club** (✉*Southwestern Taveuni* ☎*888–0444*) share a picturesque par-27, 9-hole golf course along a volcanic coastline. Nonresidents can play a 1,400-yard round of 18 for $30. The estate's grass tennis courts can be rented for $10/hour. The country club also has a swimming pool, bar, and a restaurant serving wood-fire pizzas and lighter snacks. The restaurant is open Monday–Thursday 9–6:30, Friday and Saturday 9–8:30, and Sunday 9–7:30. It does not accept credit cards.

HORSEBACK RIDING

Ride through fields of palm trees to a volcanic crater on the 1,500-acre estate **Vatuwiri Plantation Resort** (✉*Vuna Point* ☎*888–0316* ⊕*www.vatuwirifiji.com*), or to a beach on Vuna Lagoon where you can then fish. Ms. Edythe Tarte breaks in horses on this working copra plantation, owned by her family since its arrival from Europe in 1871.

SCUBA DIVING

Fiji owes the title "Soft Coral Capital of the World" in large part to the extraordinarily diverse sea life on Rainbow Reef in the Somosomo Strait between Taveuni and Vanua Levu, and on quieter Vuna Reef at the Taveuni's southern tip. While the seas in Somosomo Strait can be rough and the tides strong, divers are rewarded with brilliant colors and a huge array of fish and pelagics. Visibility is excellent year-round but is exceptional during the colder months from May to November. Different companies dive different sites and even call the same site by different names. Below are a few of the most popular sites.

Auntie's Bommie has brilliant soft coral in shades of red, purple, violet, blue, yellow, and white lining a coral head at a depth of 65 feet (20 meters). Leopard sharks are sometimes seen here among moray eels, parrot fish, basslets, and other species. **Fish Factory** is popular with beginners for its multicolor soft coral, giant clams, and tons of reef fish, including occasional stonefish and leaf scorpions, starting at a depth of just 20 feet (6 meters) and extending to around 500 feet (152 m).

The **Great White Wall** has dramatic walls covered with bright white coral from a depth of about 50 feet (15 meters) until past 200 feet (60 meters), with a tunnel from 20 feet (6 meters) to around 90 feet (25 meters). You can spot eagle rays, manta rays, lion fish, and occasionally barracuda. **Rainbow Passage** is a submerged reef starting at around 25 feet (7–8 meters) with the area's famous profusion of soft corals and fish life. It has sea fans, whips, fusiliers, hawk fish, pipe fish, barracudas, and clown fish among other species. **The Zoo** is a 100-foot (30 meter) wall dive home to big fish including barracuda, reef sharks, eagle rays, and manta rays.

★ FodorsChoice **Aqua-Trek Taveuni** (✉*Garden Island Resort, Waiyevo* ☎*888-0286* ⊕*www.aquatrek.com*) offers great packages with accommodation but will also take walk-ins if there's space. This is a country-wide favorite among serious divers for its high-quality equipment, extremely experienced and professional staff, and the diving-and-accommodation packages it offers from its base at Garden Island Resort. Because it's mainly highly experienced divers who use this operator, those taking beginner courses often get highly personalized attention. A two-dive day costs $165, an afternoon or night dive is $96, and a four-day open water course is $660.

Pro Dive Taveuni (✉*Paradise Taveuni Resort* ☎888–0125 ⊕*www.paradiseinfiji.com/diving.html*) dives the Rainbow Reef's most popular sites as well as quieter Vuna Reef. A one-tank dive with full gear rental is $135, a two-tank dive is $270, and a PADI Open Water Course is $570. Packages are available in combination with a stay at the resort.

Jewel Bubble (✉*Matei* ☎888–2080 ⊕*www.jeweldivers. com*) is owned and operated by a PADI IDC instructor and Fijian native Qiolele Morisio, the former dive operations manager at Wakaya Club in the Lomaiviti Group. A one-tank dive including everything but regulator, BCD, and wetsuit costs US$80, a two-tank dive costs US$120, and a night dive is US$90. An open-water course including equipment costs US$480.

Swiss Fiji Divers (✉*Matei* ☎888–0586 ⊕*www.swissfiji divers.com*) has two excellent dive boats, including a 40-foot (12-meter) catamaran with a bathroom and shower on board. A two-tank dive costs $150, a night dive is $60 with a minimum of two divers and an open-water course costs $600.

Taveuni Dive (✉*Taveuni Estates, Waiyevo* ☎888–0844 ⊕*taveuniestates.com/dive.htm*), based at the Taveuni Estates residential community, dives at Vuna Reef and Rainbow Reef. A one-tank dive is US$50, a two-tank dive is US$95. Night dives are US$50 and an open-water course, over three to four days, costs US$385.

Owned by a Swiss-and-German couple and based across the Somosomo Strait on Vanua Levu, **Dolphin Bay Divers** (☎992–4001 ⊕*www.dolphinbaydivers.com*) has a one-tank dive for $80, a two-tank dive for $150. A night dive costs $80 and a PADI open-water course costs $550, not including course study materials.

SNORKELING

While it shares the Rainbow Reef's beautiful coral formations and diverse sea life, the relative shallowness of some of **Vuna Reef** (✉*Taveuni's southern tip*) makes it superior for snorkeling.

SHOPPING

There are no surefire places to souvenir shop on Taveuni, though you may find handicrafts for sale in the larger villages. Matei Point has two grocery stores. Naqara, not far from Garden Island Resort in the middle of the west coast, has two supermarkets and a local produce market. There's a very small grocery store next door to Garden Island resort in Waiyevo. Most stores close in the early afternoon on Saturday and are closed on Sunday.

TAVEUNI ESSENTIALS

TRANSPORTATION

BY AIR

Air Fiji and Pacific Sun each run two daily round-trip flights between Nadi and Taveuni's Matei Airport (TVU). Most flights from the U.S. arrive in Nadi in time for passengers to connect to the early morning flight to Taveuni. Matei Airport is at Taveuni's northern tip, on the paved section of the island's main road. Nearly all accommodations arrange airport transfers.

Airlines Air Fiji (☎672–2521, 672–3189 in Nadi, 331–3666 in Suva, 877/247–3454 in U.S. ⊕www.airfiji.com.fj). **Pacific Sun** (☎672–0888 in Nadi, 310/568-8676 in U.S. ⊕www.pacificsun.com.fj).

Airports Matei Airport (☎888–2015).

BY BUS

Buses make three round-trips on two routes weekdays, one covering the northern half of Taveuni, the other the southern half. The routes have one bus each on Sunday. The first leaves Lavena at 5:45 AM and the last returns at 6:30 PM. A trip from one end of the island to the other over increasingly rough roads as you head south is two hours and 20 minutes one-way. At the stop in front of the supermarket in Naqara, you'll likely see locals loading supplies to send south. Plans to pave the southern end of the road were interrupted by the last coup.

BY CAR

Taveuni is a good place to rent a four-wheel-drive if you plan on visiting Des Voeux Peak and Vuna Point in the south while staying in the north. Otherwise the buses, though somewhat unpredictable, are a great way to meet locals. You may be able to rent a taxi with a knowledgeable driver to guide you for around $150 a day. Budget Rent A Car in Naqara is open weekdays 8–5.

Contacts **Budget Rent A Car** (☎888–0291 or 672–2636).

BY FERRY

On Taveuni, all ferries depart from two wharfs located between Waiyevo and Naqara. Bligh Water Shipping operates ferries between most of Fiji's major destinations, including Savusavu, Taveuni, Lautoka, and Suva. Check the Web site for schedules.

For a long but wonderfully scenic journey from Vanua Levu, Grace Shipping runs a 3½-hour bus over the lush, mountainous (and rough) Hibiscus Highway to the village of Napuka on Buca Bay, where it meets a ferry for the hour-long crossing to Taveuni. The trip costs around $15. Look for the bus marked "Taveuni" departing the Savusavu station on Vanua Levu around 8 AM. The return trip leves from Naqara on Taveuni.

Contacts **Bligh Water Shipping** (✉Agent is Tima Limited, Waiyevo ☎888–0261 ⊕www.blighwatershipping.com.fj).

CONTACTS & RESOURCES

BANKS & EXCHANGE SERVICES

Taveuni's only bank is in Naqara. It has an ATM.

Bank Info **Colonial Bank** (✉Garden State Price Point Bldg., Naqara ☎888–0433).

Kadavu
Group

WORD OF MOUTH

"We stayed at a very small, remote eco-resort called Papageno on the little-known island of Kadavu. This place was very special: amazing food, wonderful locals, and very natural. [Kadavu] is the place that we had the most "National Geographic" type moments, for example, the time I was kayaking over to the mangroves and a school of slender, silver fish "flew" in front of the kayak—unreal."

—Connie

Written
by Robert
Brenner

FROM ITS ABUNDANCE OF UNINHABITED COVES and lush volcanic peaks to its lack of roads and retail, this rugged 58-km-long (36-mi-long) island is the stuff of an adventurer's dreams. Kayakers can make a day trip out of exploring coves, trekkers (and walkers) reach waterfalls and breathtaking ridge-top views, surfers get their breaks, and those drawn to the deep are smitten with the relatively unexplored sites of the famous Great Astrolabe and fringing reefs.

Despite the jungle-clad mountains balancing on pristine bays—a visual feast to satisfy any South Pacific romantic—most visitors come for the kind of vistas, which can only be found below sea level. The Great Astrolabe Reef, off the island's northern tip, is the world's fourth-largest barrier reef. Divers are treated to everything from a plethora of species of reef fish on up to barracuda, sharks, and 5-meter-wide manta rays swooping amid daring swim-throughs and rainbowlike coral walls.

The island group's culture is also easily accessible, as you come to know staff in boutique resort settings and are welcome to visit nearby villages where you can tour schools, experience kava ceremonies, and attend Sunday church services. Should you witness the stir created by the weekly arrival of the ferry from Suva, you'll understand your local hosts' genuine excitement at the opportunity to share a few hours with people from afar. This is Fiji's least-touched and most demanding tourist-friendly destination. Lend your energy and spirit to Kadavu and it will generously repay you.

ABOUT THE HOTELS

Resorts on the island range from basic to remote-chic and all are small and encourage swapping stories of the days' adventures between guests at meals. Each resort is keen on activity, with emphases on diving, fishing, kayaking, hiking, and often all of the above. At last count, there were a total of four televisions among the seven resorts recommended here. Divers may want to pick somewhere near the Great Astrolabe Reef. Those looking for luxury will find pleasing accommodations but should not expect sophisticated international cuisine. Partly based on principle and partly out of necessity, your resort will treat you to fruits and vegetables from organic gardens, solar power…you might even see the term "free-range" vividly illustrated as you narrowly avoid stepping on a fresh-laid egg. Staff here are invariably friendly—in some cases remarkably so, and management is often eager to get to know their guests.

WHAT IT COSTS IN FIJI DOLLARS (\$F)			
$	$$	$$$	$$$$
RESTAURANTS			
under \$F10	\$F10–\$F20	\$F20–\$F30	over \$F30
HOTELS*			
under \$F200	\$F200–\$F400	\$F400–\$F700	over \$F700
HOTELS**			
under \$F300	\$F300–\$F500	\$F500–\$F800	over \$F800

*EP, BP, CP **AI, FAP, MAP; Restaurant prices are per person for a main course at dinner. Hotel prices are per night for a double room in high season and may not include a 12.5% Value-Added Tax (V.A.T.) or a 5% hotel turnover tax. Hotel prices are in U.S. dollars where noted.

EXPLORING KADAVU

7

Kadavu's Vunisea airstrip is toward the middle of the island, at its narrowest point. From there, it's a short walk to a harbor that's dwarfed by the ferry from Suva when it makes its call each week. The only things on Kadavu worth exploring on your own are the delicious and inexpensive treats sold by the lady at the airstrip's snack counter. A hospital, post office, and police post are also nearby, but after your midday arrival, you'll probably be as eager as your hosts to get to your accommodation. The boat ride can take between 15 minutes and 3 hours depending on which resort you're destined for and the weather conditions. The cost of that ride along the magnificent coastline can be up to $50 each way; some build it into the nightly rate and others waive the fee over a longer stay (check with you resort).

Villages on Kadavu are extremely welcoming to visitors, perhaps even more so than elsewhere in the country owing to their isolation. The opportunity to visit one and take a glimpse into the communal lifestyle that inspires the Fijians' friendly and hospitable ways should not be missed. An excellent time to visit is on Sunday morning, when you can attend a church service. Believers and nonbelievers

Kadavu

KEY
① Hotels

Hotels
Bai's Place, **6**
Matana Beach Resort, **1**
Matava, **7**
Oneta Resort, **3**
Papageno Resort, **2**
Tiliva Resort, **4**
Waisalima, **5**

KADAVU'S TOP 4

Dive the Great Astrolabe. Duck into a swim-through past brilliant coral, be the wingman (or woman) of a huge manta ray or rubberneck at eels and reef sharks.

Kayak the Coves. Take a paddle to the serene inlets created by Kadavu's winding coastline.

Village Visits. Kadavu's villages are extremely welcoming and friends you make among the resort staff offer quick entrée to the islanders' particularly traditional way of life.

The View. Look around—you're in the setting of rugged South Pacific dreams. A sense of mystery and the past lingers in the island's untamed mountains and underwater depths, something that's harder to come by in the country's more accessible, sandier settings.

alike invariably marvel at the locals' beautiful a cappella style of singing. ■TIP→ **Modest dress is required when visiting a village at any time.** Cover the shoulders and waist and, out of respect, do not wear sunglasses or anything on top of your head.

Great Astrolabe Reef. The world's fourth-largest barrier reef traces the northern tip of the island group. Many resorts dive the site frequented by manta rays with wingspans of up to five meters. Those resorts nearest the Great Astrolabe explore more of its intricate coral-ways, while other resorts have uncovered excellent sites on the island's fringing reefs. Sea life across the group includes pipefish, sea horses, triggerfish, a variety of eels and wrasse, barracuda, reef sharks, occasional hammerheads, grouper, stone fish, octopuses, turtles, and spinner dolphins among many other species, all set amid a vast network of soft and hard coral formations including swim-throughs and mazes to impress the most experienced divers.

Nabukelevu (Mt. Washington). Rising at the southwestern end of Kadavu, as if a terrestrial balance to the submerged Astrolabe Reef in the northeast, is the 805-meter-high (2,641-foot-high) inactive volcano, Nabukelevu. From pottery pieces discovered within avalanche debris, scientists conclude that the last eruption occurred within the last 3,000 years. At the volcano's base are good diving and a pretty white-sand beach.

WHERE TO STAY & EAT

$ ☲ **Bai's Place.** Extremely rustic accommodations on a small island 25 minutes' from Kadavu's airstrip allow you a fantastic glimpse into Fijian life. Bai's paternal ancestor arrived from Boston as a handyman on one of the U.S.'s first voyages to Fiji in the 19th century and his descendants have lived here ever since. Bai will teach you to spearfish, free-dive for lobsters and scuba dive, and will educate you concerning village life and sustenance using his lush garden of sugarcane, avocadoes, and other fruits. Snorkeling (bring your own equipment), hiking, bird-watching and, of course, village visits are close at hand. One bure has a double bed and its own toilet and shower, another has two very small double bedrooms sharing a nearby outdoor shower and outhouse toilets. Over a hill is a 12-bed dorm with cooking facilities and a separate bathroom set on a beautiful white-sand beach. A meal plan including hearty curries, Fijian dishes, and plenty of vegetables is $15 per day. **Pros:** Fantastic opportunity to discover the local lifestyle; gain local knowledge. **Cons:** Private bures are set on a poor beach; extremely basic facilities. ⊠*Galoa Island* ☎*362–0139* ✐*whippywb@yahoo.com.au* ⇌*2 bures, 1 dorm* ⚴*In-room: no a/c, no phone, no TV. In-hotel: restaurant, beachfront, diving, water sports, airport shuttle* ▤*No credit cards* ⦿*FAP.*

$$ ☲ **Matana Beach Resort.** Better known as "Dive Kadavu" after its in-house dive shop, the emphasis here is on relaxation and the reefs. Matana's three covered dive boats hit 24 sites including the hangout of giant manta rays on the Astrolabe Reef, another with shark feeding, and one with a dive to 120 feet with a big swim-through. Shore dives are free. Set both on the beach and a bit uphill, the 10 simply appointed studio-style bures sleep from two to six. Bures 9 and 10, designed for couples, have king beds and are set right on the lovely beach, as are a few of the larger, family-oriented bures. When not submerged, you might trek up the ridge behind the resort for fantastic ocean views, take a boat to a local waterfall or another beach for a picnic or a sunset booze cruise. The included food is good and there's plenty of it, with predinner hors d'oeuvres served at the beach bar. **Pros:** Great dive staff; beautiful beach. **Cons:** Next door to village; underwhelming decor. ⊠*Kadavu Island* ☎*362–3502* ⊕*www.matanabeachresort.com* ⇌*10 bures* ⚴*In-room: no a/c, no phone, safe. In-hotel: restaurant,*

GREAT ITINERARIES

Budget, desired resort ambience and reef proximity (if diving) should be the deciding factors in planning a Kadavu Group itinerary.

IF YOU HAVE 3, 5, OR 7 DAYS

Owing to its lack of infrastructure and relatively few resorts spread over a 58-km-long (36-mi-long) island, all activities in Kadavu are resort-based. Because it can be pricey and time-consuming to commute between resorts, it's best to pick one for stays of three or four days. If staying for longer, consider pairing a resort with a particular strength (such as diving or fishing) with one in another part of the island offering a dissimilar level of comfort and thus a different perspective on the Kadavu experience. Divers may want to spend some of their time based at a resort on the northern end, where they can best explore the Great Astrolabe, and some in the hands of another dive operation, discovering the island's fringing reef.

bars, diving, water sports, laundry service, public Internet, airport shuttle ▤AE, DC, MC, V ⦿FAP.

$$ ⌧**Matava.** Divers and snorkelers, game-fishers, and kayakers not married to "the finer things" will find this eco-friendly resort a worthy base camp. The resort dives nearly 30 sites on the famed Astrolabe Reef, including one known for its enormous manta rays. A nice sand beach within view is a long swim or one-minute boat ride away. Remodeled in mid-2008, the studio-style bures are well-spaced on a steep hillside and have simple, white-tiled bathrooms and excellent, unobstructed views of the ocean. Honeymoon bures, commanding even better views from near the top, are a bit roomier with king-size beds. A new waterfront deck with wood-fire oven and daybeds is due by 2009. The included meals are very good though not exceptional and feature vegetables from an extensive organic garden and the occasional yellowfin tuna caught that day. **Pros:** Fantastic diving and fishing; personable staff; great views. **Cons:** No beach; no selection at meals. ✉*Kadavu Island* ☎*333–6222* ⊕*www.matava.com* ⇌*12 bures* ⌂*In-room: no a/c, no phone, no TV. In-hotel: restaurant, bar, diving, water sports, laundry facilities, public Internet, airport shuttle* ▤*AE, MC, V* ⦿*FAP.*

7

$$ ⊡**Oneta Resort.** Adventure-meets-intimacy-meets-science at Kadavu's newest addition, opened in summer 2008 on Ono Island. Practically surrounded by the Astrolabe Reef, the six-bure all-inclusive is owned in part by two northern Italian marine biology professors who will occasionally teach courses and conduct research at the resort's small lab. The emphasis is naturally on diving and fishing, led by two fast boats and an in-house dive operation that frequents sites on the Astrolabe not visited by any other resort. A single tank dive is $90, a two-tank dive is $160. Full- and half-day kayaking trips are also offered. Bures—two for honeymooners, three standards, and one six-bed for groups—were not yet ready at this writing. Honeymoon bures will have king-size beds, dual sinks, outdoor showers; one also has an indoor shower, and a TV with VCR. The cuisine is a fusion of traditional Fijian fare and Italian classics made with ingredients including organic vegetables and homegrown chicken and pork. **Pros:** Closest resort to the Astrolabe Reef; personalized experience; privacy. **Cons:** Seclusion. ⊠*Ono Island* ☎*603–0778* ⊘pieropiva@gmail. com ⇋*6 bures* ⛵*In-room: no a/c, no phone, no TV (some). In-hotel: restaurant, bar, beachfront, diving, water sports, airport shuttle* ☐*MC, V* ⊙*FAP.*

$$ ⊡**Papageno Resort.** Kadavu's most stylish bures and a
☾ carefully crafted ambience set this extremely ecofriendly
★ resort apart as the island's finest. Its generous white-sand beach is dotted with hammocks and edged by the five Ocean Bures designed for families with teenagers. There are bures for everyone—including a 12-capacity Royal Bure for corporate retreats and a "Kinder House" with a kitchen for very young families—and four Garden Rooms sharing a deck, each with a double and two single beds. All bures are furnished with beautiful Pacific Green–brand leather furniture, lavish bed spreads, and pretty bathrooms. Among the most popular activities are a day trip to Mt. Nabukelevu including fishing and diving at the volcano's base, and a picnic. A village tour with a kava ceremony and a day-cruise around the northern Astrolabe Reef are also guest-favorites. Meals in the comfortable main bure are designed for guests' preferences; lunch and dinner are communal. The resort is planning to open a down-scale resort on Long Beach, the island's lengthiest patch of land in the summer of 2008. **Pros:** Fantastic beach; beautifully appointed bures; nitrox diving. **Cons:** Lots of mosquitoes; no selection at meals; Garden Rooms a bit tight for four.

IF YOU LIKE

DIVING & SNORKELING

The world's fourth-largest reef is home to huge manta rays and an array of soft coral rivaling, if not surpassing, that of any other reef in the world. And if visitor traffic is anything to go by, it's *sorely* underappreciated. There are also great sites on the fringing reef, mostly off the southern coast of the island, including shallow spots ideal for snorkeling just off-shore.

FISHING

From feisty marlins to yellowfin with plenty of fight, there's big game to be had in and around the reef. Matava and Oneta have great boats and particularly strong expertise, and a number of resorts will take guests trolling into the gorgeous clear blue.

KAYAKING

Kadavu's rugged terrain and lack of roads lend themselves to an active, water-based holiday, epitomized by a good journey by kayak. Fantastic views are motivation enough and the small, pristine beaches are bonuses.

ECO-FRIENDLINESS

Solar power, organic gardens, compost piles, water recycling, and marine protected areas are the name of the game at these remote resorts invariably founded by green-minded people. You can take a tour, help garden, or simply savor the fruits of your hosts' labor.

✉ *Kadavu Island* ☎ *603–0466* ⊕ *www.papagenoresort.com* ⇙ *4 rooms, 7 bures* ⌂ *In-room: no a/c, no phone, refrigerator, no TV. In-hotel: restaurant, laundry service, public Internet, airport shuttle* ▭ *MC, V* �|○|*FAP.*

$$ ▣ **Tiliva Resort.** Six high-ceilinged, tropically appointed bures set far apart allow couples and families plenty of space at this boutique resort on Kadavu's eastern tip. It's run by Kemu "Kim" Yabaki, who grew up in nearby Tiliva Village, left to travel the world at 17, and returned 38 years later with wife Barbara to build a resort. When you aren't relaxing or diving with the operation at nearby Waisalima, you can kayak, trek through the mountains, or picnic on Ono Island's beaches a short boat-ride away. From the bures, it's a quick walk down the hill to the resort's beautiful strip of beach or up to the dining bure's large, comfortable outdoor deck overlooking the water. Lunches usually include a salad and fish-and-chips, and you're often asked whether you prefer chicken, meat, or fish for an entrée for that evening's Continental-style dinner. **Pros:** Privacy;

personalized experience; great beach. **Cons:** Only partial views to water through trees; bures set back from the beach. ✉*Kadavu Island* ☎*333-7127* ✺*www.tilivaresortfiji.com* ⟿*6 bures* ⚏*In-room: no a/c, no phone, no TV. In-hotel: restaurant, bar, beachfront, diving, water sports, airport shuttle, no kids under 3* ▤*MC, V* ⎁*FAP.*

$ ▦**Waisalima Beach Resort.** Guests make quick friends with staff and villagers at this simple, intimate resort on Kadavu's eastern tip. Painter Maureen Riggs moved her family here to escape the high-rise development of Australia's Gold Coast and the resort's ties with the local community make it clear that this is a home first, a resort second. Many guests come for the on-site dive shop, which offers highly personalized instruction (sometimes one-on-one); other popular activities include day trips to waterfalls and snorkeling trips to a nearby beach with picnic lunches, and visits to a nearby village. Bures were built and existing ones renovated in 2008. Two are right on the water and each is basically appointed with a double and two single beds, a simple bathroom and covered deck. There are also three dorm-bures that each sleeps three. Hearty Fijian-influenced fare is served buffet-style in an open dining room, the floor of which is a stunning tiled mosaic of the island. Eggs for breakfast are found wherever the truly "free-range" chickens decide to lay them. **Pros:** Personalized diving; great staff; excellent access to local culture. **Cons:** Poor beach; no selection at meals. ✉*Kadavu Island* ☎*603-0486* ✺*www.waisalimafiji. com* ⟿*8 bures, 3 dorms* ⚏*In-room: no a/c, no phone, no TV. In-hotel: restaurant, bar, beachfront, diving, water sports, laundry service, public Internet, airport shuttle* ▤*MC, V* ⎁*FAP.*

SPORTS & THE OUTDOORS

BOATING

Aboard the 36-foot luxury sloop of **Safari Charters** (✉*Matava* ☎*333-6222* ✺*www.matava.com*), you choose exactly where you go and what you do, be it island-hopping, high-speed adventure sailing, fishing, or a surfing trip. The yacht can take up to seven passengers on half- and full-day trips, and a single couple for live-aboard voyages of up to seven days. Prices start at $550–$650 for a day trip for up to four people and $900 per night for two including three meals.

It's Easy Being Green

In the realm of Fiji, 100 km (62 mi) can be a long way to go. So long, in fact, that the weekly ferry from Suva takes between seven hours and 1½ days to reach Kadavu's Vunisea harbor, depending on the weather. The ferry brings in the island's building materials, grocer- ies, dry goods, and even farm animals (and the occasional tourist). Because no guest likes to be told that the replace- ment generator part needed to power a hot shower is "on its way" or that the star ingredi- ent in that evening's chicken *cordon bleu* is still in steerage somewhere in the South Pa- cific, most resorts on Kadavu use sustainable "green" tech- nology and practices that allow them to be largely self-suf- ficient. There's also the not-so- small matter of preserving the magnificent rain forests, reefs, and beaches to which resorts in-part owe their livelihood and many eco-adventurers owe their bliss.

Solar energy is what keeps Matava's office and several of its bures powered. The resort was intentionally built next to a natural source of limestone- filtered spring water, has an organic garden, and builds its structures using locally grown pine and hardwoods. It composts waste, feeds food scraps to its pigs, and funnels grey water out to the plants on its grounds. Its game- fishing operation enforces a tag-and-release policy on all fish that aren't national or world records—or designated to become dinner. The resort supports a local village in exchange for protection of the resort's foreshore as a marine reserve (no-fishing zone) and has similar arrangements with villages near favored dive sites.

Papageno Resort's power is a combination of solar, micro- hydro, and a back-up diesel generator (the latter if needed), with plans to add solar panels. It grows organic produce in an extensive garden and composts its organic waste. By 2009 all Waisalima's bures will be solar- powered and at both Papageno and Waisalima, vigorous free- range chickens supply the eggs. Papageno recycles its bottles, cans, plastics, and used batter- ies in Suva, and other resorts ask that guests take these items back to the mainland with them for proper disposal.

FISHING

The resort **Matava** (⊠*Kadavu Island* ☎*333–6222* ⊕*www. matava.com*) offers big-game and sport fishing on and around the Great Astrolabe Reef. A 31-foot purpose-built boat goes after billfish using switch and bait techniques. A

17-foot boat is used to fish for trolling for wahoo, yellow fin, mahimahi, and others using high-quality rods and reels. Contact the resort for pricing.

HIKING

Most resorts have trails leading to stunning views, waterfalls, local villages, or up the sides of volcanoes. These can be short walks up the ridge behind the resort or day trips with stops for lunch and swimming along the way. Some of the trails are thin slices through the dense rain forest, others are subject to tides and all can be increasingly difficult to traverse following heavy rains.

KAYAKING

Regardless of where you stay, you'll find rain forest–edged coves to wind your way in and out of, dipping your oars into a dazzling turquoise sea. Paddle far enough and you're certain to come across at least one white sandy patch suitable for a sunbathing break or as a base for a swim. The water can be rough at times; resort staff will advise you on conditions.

SURFING

Off the southwestern tip of Kadavu are two of Fiji's better breaks, the **King Kongs:** King Kong Left and King Kong Right. King Kong Left is accessible to moderately skilled surfers. Long rides on generally 3- to 5-foot waves take off in deep water, keeping surfers safe from coral. King Kong Right is a fast tube for advanced surfers. There are also several beginner breaks nearby. If you're visiting Kadavu purely to surf, **Nagigia Island Resort** (⊕*www.fijisurf.com*) bills itself as a surf camp and is right next to the King Kongs.

Matava runs trips to two left-hand reef breaks at Soso and Vesi Passages, and one left- and–right-hand reef break at Naigoro Passage, all roughly 10- to 20-minutes from the resort. The waves can be up to 12-feet and require intermediate-to-advanced skills. There are also a few breaks outside the reef. The waves here are best December through March.

KADAVU ESSENTIALS

TRANSPORTATION

BY AIR

Pacific Sun runs a daily round-trip flight at midday between Nadi and Kadavu. Air Fiji follows soon after in the day with a daily flight between Suva and Kadavu. The two airlines share a phone number at the Vunisea Airstrip (KDV). All resorts meet their guests at the Vunisea airstrip for the trip by car and then boat to their accommodations. This transportation can cost between $20 and $50, although some resorts waive the fee for guests on longer stays.

Pacific Island Seaplanes offers chartered seaplane flights between Nadi and anywhere in Fiji and will land right in front of the resort.

Airlines **Air Fiji** (☎333–6042 ⊕www.airfiji.com.fj). **Pacific Island Seaplanes** (☎672–5644 ⊕www.fijiseaplanes.com). **Pacific Sun** (☎333–6042 ⊕www.pacificsun.com.fj).

BY FERRY

Venu Shipping runs a ferry service between Suva and Kadavu. However, the service can take anywhere from 8 to 36 hours; you may miss your resort transfer from Vunisea if the ferry is late, and fellow passengers might include livestock.

Contacts **Venu Shipping** (☎339–5000).

CONTACTS & RESOURCES

BANKS & ATMS

There are no banks in the island group. Bills can be settled by credit card at all resorts except Bai's Place, which only accepts cash.

FIJI VOCABULARY

Fijian is a classic example of a South-Pacific, vowel-centric language. In devising a written form of the language, English missionaries successfully matched all of its sounds to letters within our alphabet. However, there are a few simple but significant deviations:

The sound "d" is said as if preceded by an "n," so Nadi is pronounced *Nandi,* and Kadavu is *Kandavu*"; "b" is pronounced with a soft "m" in front of it, as in *mmbula*; "j" is "ch" as in *cherish*; "g" is "ng," so Sigatoka is pronounced *Singatoka*; "c" is "th" so Mamanuca is *Mamanutha*; "q" is "g" as in *good*.

FIJIAN GLOSSARY

archipelago	group of islands
atoll	a coral reef surrounding a lagoon
bilibili	bamboo raft ride
bilo	a kava drinking cup made from a coconut shell
bure	house
drua	double-hulled canoe used for war
dua	one
dua tale	one more
gunu	drink
kana	eat
kerekere	shared property
koro	village
lavalava	a singular rectangular cloth worn like a kilt or skirt
marama	lady
meke	traditional song and dance
rara	village green
rua	two
sevusevu	literally "presentation," ceremonial gift
sitoa	shop
sulu	the national dress of Fiji. It resembles a skirt and is commonly worn by both men and women

tanoa	kava-bowl
tapa	cloth made from the bark of the paper mulberry tree
turaga	man
teitei	a garden
vale lailai	toilet
vaka lailai	little
vaka levu	plenty
vaka totolo	quickly

FIJIAN FOOD GLOSSARY

copra	dried coconut meat used to produce coconut oil, cosmetics, soaps, and margarine
dalo	*see taro*
ika	fish
kava	both a plant and its beverage byproduct, which has intoxicating effects
kokoda	raw fish marinated in lolo and lime juice, spiced with pepper, onion, and tomato (often described as Fijian ceviche)
lolo	coconut milk
lovo	a traditional Fijian feast of fish, chicken, and pork (sometimes) wrapped in banana leaves and cooked on heated rocks in an underground oven
niu	coconut
pawpaw	papaya
taro	a starchy tuber cooked like a vegetable or ground into a flourlike substance; a staple food
tavioka	cassava
yaqona	a ground pepper plant used to make kava

FIJIAN ESSENTIALS

Hello	bula
Good morning	ni sa yadre
Good-bye	ni sa moce (ni sa mothey)
Thank you	vinaka
You're welcome	sega na leqa
Yes	io (ee-o)
No	seqa (senga)
Please	yalo vinaka
Excuse me	tulou (too low)
Where is…?	I vei…?
What's this?	na cava oqo?
What's your name?	kocei na yacamu?
Help	oilei!
I am lost	au saa sese
I want…	au vinakata (aoo vina kahta)

FIJI-HINDI ESSENTIALS

Hello	namaste
Thank you	dhanyabaad
How much?	Kitna?
How are you?	Kaise hai?
I'm fine	Theek bhai
Yes	Haan
No	Nahi
Good (also used for thank you)	achhaa
Where is the…?	Kaha hai?
What's your name?	Aapke naam kaa hai?
Help!	Hame madad karo
What's this?	Yeh kia hai?
Excuse me	maaf kijye ga

Travel Smart Fiji

GETTING HERE & AROUND

The main islands of Viti Levu and Vanua Levu are similar to Hawaii's islands. There's a coastal road circling the perimeter of the island, with few roads venturing into the lush, highland interior. The islands are studded with a few major cities, with smaller villages scattered in between. Travel times, therefore, can often be double what you'd expect, due to road conditions, unexpected detours, and lack of infrastructure. In the outer islands, even Kadavu, which is the fourth-largest island, there's even less infrastructure—Kadavu only has one road, so travel is primarily by boat.

■TIP➔ **Ask the local tourist board about hotel and local transportation packages that include tickets to major museum exhibits or other special events.**

▮ BY AIR

Fiji is a collection of more than 300 islands scattered about the South Pacific. Like Hawaii, Fiji is one of the main travel hubs in this vast expanse of ocean. Most travelers fly into Nadi International Airport on the island of Viti Levu, although the Nausori airport near the capital of Suva also hosts a few international flights. Because of Fiji's location, it's serviced by a variety of air carriers, from Air New Zealand and Qantas, to the more destination-specific airlines like Air Vanuatu.

Air Travel Resources in Fiji Airports Fiji Limited Customer Service (☎672–5777 ⊕www.afl. com.fj) has answers regarding consumer service complaints at the islands airports.

AIR PASS
Air Fiji offers a 30-day, four-flight air pass for $270. Additional flights are $90, children under 12 pay 75% of the fare, and children under two pay 10%. The passes are only sold overseas or via their Web site. Changes in reservations are free of charge, and some refunds apply before departure (visit the Web site for full details).

Air Pass Info Air Fiji (☎877/247–3454 toll-free U.S. number through Fiji Travel Alliance Management ⊕www.airfiji.com.fj).

AIRPORTS
Nadi International Airport (NAN) is the major gateway airport in Fiji, about 6 mi north of the city center of Nadi. It has good facilities, including accommodation, travel agency, and car rental representatives, a 24-hour bank with currency exchange, cafés, a post office, shops, a small bookstore, and luggage storage (about $6 per day). As with everything in Fiji, airlines also experience delays and don't always run on time, so make certain that you arrive in plenty of time to sort out any potential problems, and then settle in for what could be a long wait. Transport between the airport and the center of Nadi is

readily available, should you need to find lodging for another night or have a lot of time to kill.

Nausori Airport (NFNA), which is about 14 mi from downtown Suva, is smaller and less busy than Nadi, servicing mostly domestic transfers. Although the airport offers some creature comforts, plans are afoot for a major renovation to make it more of an international gateway airport, like Nadi.

There are domestic airstrips/airports in Mana Island, Vanua Balavu, Kadavu, Lakeba, Moala, Labasa, Savusavu, and Taveuni. These "airports" often consist of one building with a ticket counter, a soda machine, possibly a sandwich shop, a toilet, and an airstrip for the smaller planes used in domestic transfers. As Fiji Time prevails in the outer islands, it's best to come prepared: pack snacks, water, toilet paper, and a good book.

Airport Information Nadi International Airport (NAN) (☎672-5777 ⊕www.afl.com.fj). **Nausori Airport** (NFNA) (⊕www.afl.com.fj).

GROUND TRANSPORTATION

Both Nadi International Airport and Nausori Airport are well serviced by taxis, buses, car rental agencies, and accommodation transport. If you're booking your accommodation in advance, ask about airport transfers, which can usually be arranged. Otherwise, approach any taxi or bus driver to discuss routes and fares. If you have questions or are facing difficulties, speak to the Visi-

tors Bureau staff, who should be able to assist you.

FLIGHTS

Island-hopping by plane is usually affordable and fast. If you can handle the occasional light-plane turbulence, you'll be rewarded with scenic views of the islands and reefs. Note that your luggage may fly separately (due to space availability or weight issues), arriving just before or after you. Flights are usually reliable and more or less on time, but book in advance if you want to secure a seat.

Planes tend to be small, with one or two seats on either side of the aisle, specific weight requirements (you'll have to weigh yourself and your luggage before the flight), no bathrooms, and definitely no in-flight service.

Fiji, like Hawaii, is one of the major destination hubs in the South Pacific, and many people traveling from the U.S. to Australia or New Zealand prefer to stop in Fiji en route. Air New Zealand and Qantas fly direct from the west coast to Fiji, with a travel time of about seven hours. Air New Zealand currently operates three flights per week from L.A. to Fiji, although that might change in April 2008, when a code-sharing service with Air Pacific would see those flights upped to six times per week.

Domestic Airline Contacts Air Fiji (✉Nadi ☎672-2521 ⊕www.airfiji. com). **Air Pacific** (✉Nadi ☎672-0777 ⊕www.airpacific.com.au). **Pacific Sun** (✉Nadi ☎672-0888 ⊕www.pacificsun.com.fj).

International Airline Contacts
Air New Zealand (☎800/262–1234 ⊕www.airnz.com).
Qantas (☎800/227–4500 ⊕www.qantas.com.au). **United Airlines** (☎800/538–2929 ⊕www.united.com).

CHARTER FLIGHTS

Travelers to Fiji like to island-hop and there are several charter flight companies to choose from. Island Hoppers has more than 30 years of experience in Fiji and an extensive knowledge of the islands. Pacific Island Seaplanes offers everything from island transfers to scenic tours and Turtle Airways, which has been operating for 25 years, was the first float-plane service in Fiji.

Scenic flights over Fiji's spectacular mountain ranges and gorges are offered by both helicopter and plane, usually around $200 for 20 minutes. Seaplanes and planes offer both scenic flights and island transfers for around the same price.

Contacts Island Hoppers (✉Nadi ☎672–0410 ⊕www.helicopters.com.fj). **Pacific Island Seaplanes** (✉Nadi ☎672–5644 ⊕www.fijiseaplanes.com). **Turtle Airways** (✉Nadi ☎877/327–5263 in U.S., 672–1888 ⊕www.turtleairways.com).

▌ BY BOAT & FERRY

Since Fiji is surrounded by water, boat travel is one of the primary means of transport. In some of the more remote areas (Kadavu, for example), boats are often the only means of transport, and many resorts have their own. Boat travel can be rustic, so use your best judgment if you're uncertain about the weather conditions. Ask about the safety of the boat, look to see if it has a radio or phone, and find out how long it will take to reach your destination before making your decision.

Island-hopping is a favorite pasttime of visitors to Fiji, and interisland ferry trips and sightseeing tours have increased because of this. Regular ferries service Viti Levu with Vanua Levu, Ovalau, and Taveuni, while there are not-so-regular ferries among Suva, Lau, Rotuma, and Kadavu. Many ferries transport people, cars, and cargo, and have café food or snacks available. However, they're often on Fiji time, not running on scheduled timetables or not running at all, and it's a good precaution to bring your own water and toilet paper. The Yasawas and Mamanucas have made a solid business from islandhopping tours, so speak to your resort or lodging about options and passes.

Contacts Awesome Adventures (☎675–0499 in Nadi ⊕www.awesomefiji.com). **Beachcomber Cruises** (☎666–1500 in Lautoka, 885–0266 in Savusavu ⊕www.beachcomberfiji.com). **Consort Shipping** (☎330–2877 in Suva). **Patterson Brothers Shipping** (☎331–5644 in Suva, 666–1173 in Lautoka). **South Sea Cruises** (☎675–0500 in Nadi ⊕www.ssc.com.fj).

▍ BY BUS

Bus is the most common form of transport in Fiji, and nearly every town or village (with a major road or road infrastructure) has bus service. Traveling this way is inexpensive and the larger islands have extensive services, plus it's a great way to enjoy a local experience; buses are usually noisy and full of laughter, windows down, with rolled-up canvas flaps in case of a rainstorm. In the major cities you can find air-conditioned, scheduled, nonstop bus service, but most buses are on Fiji Time. Ask the locals at the bus-stop or your hotel for a timetable and expect delays; you can often flag buses down at nonscheduled stops.

Pacific Transport and Sunbeam Transport are the two major carriers and advance reservations aren't required for either. Pacific Transport has six to eight express buses that run daily between Nadi and Suva for approximately $8. Sunbeam Transport Limited offers three or four express buses that also run daily between Lautoka and Suva for approximately $10.

Coral Sun Fiji has a variety of transport services offering airport transfers as well as service between Nadi and Suva. Transport is in modern, air-conditioned coaches for between $11 and $70, depending on the tour and the number of stops. You can purchase a variety of transport options from Feejee Experience, including bus passes and multiple-stop fares. United Touring Fiji has two modern, air-conditioned buses that run daily between Nadi and Suva for approximately $30.

Contacts Coral Sun Fiji (☎672–3105 in Nadi ⊕www.coralsunfiji.com). **Feejee Experience** (☎672–0097 in Nadi ⊕www.feejee experience.com). **Pacific Transport Limited** (☎670–0044 in Nadi, 330-4366 in Suva). **Sunbeam Transport Limited** (☎927–2121 in Nadi, 338–2122 in Suva). **United Touring Fiji** (☎672–2811 in Nadi).

▍ BY CAR

Fijian drivers have their own rhythm, and road signs are often disregarded. So be aware of what's going on around you.

A valid driver's license from an English-speaking country or an international driving permit is needed to drive in Fiji, both of which need to be obtained in your home country before traveling to Fiji. The minimum driving age is 21, regardless of what it is in your home country. Roads are a mixture of paved and unpaved; the majority are two lanes, but locals often disregard this when overtaking other vehicles.

GASOLINE

On Viti Levu and Vanua Levu, petrol stations (as they're called) are easy to find and are competitively priced. However, once you start driving out of the city, petrol stations are few and far between. Plan ahead and make sure you have a full tank before heading out to explore, especially if you are heading into the island's interior or highlands.

Petrol is sold by liters, and the cost can range widely from $1.50 per liter in the major cities to $12 per liter in the outer islands. Cash is usually the only payment accepted, and most stations are self-service, although the attendants are usually happy to come out for a chat and help if business is quiet.

PARKING

Parking tends to be ad hoc: on the street, where you can find it, but don't park in front of an entrance or block anyone in. Parking fines tend to be around $2, and towing tends to be on Fiji Time: you should have time to return to your car if you've made a mistake, but asking the locals or nearby shops/hotels will save you the worry.

RENTAL CARS

Renting a car can be expensive in Fiji, but if you're staying on one of the main islands—Viti Levu and Vanua Levu have 90% of Fiji's roads—it can be an efficient means of exploration, especially if you're traveling in a group or with your family. The rule of thumb is the longer the hire, the cheaper the rate. Daily rates for a week or more start around $75 per day (excluding tax); expect to use a credit card to pay the deposit. Nadi International Airport on Viti Levu is the easiest place to rent cars, although most companies have desks at major resorts/hotels or in town. Delivery and collection are often included in the price of the rental car, so make certain you ask.

Contacts **Avis** (☎672–2233 Nadi Airport, 347–8963 Suva's Nausori Airport, 800/331–1084 in U.S., ⊕www.avis.com.fj). **Budget** (☎672–2735 Nadi Airport, 331–5899 in Suva, 800/472–3325 in U.S. ⊕www.budget.com.fj). **Europcar** (☎672–5957 Nadi Airport, 337–2050 Suva ✉Lot 5, Karsanji Rd., Vatuwaqa, in Suva ⊕www.europcarasia.com). **Hertz** (☎672–3466 Nadi, 338–0981 Suva, 800/654–3001 in U.S. ⊕www.hertzfiji.net). **Khans** (☎672–3506 Nadi Airport, 338–5033 Suva ⊕www.khansrental.com.fj). **National Car Rental** (☎800/227–7368 ⊕www.nationalcar.com).

RENTAL CAR INSURANCE

Insurance is added to the daily rental rate, and it's necessary, as is personal accident insurance. But car theft (which isn't common in Fiji, but can occur, especially around the major cities) isn't usually covered by insurance, and neither is windshield or underbody damage. Also, many rental agencies will not insure their cars to be driven on unpaved roads in Fiji, which most travelers will find limiting. Make certain you have a clear understanding with the rental car company of what you can and can't do before setting off.

ROADSIDE EMERGENCIES

Discuss with the rental car agency what to do in the case of an emergency, as this sometimes differs between companies. Make sure you understand what your insurance covers and what it doesn't, and it's a good rule of thumb to let someone at your accommodation know where you are heading and when you plan to return. If you find yourself stranded, hail a bus or speak to the locals, who may have some helpful advice about finding your way to a phone or a bus stop. Keep emergency numbers (car rental agency and your accommodation) with you, just in case. Hitching is common in Fiji, but it's never a safe option, and muggings do happen.

ROAD CONDITIONS

Generally speaking, most of Viti Levu's perimeter road is paved. The more you venture into the interior, the more likely you are to be traveling on dirt roads. Often a 4WD is the only safe way to travel. (Vanua Levu is the same, only no paved roads.)

RULES OF THE ROAD

Driving is on the left-hand side of the road, although many locals ignore this, especially when overtaking other vehicles or speeding around bends. Fijian drivers have their own rules of the road, stopping frequently and without warning, speeding, and passing around blind corners. Seat belts are required by law, and the average speed limit is 80 kph, which drops to 20 kph in the villages. Pay attention to the speed limit, especially in villages, where children and dogs are often found close to the road. Also watch for sugar trains, which are not only slow-moving, but they have the right of way. Signs are in English and easy to understand, although roads aren't always well-marked.

▌ BY TAXI

Taxis are plentiful and reasonably priced. For the most part, they're a safe means of transportation, though some of the vehicles are a bit past their prime, and some of the drivers more than enthusiastic. You'll find taxis on Viti Levu, Vanua Leu, Ovalau, and Taveuni by bus station depots or major intersections. Taxis are reasonably priced—$2.50 will take you almost anywhere you need to go. Drivers are usually Indo-Fijian, friendly, and English-speaking. They're also keen to cut deals: you can save money on other trips if you allow them to pick up extra passengers and you can negotiate a daily rate (think personal chauffer service).

Make certain you negotiate a price before starting out, or make certain the meter is on—many drivers won't use it if they don't have to. Also, if you're traveling to a remote area, ask whether it's a return taxi so you aren't stranded.

ESSENTIALS

▌ ACCOMMODATIONS

Fiji's accommodation options are seemingly endless, and though there's a wide range of price options, accommodation is likely to be your greatest expense in Fiji. Compared to other destinations, the country doesn't provide the best value for money. However, if you're prepared for this, you can find some unique and memorable lodging experiences.

■TIP➔**Assume that hotels operate on the European Plan (EP, no meals) unless we specify that they use the Breakfast Plan (BP, with full breakfast), Continental Plan (CP, Continental breakfast), Full American Plan (FAP, all meals), Modified American Plan (MAP, breakfast and dinner) or are all-inclusive (AI, all meals and most activities).**

For lodging price categories, consult the price charts found near the beginning of each chapter.

APARTMENT & HOUSE RENTALS

Long-term rentals are primarily available in the major cities of Suva and Nadi. If you're looking for rentals in the more remote areas, ring local lodges and ask the owners if they know of any available options.

Renting is a good option if you want to base yourself somewhere, or if you're planning on staying for a long period of time—they're not ideal if you're staying short-

FODORS.COM CONNECTION

Before your trip, be sure to check-out what other travelers are saying in Talk on www.fodors.com.

term but are if you're looking to save money, say, with cooking your meals. Accommodation options with kitchen facilities end up being the better deal.

Fiji Travel Maxia is a Web site that features home and villa properties available for rent in Fiji, and Fiji Hotels is a Fiji-based reservation service that lists everything from holiday homes to hostels.

Contacts **Fiji Hotels** (☎672–4244 ⊕www.fiji-hotels.com.fj). **Fiji Travel Maxia** (⊕www.fiji.travel-maxia.com). **Forgetaway** (⊕www.forgetaway.weather.com) **Home Away** (☎512/493—0382 in U.S. ⊕www.homeaway.com). **Villas International** (☎415/499–9490 or 800/221—2260 in U.S. ⊕www.villasintl.com).

CAMPING & VILLAGE STAYS

These are excellent options, as they are cheap and provide unique local experiences, but you'll need local permission or an invitation to stay at a village. If you show up at a village uninvited, ask the first person you see for an introduction to the chief—don't wander around or

TIPS FOR STAYING 🏠

Avoid peak season (May through October). Rates are about 15% higher and accommodation tends to fill up quickly.

Book in advance. You may be traveling to remote areas where transport is primarily by boat (i.e., Kadavu). Booking in advance allows you and your hosts to plan for your arrivals and departures so you're not left stranded.

Walk-in deals exist. If you're not traveling during peak season, you could end up saving a lot of money by walking in and requesting rates and availability.

Use caution when booking online. A lot of the cheaper accommodations aren't familiar with the threat of identity fraud. Often complete credit card numbers are quoted back in e-mail confirmations, or you'll see them displayed on your bill. If a credit card number is required for a reservation, request that the number isn't included in any of the paperwork.

Know the terminology. The term "guesthouse" is often used to describe a house of ill-repute, and "bure" can be anything from a traditional thatched house to a touristy imitation.

Consider your options. Decide ahead of time what you want from your Fijian holiday. Resorts are luxurious, but they're often self-contained. Remote bures can be romantic *and* isolated. Village stays are a wonderful cultural experience, but there's no relaxing beach time.

take photographs until you're officially invited to do so.

You'll most likely visit a village with a tour group or guide as most operators include a village visit or stay in the itinerary. If you're interested in staying longer or returning to the village, or if you're an independent traveler wishing to gain advance permission to visit a village, speak to a tour operator—they'll have local contacts and often it may be as simple as following instructions to "call Moses." You'll probably have to negotiate a price for the information, but most tour operators can help you.

There are strict cultural rituals and protocol to observe when visiting a village. All visitors need to present the chief with a *sevusevu*, or gift. The most common and appropriate gift is *yaquona* (kava root). Gifts of canned goods or staples like tea, flour, or kerosene are also appreciated. *See The Kava Ceremony box, in Chapter 1 for more information.*

Your village hosts will be happy to welcome you into their community, but make certain you look after them, as well: observe local customs (conservative dress, etc.), participate in games if you're asked (volleyball, touch rugby, etc.), and pay for any extras—F\$10 (Fijian dollars) is usually sufficient if you hire guides or horses from the village. If you would like to make a donation to the village in thanks for the hospitality, offer F\$15 or F\$20.

Contacts Bula Fiji (⊕www.bulafiji.com). **Fiji Bure** (⊕www.fijibure.com).

HOSTELS OR BACKPACKERS

Hostels or backpackers are the terms commonly used in Fiji for, well, backpackers or low-budget establishments—they aren't referred to as youth hostels, though, just hostels.

Budget accommodation is becoming increasingly popular as Fiji attracts more and more backpackers, so travelers at these lodgings tend to be younger, and the facilities geared to them with Internet access, bars, movie nights, and pool-side parties (although amenities tend to diminish in the outer islands). Always ask if meals are included in the price, and if there's a restaurant either in the accommodation or nearby. Some budget lodgings give discounts for Hostelling International cards, and it's best to call the lodging the day before to confirm any bookings you may have made: administration can be lax in Fiji, and often reservations go missing.

Expect to pay around $25 for a dorm bed, $60 for a single, and $75 for a double. Facilities tend to be shared and moderately clean. However, Fiji does respond well to word-of-mouth: if you're unhappy with the quality of service or cleanliness, voice your concerns—they're usually responded to.

Contacts **Hostelling International—USA** (☎301/495–1240 ⊕www.hiusa.org).

HOTELS

Motels and hotels occupy the majority of Fiji's accommodation options. Prices range from around $150 for a single to $400 for a double, depending on quality, although there's no roof to tariffs when you get to the higher-end establishments or farther islands. Most motels and hotels offer some combination of in-room bathroom facilities, tea/coffeemakers, TVs, and sometimes kitchens and Internet access, as well as shared facilities of bars, restaurants, pools, and occasionally shopping. Book well in advance during the peak season (May through October), but don't forget to ask about walk-in rates if you haven't made a reservation. Often these provide the best bargains.

Contacts **Bula Fiji** (⊕www.bulafiji.com). **Fiji Budget.** (⊕www.fijibudget.com). **Fiji 4 Less** (⊕www.fiji4less.com). **Fiji Hotels** (⊕www.fiji-hotels.com.fj). **Fiji Travel Maxia** (⊕www.fiji.travelmaxia.com). **4 Hotels** (⊕www.4hotels.co.uk/fiji).

LUXURY RESORTS

If you can afford to stay in a luxury resort—top-end resorts can top $2,000 per night, all inclusive—we suggest you do as staying in a luxury resort in Fiji is like stepping into a dream that's filled with white-sand beaches, blue oceans, palm trees, warm-weather ocean views, wraparound decks, open-air verandas, fresh fruit, and seafood. Resorts and resort packages vary widely, from the privacy of your own island, to deluxe spa treatments on the beach, to private helicopter tours. Even the "lower-end" resorts offer a variety of both local and international cuisine and a room with a view.

LOCAL DO'S & TABOOS

CUSTOMS OF THE COUNTRY

Fijians are laid-back about time and expect the same from their visitors. Getting upset over delays will get you nowhere.

Public drunkenness and public displays of affection are offensive. If you're traveling with a partner, keep the touchy-feely displays to a minimum, especially if you're gay. Attitudes are changing, but slowly. Never touch a Fijian's head or hair, as the head is considered sacred.

Fijians are curious and ask many questions. It's proper etiquette to ask questions in return. ⚠ **Due to the unstable political situation in Fiji, political discussions can be explosive, even if you're only asking someone's opinion.**

A village experience is unique and shouldn't be passed by, but make certain you follow a few simple rules. Always be invited into a village. If you show up unannounced, ask the first person you see whether you're allowed to visit their village. As a guest, you'll most likely be invited into the villagers' homes. It's proper to bring a *sevusevu* (gift), which will be presented to the chief; yaqona root is a good gift. *See The Kava Ceremony box, in Chapter 1 for more information the ceremony.*

Always accept food, even if the family seems poor; it's rude to refuse. It's also rude to camp outside if you've been offered a place to sleep—your host family will think their bure isn't good enough.

Dress appropriately, even in resorts, as displaying too much skin is offensive. Wear a sarong over swimwear; never wear a hat or sunglasses; and carry your bags in your hands, not over your shoulder. Avoid showing off expensive or favorite items. The custom of *kerekere* (shared property) means that if you're asked for something, it's polite to hand it over; you can usually get out of it by explaining you can't do without it. Conversely, be careful of openly admiring something that belongs to a Fijian as they will feel obligated to give it to you.

GREETINGS

Bula (hello) and *Yadra* (good morning) are words you'll hear frequently, and repeating them back is a proper response. You may also hear *Kaise* (how are you?) or *Namaste* (formal greeting) in Fiji-Hindi, to which *Tik* (fine) or *Namaste,* respectively, are the polite returns. However, avoid any hugging or handshakes unless initiated by the other person.

LANGUAGE

Fiji has two main languages: Fijian and Fiji-Hindi. English is also widely spoken and most signs, forms, and menus are in English, even in the outer islands. Also, Fijians rarely refer to the compass when discussing directions. Words like "north" and "south" are replaced by more practical references, like "sea-side," "inland," or "this side," which makes perfect sense, especially if you happen to have a map handy.

Whether it's luxury or privacy offered, you're sure to get your money's worth, as these are truly paradisiacal experiences. Prices and packages are wide-ranging, often including everything the motels/hotels offer, as well as meal plans and access to activities like diving trips, Jet Skis, island-hopping, and fishing. Some of these activities may be included in the price, and some may need to be paid for in advance, so ask the individual resort. Resorts are often a good option for families, as they're usually all-inclusive, have Kids Clubs, and have self-contained units.

▌ COMMUNICATIONS

INTERNET

Internet access around Fiji is spotty. You can usually get access (whether you're on your own laptop or on a shared computer) in the major cities—Suva, Lautoka, and Nadi—which all have a number of Internet cafés, and most accommodation (from backpackers to resorts) have access. In these areas, access is cheap; usually about 10¢ per minute. Outside of the cities, especially in the outer islands, access is more difficult to come by and you'll pay for the privilege; the fees nearly double the price of that in urban areas.

For travelers carrying their own laptop, it makes sense to create a dial-up account with a service provider like Connect or Unwired Fiji.

Contacts Connect (⊕www.connect. com.fj). **Cybercafes** (⊕www. cybercafes.com). **Unwired Fiji** (⊕www.unwired.com.fj).

PHONES

The good news is that you can now make a direct-dial telephone call from virtually any point on earth. The bad news? You can't always do so cheaply. Calling from a hotel is almost always the most expensive option; hotels usually add huge surcharges to all calls, particularly international ones. In some countries you can phone from call centers or even the post office. Calling cards usually keep costs to a minimum, but only if you purchase them locally. And then there are mobile phones (⇨*below*), which are sometimes more prevalent—particularly in the developing world—than land lines; as expensive as mobile phone calls can be, they are still usually a much cheaper option than calling from your hotel.

Fiji's country code is 679.

CALLING WITHIN FIJI

The best option for making phone calls in Fiji is to use a phone card and dial direct, as it's usually the cheapest and the most reliable. Phones are available in most hotels and resorts. Local calls are usually free, and you can use a phone card for the international calls. Public phones are scattered throughout the city, but they're rarely in working order. In the outer islands, satellite and cable systems provide some phone access, but it's spotty at best, and calls tend to be more expensive than calling from the major cities.

CALLING OUTSIDE FIJI

When calling from Fiji, put 00 before the number. International directory assistance in Fiji is 022.

CALLING CARDS

The cheapest way to phone home is by using a phone card to dial direct. You can buy phone cards at post offices, news agents, dairies, and some pharmacies and petrol stations.

MOBILE PHONES

If you have a multiband phone (some countries use frequencies different from those used in the United States) and your service provider uses the world-standard GSM network (as do T-Mobile, Cingular, and Verizon), you can probably use your phone abroad. Roaming fees can be steep, however: 99¢ a minute is considered reasonable. And overseas you normally pay the toll charges for incoming calls. It's almost always cheaper to send a text message than to make a call, since text messages have a very low set fee (often less than 5¢).

If you just want to make local calls, consider buying a new SIM card (note that your provider may have to unlock your phone for you to use a different SIM card) and a prepaid service plan in the destination. You'll then have a local number and can make local calls at local rates. If your trip is extensive, you could also simply buy a new cell phone in your destination, as the initial cost will be offset over time.

■ TIP➔**If you travel internationally frequently, save one of your old mobile phones or buy a cheap one on the Internet; ask your cell phone company to unlock it for you, and take it with you as a travel phone, buying a new SIM card with pay-as-you-go service in each destination.**

Vodafone is the primary mobile phone company in Fiji; Mobal and Planet Fone also have coverage. You can rent a phone for approximately $5 per day. Check out the Web site for more information. If you bring your own mobile phone, ask your company about rates in Fiji as you may end up paying international rates for local calls.

Contacts **Mobal** (☎888/888–9162 ⊕www.mobalrental.com). **Planet Fone** (☎888/988–4777 ⊕www.planetfone.com). **Vodaphone** (⊕www.vodafone.com.fj.com).

▌CUSTOMS & DUTIES

Travelers to Fiji are not allowed to take any of the following out of the country: whale bone or teeth, turtle shells, trochus shells (a spiral shell with a flat base), and coral. Wood, shells, food, and anything made from hides or plants may also be confiscated either leaving Fiji or arriving into your home country, so be careful with your purchases. Travelers can leave Fiji with $400 (per person) of duty-free goods without incurring the V.A.T. tax.

FIJI INFORMATION

Fiji Government (⊕www.fiji.gov.fj).

U.S. INFORMATION

U.S. Customs and Border Protection (⊕www.cbp.gov).

▌ EATING OUT

Food is a big part of daily Fijian life, and consequently the country has a wide variety of dining options, from markets to upscale restaurants. Most dining, however, is casual and represents a wide cultural mix: indigenous Fijian, Chinese, Indian, etc. Nadi and Suva have the most options to choose from; food tends to be more traditional in the more remote areas.

Breakfast is usually served early, and tends to be bread, fruit, and sometimes fish. Fijians snack regularly throughout the day, and markets are a great place to find a morning snack. Nearly every sizable town in Fiji has a local market that sells fruits, vegetables, and cooked-on-the-spot snacks like roti parcels (Indian flat-bread wrapped around curried meat or vegetables) or salted peas. ■TIP→**Saturday markets are especially colorful and worth the trip.**

Lunch and dinner depends on where you're dining: you'll find excellent seafood in the top-end waterfront restaurants, or spectacularly spicy traditional Indian cuisine. Restaurants tend to be good value for money—around $20 for dinner and one drink in a mid-range restaurant—but they also tend to close early—usually around 9 PM.

Traditional dining (particularly in the outer islands) is a unique experience. Foods include baked or boiled fish, dalo (taro root), lolo (coconut milk), corned beef, and tavioka (cassava). Two Fijian specialties include *kokoda* (raw fish

marinated in lolo and lime juice) and *lovos* (chicken, pork, dalo, and lolo wrapped in banana leaves and steamed on hot stones in an underground oven). Meals are communal, with men and guests eating first, and food tends to be eaten with the hands while seated on mats on the floor. If you're dining with a family or in a village, don't start serving yourself or eating until your host asks you to. Many Fijians are religious and may want to pray first.

Being vegetarian in Fiji is easy, as most of the traditional food tends to be starchy carbs or fresh fruits and vegetables. Most of the Indian food is vegetarian, as well. The only place it gets tricky is in villages, as your host may not understand the concept—it's easier to use health reasons or religious beliefs as an explanation.

Kids, also, can feast on their fill of breads and fruit. Baby food is available in supermarkets, and fast-food options can be found in Nadi or Suva. Make certain you use bottled (or boiled) water for infants.

One trick of traveling in the islands: drinking hot tea helps to both warm you up and keep you cool. In some of the outer islands (Kadavu, for example) there is a native drink called "lemon leaf tea," a local lemon-tasting tree leaf dunked in boiling water, that is refreshing and rejuvenating.

Unless otherwise noted, the restaurants listed in this guide are open daily for lunch and dinner.

FIJIAN CUISINE

Along with the regular cuisine types that you'll find in most guides, we've introduced two Fiji specific cuisines in this book. **Pacific Rim** is a fusion of cuisines from Hawaii, the Pacific Islands, and the countries of Southeast Asia that feature seafood, tropical fruits, and vegetables. Examples (from celebrity chef Emeril) include lobster spring rolls, chile-baked crabs, and salmon teriyaki.

Fijian cuisine features seafood and fish, usually cooked in coconut milk (lolo in Fijian) and/or lime juice, as well as carbohydrate-heavy native vegetables including the potatolike cassava (often fried), yams, breadfruit, and the taro root ("dalo") and its spinachlike leaves (rourou). Pork, chicken, and beef are also featured and traditionally cooked in a shallow underground oven as part of a large special-occasion meal (lovo). The most well-known Fijian dish is kokoda (pronounced "kokonda"), a cevichelike dish of raw fish marinated in coconut milk and lime juice.

PAYING

Most major credit cards (Visa, American Express, and Master-Card) are accepted in restaurants.

For dining price categories, consult the price charts found near the beginning of each chapter. For guidelines on tipping see Tipping, below.

RESERVATIONS & DRESS

As a whole, dining in Fiji is pretty casual, but if you're going to an upscale resort restaurant, it pays to ask if a reservation is required. We only mention reservations when they are essential (there's no other way you'll ever get a table) or when they are not accepted. The country is pretty casual about dress, too, but too much skin is a cultural don't, so make certain you cover up, whether you're visiting a village or lounging pool-side at a backpacker's. We mention dress only when men are required to wear a jacket or a jacket and tie.

WINES, BEER & SPIRITS

Alcohol is widely available: it's sold in most restaurants, bottle shops, and some supermarkets. Fiji Bitter and Fiji Gold are two quality local beers, sold for around $4 a glass. Wine is usually imported from New Zealand or Australia, with a decent bottle averaging $15. A 750ml bottle of Fijian rum runs about $40.

▌ ELECTRICITY

Fiji's electricity is supplied at 240-volts, so appliances require a flat two- or three-pin plug, similar to Australia or New Zealand. On the more remote areas, power generators are often used, and power supplies can be unreliable.

EMERGENCIES

The emergency number in Fiji is 911. The response time can vary widely, depending on where you are and how difficult it is to reach you. Hospital and clinic care tends to be clean and good, if a bit rustic, so don't delay getting help if you need it.

Due to the current political climate in Fiji, police and the military are on edge, and it wouldn't be wise to push your luck. Remember that you're bound by Fiji's laws. If you're arrested, you have the right to contact your embassy or consulate, but the rule of thumb is that your embassy can't do much if the problem is one of your own making. Carry the number of your embassy with you at all times.

FOREIGN EMBASSIES
American Embassy (⊠31 Loftus St., Suva ☎331–4466 ⊕suva. usembassy.gov). **Fiji Embassy** (⊠2233 Wisconsin Ave. NW, Suite 240, Washington, D.C. ☎202/337–8320 ⊕www.fijiembassy.org).

HEALTH

Health hazards in Fiji include the standard heat-induced problems (dehydration, prickly heat, heatstroke, fungal infections, heat exhaustion, and sunburn), stomach disorders (diarrhea and food poisoning), environmental hazards (coral cuts and jellyfish stings), and mosquito-transmitted diseases (including dengue fever). Although

> ### WORD OF MOUTH
>
> "Don't drink the water in Fiji without boiling it first, even to brush your teeth—this is from experience!" —wilees

the list may seem long and full of peril, most people leave Fiji healthy, except for a few mosquito bites and mild sunburn.

The best offense, of course, is a good defense, so be prepared. The water in Fiji's major cities is generally safe to drink, but be cautious in the more remote areas. Boil water, drink bottled water, or use water purifying tablets, and use caution while brushing your teeth, drinking water while you shower, or eating ice cubes. Fruits and vegetables should be peeled, and be careful of uncooked meat.

Wash your hands frequently, and treat cuts with extra caution: a small skin puncture can quickly turn septic in the tropics. Wash the injury well, and treat with an antiseptic ointment. Keep the wound as dry as possible (so no bandages or Band-Aids). If the wound is starting to spread, or if it isn't healing, see a doctor.

With mosquitoes, the simplest solution is to keep as much skin covered as possible with long-sleeved shirts and trousers. Avoid perfumes or scented lotions, use mosquito repellent containing DEET, and use a mosquito net or coil when sleeping, if possible.

Health care in Fiji can seem a bit rustic, but most clinics and hospitals are clean and well-staffed. If you're experiencing a health problem, do not wait to return to your home country. You'll have to pay for any treatment up front, so make certain you have adequate health insurance. (If you need a prolonged hospital stay, often your insurance company can work something out with the local hospital.)

OVER-THE-COUNTER REMEDIES

Pharmacies in Fiji carry most of the over-the-counter medications that you'll need for headaches, upset stomachs, minor aches and pains, and cuts and bruises. They also provide a selection of basic cosmetic and health care products (like shampoo and toothpaste), sunscreen, and mosquito repellent and coils. Most of the supplies are similar to those in the U.K., New Zealand, or Australia. (For example, Tylenol is called paracetomol.) If you can't find what you're looking for, or have any questions, your accommodation hosts should be able to help you. Make certain you stock up on anything you need before traveling to the outer islands, as supplies are more difficult to come by.

SHOTS & MEDICATIONS

About six weeks before your departure to Fiji, make certain all your standard immunizations have been covered: influenza, chicken pox, polio, measles, mumps, rubella, diphtheria, tetanus, hepatitis A and B, and typhoid. Also, note that a yellow fever certificate is required for all travelers (over one year of age) who are entering Fiji within 10 days of having stayed overnight in an area at risk from the disease.

Although diseases can be picked up anywhere at anytime, the only real threat in Fiji is dengue fever, a virus spread by mosquito bites. The fever causes headache and muscle pains, and danger signs include a rash and prolonged vomiting. There is no vaccine or prevention for dengue fever, and treatment includes rest, fluids, and paracetamol—not aspirin.

Health Warnings **National Centers for Disease Control & Prevention** (CDC ☏877/394–8747 international travelers' health line ⊕www.cdc.gov/travel). **World Health Organization** (WHO ⊕www.who.int).

▌ HOURS OF OPERATION

Adhering to business hours in Fiji can be frustrating, as everyone is on Fiji Time. Generally, banking and post office hours tend to be between 9 AM and 4 PM, although offices might close earlier on Friday afternoons; there's a 24-hour bank at Nadi International Airport if you're in a bind. Shops tend to be open weekdays from 9 to 5, and 8 to 1 on Saturday. (If you aim for the hours of 9:30 AM to 3 PM, you'll be safe, though many places close for lunch between 1 and 2.) Cafés open around 9, and restaurant hours generally run 11 AM to 10 PM. Sunday is a day for family, religion, and rest in Fiji, and very little is open.

HOLIDAYS

In Fiji, official holidays include New Year's Day, Good Friday, Easter Monday, Prophet Mohammed's Birthday (April), National Youth Day (May), Ratu Sir Lala Sukuna Day (1st Monday in June), Queen's Birthday (mid-June), Birth of Lord Krishna (August/September), Fiji Independence Day (early October), Diwali Festival (October/November), Christmas Day, Boxing Day (December 26).

MAIL

Fiji has post offices scattered throughout the country, with Nadi and Suva being the main hubs. Delivery is usually reliable, although service can be painfully slow. Surface mail tends to be the cheapest, but its arrival is prolonged and unpredictable. Airmail to New Zealand or Australia usually takes about three days, and to Europe or America it's about a week. It's possible to receive mail in all major post offices, and mail can be held for two months without charge. It's also possible to send and receive faxes at major post offices. Often, top-scale resorts and hotels offer postal services, so check with the front desk to see if they can help you.

SHIPPING PACKAGES

Shipping packages and purchases to and from Fiji can be an adventure. FedEx operates in Fiji and is usually the safest bet. Some stores will offer to ship purchases home for you, but use your judgment: if the process seems smooth, chances are the store does this often. If forms can't be found, or there seems to be complications or questions, best to deal with the post office, FedEx, or even your accommodation host.

Shipping Options FedEx (⊕www.fedex.com/fj). **Post Fiji** (⊕www.postfiji.com.fj).

MONEY

Like most Pacific countries, Fiji will seem to be both feast and famine. Some things (such as locally grown produce, gold jewelry, and tours) are great value for money. Other things (like petrol, cosmetics [i.e., shampoo], and anything else that needs to be imported) can seem shockingly expensive, and they only get more so in the more remote areas. Bus fare from Nadi to Suva is US$8; a bottle of shampoo costs about the same. One liter of bottled water or one liter of petrol is about US$2. A piece of fruit in the market is about 50¢.

Credit cards and Fijian dollars are the most universal form of currency, although traveler's checks can still be used in more touristy areas. Hotels and banks are still the best bets for a good exchange rate, and U.S., Australian, and New Zealand dollars are the easiest to exchange, although Fijian currency is what is accepted in day-to-day use. Major international banks in Fiji include ANZ (Australia and New Zealand Banking Group Ltd) and Westpac, and their ATMs will accept nearly every international debit card. As always, protect your pin number when withdrawing money.

When heading to the outer islands, make certain you bring enough local currency, as ATMs are difficult to come by outside of city centers (and are often out-of-service). Check with your lodging to see what is available, and what form of payment they accept.

Prices throughout this guide are given for adults. Substantially reduced fees are almost always available for children, students, and senior citizens.

■TIP➔ **Banks never have every foreign currency on hand, and it may take as long as a week to order. If you're planning to exchange funds before leaving home, don't wait till the last minute.**

ATMS & BANKS
ATMs can be found in most banks, which are found in most cities. Banks become fewer and far between in the outlying islands, unless you're staying at a major resort. PIN numbers in Australia, New Zealand, and the South Pacific need to be four digits.

CREDIT CARDS
Throughout this guide, the following abbreviations are used: **AE,** American Express; **DC,** Diners Club; **MC,** MasterCard; and **V,** Visa.

It's a good idea to inform your credit-card company before you travel, especially if you're going abroad and don't travel internationally very often. Otherwise, the credit-card company might put a hold on your card owing to unusual activity—not a good thing halfway through your trip. Record all your credit-card numbers—as well as the phone numbers to call if your cards are lost or stolen—

in a safe place, so you're prepared should something go wrong. Both MasterCard and Visa have general numbers you can call (collect if you're abroad) if your card is lost, but you're better off calling the number of your issuing bank, since MasterCard and Visa usually just transfer you to your bank; your bank's number is usually printed on your card.

If you plan to use your credit card for cash advances, you'll need to apply for a PIN at least two weeks before your trip. Although it's usually cheaper (and safer) to use a credit card abroad for large purchases (so you can cancel payments or be reimbursed if there's a problem), note that some credit-card companies *and* the banks that issue them add substantial percentages to all foreign transactions, whether they're in a foreign currency or not. Check on these fees before leaving home, so there won't be any surprises when you get the bill.

■TIP➔ **Before you charge something, ask the merchant whether or not he or she plans to do a dynamic currency conversion (DCC). In such a transaction the credit-card *processor* (shop, restaurant, or hotel, not Visa or MasterCard) converts the currency and charges you in dollars. In most cases you'll pay the merchant a 3% fee for this service in addition to any credit-card company and issuing-bank foreign-transaction surcharges.**

Dynamic currency conversion programs are becoming increasingly widespread. Merchants who participate in them are supposed to ask whether you want to be charged in dollars or the local currency, but they don't always do so. And even if they do offer you a choice, they may well avoid mentioning the additional surcharges. The good news is that you *do* have a choice. And if this practice really gets your goat, you can avoid it entirely thanks to American Express; with its cards, DCC simply isn't an option.

Credit cards are widely used in Fiji. Most hotels, restaurants, shops, and travel agents accept major credit cards, although some hotels add a 5% surcharge if you pay with one (check with your accommodation hosts before paying). When heading to the outer islands, bring your credit card, but bring enough cash to cover you if credit cards aren't accepted. (Most banks in large towns will provide cash advances through credit cards.)

Reporting Lost Cards American Express (☎800/528–4800 in U.S., 336/393–1111 collect from abroad ⊕www.americanexpress.com). **MasterCard** (☎800/627–8372 in U.S., 636/722–7111 collect from abroad ⊕www.mastercard.com). **Visa** (☎800/847–2911 in U.S., 410/581–9994 collect from abroad ⊕www.visa.com).

CURRENCY EXCHANGE

At the time of this writing, US$1 equaled $1.50 Fijian dollars. The local currency is split into bank notes (50, 20, 10, 5, and 2) and coins (1, 50¢, 20¢, 10¢, 5¢, 2¢, 1¢). Currency is the same throughout the islands, although prices tend to increase in the more remote areas. Fijian dollars is the currency that is widely accepted; occasionally some major hotels or restaurants will accept U.S. dollars, but don't count on it.

■TIP➔ **Even if a currency-exchange booth has a sign promising no commission, rest assured that there's some kind of huge, hidden fee. (Oh…that's right. The sign didn't say no *fee*.) And as for rates, you're almost always better off getting foreign currency at an ATM or exchanging money at a bank.**

Currency Conversion Google (⊕www.google.com). **Oanda. com** (⊕www.oanda.com). **XE.com** (⊕www.xe.com).

▌ PACKING

Large cities like Suva, Nadi, and Latoka should have anything you may have forgotten, but in Fiji it's best not to count on that—especially with prescription medicine. The farther you travel outside of the major cities, the less likely you are to find what you're looking for, so stock up before you leave.

Make sure you have plenty of bug spray and sunscreen, proper reef shoes—flip-flops won't stand up to coral reefs or sink holes—seasickness tablets, a tropical wardrobe that includes layers—it can get chilly on the water—an underwater camera, and a snorkel and mask if you consider taking a dip.

PASSPORTS & VISAS

Whether arriving by sea or air, travelers to Fiji need to have a passport that's valid for at least three months beyond their departure date, as well as an onward ticket in order to receive a free four-month tourist visa to Fiji. This visa's open to citizens of more than 100 countries; for a complete list visit the Fijian government's Web site. Countries that are excluded from the list will have to apply to the Fijian embassy for visas prior to arrival.

If you're a journalist or traveling to Fiji for business (or reasons other than a holiday), you'll need to declare this on your arrival card in order to receive your 14-day visa. Any extensions beyond these two weeks will need to be applied for. If you wish to live or work in Fiji for more than six months, you can apply for a work visa before you arrive in Fiji. These can take several months (and quite a few headaches) to arrange, so make certain you plan ahead. As unemployment is a problem in Fiji, you'll most likely need to provide proof of employment that no skilled laborer in Fiji can fill. Contact the Fijian embassy in your area for more information and forms.

Info Fiji Embassy (✉Washington, D.C. ☎202/466-8320 ⊕www.fiji embassydc.com). **Fiji Government** (☎877/235-5467 ⊕www.fiji.gov.fj).

RESTROOMS

Facilities in Fiji range from the rustic to the swank, depending on where you are and how evolved the infrastructure is. On a whole,

though, bathrooms are clean, and the use of them (in restaurants, gas stations, etc.) is never a problem, although having your own stash of toilet paper or tissues can come in handy. Since Fijians are such good hosts, it's good manners to return the favor for them. For example, if you use the facilities at a gas station, buy a bottle of water or even a pack of gum as an acknowledgement of thanks.

Find a Loo **The Bathroom Diaries** (⊕www.thebathroomdiaries.com) is flush with unsanitized info on restrooms the world over—each one located, reviewed, and rated.

SAFETY

Theft isn't a pervasive problem in Fiji, but opportunists are everywhere, so be smart. Keep an eye on your luggage at all times, or store it in Nadi International Airport (approximately $6 per day) or in a secure room at your accommodation. Keep your doors locked at night, store your valuables in a safe, don't walk alone at night or hitchhike, and don't overtly flaunt anything expensive—money, jewelry, cameras, etc. Travel insurance and common sense are the best defense against thieves. Also, keep aware of your surroundings: Fiji has the potential to erupt into a political or environmental storm, so have a game plan that will take you to safety. Don't cause your own trouble, either: it's illegal to drink and drive in Fiji, and all drugs (marijuana included) are also illegal. If you're arrested for drug use or possession, you could be imprisoned in a mental hospital, so the risk is high. Sodomy and homosexual acts are also illegal, although the attitude toward gay and lesbians is slowly changing. Fijians are uncomfortable with public displays of affection from any couple, but overt homosexual behavior can be a magnet for trouble.

"Sword sellers" are something of a Fijian legend: an over-friendly person will approach you on the street, ask you a few questions, and start carving your name on a block of wood. They will then try to sell you this personal "sword" and will get belligerent if you don't pay for the ridiculous souvenir. If you encounter one of these charlatans, just walk away.

■TIP→ **Distribute your cash, credit cards, IDs, and other valuables between a deep front pocket, an inside jacket or vest pocket, and a hidden money pouch. Don't reach for the money pouch once you're in public.**

Contact **Transportation Security Administration** (TSA; ⊕www.tsa.gov).

GOVERNMENT ADVISORIES
Fiji is fond of coups. In December 2006, Fiji's military commander deposed the elected government in the fourth coup since 1987. Although the situation appears calm on the surface and hasn't negatively affected travelers, journalists have been deported, and it has seriously impacted the economy and tourism, leaving the country in a deep state of uncertainty. At the time of this writing, there aren't any travel warnings for Fiji, but travelers would be

smart to do their homework and keep their wits about them, as basic rights are uncertain and the situation could deteriorate rapidly and unexpectedly. Know where your exits are, avoid discussing politics (especially in major cities like Nadi or Suva), and stay away from demonstrations.

General Information & Warnings
Australian Department of Foreign Affairs & Trade (⊕www.smartravel-ler.gov.au). **Consular Affairs Bureau of Canada** (⊕www.voyage.gc.ca). **U.K. Foreign & Commonwealth Office** (⊕www.fco.gov.uk/travel). **U.S. Department of State** (⊕www.travel.state.gov).

▌ TAXES

Fijian departure tax is $40, payable at the airport in local currency before passing through immigration. Sometimes the departure tax is included in the price of the flight, so check your booking before arriving at the airport. The local value-added tax (V.A.T.) is set at 12.5% and is levied on all goods in excess of concessions. Most accommodation includes the V.A.T. in the rate, but ask to be certain.

▌ TIME

There are approximately 70 countries in the world that use Daylight Saving Time in one way or another, but unfortunately Fiji is not one of these, having stopped the practice a few years ago. Fiji is 12 hours ahead of GMT. Therefore, when it's noon in Suva, it's 5 PM in L.A. on the previous day and 8 PM in New York City on the previous day. When these countries are experiencing Daylight Saving Time, subtract one hour from the time.

Time Zones Timeanddate.com (⊕www.timeanddate.com/worldclock).

▌ TIPPING

Fiji is a culture of gift exchanges on important occasions: food, kava, necessities, and money (during prominent social events). The practice of tipping isn't customary, but you'll see locals tipping, and that little extra is welcome if you feel the service was exceptional. In restaurants, 10% of the bill is fine; in resorts, speak to the manager on duty—often there's a general fund you can contribute to if the overall service exceeded your expectations. If you would like to tip an individual staff member, again, best to speak to the manager first. Often, directly handing money to an employee can cause confusion or embarrassment, and there may be a more discreet way of rewarding the employee for his or her good service.

▌ TOURS

Since Fiji is comprised of a few hundred islands scattered around the South Pacific Ocean, package tours are not the forced marches that people have in mind. They're often an efficient way to see as much as you can as cheaply as you can, consolidating air and water transfers, island-hopping, and village stays into one easy experience.

A seven-day all-inclusive kayaking tour around the island of Kadavu with Tamarillo Tropical Expeditions, for example, is about US$1,705. The "Lei Low" travel package with Feejee Experience is a six-day tour around Viti Levu, including sandboarding, a village visit, snorkeling, and a visit to Beachcomber Island for US$380.

TOUR OPERATORS

Fiji is an outdoor playground, and tour companies thrive on marketing what the country has to offer. Whether it's bird-watching or diving, Fiji has something for everyone.

Tamarillo Tropical Expeditions, run by a New Zealander, an Italian, and a Fijian chief, offers unique kayaking tours around the island of Kadavu, overnighting at local beachfront resorts and villages. Since Fijians co-own the company, there's a wealth of local knowledge and a vested interest in giving back to the community.

Feejee Experience has a lively, backpacker-vibe to it. The company specializes in three- to four-day trips around Viti Levu and Beachcomber Island. It's a great deal for backpackers or travelers on a budget.

Fiji Adventures offers tour packages ranging from diving, to spas, to adventure tourism. There literally is something for everyone.

Recommended Companies
Feejee Experience (☎672–5950 ⊕www.feejeeexperience.com). **Fiji Adventures** (☎866/755–3452 in U.S. ⊕www.fijiadventures.com). **Tamarillo Tropical Expeditions** (☎877/682–5433 in U.S. ⊕www.tamarillo.co.nz).

TRIP INSURANCE

Comprehensive travel policies typically cover trip-cancellation and interruption, letting you cancel or cut your trip short because of a personal emergency, illness, or, in some cases, acts of terrorism in your destination. Such policies also cover evacuation and medical care. Some also cover you for trip delays because of bad weather or mechanical problems as well as for lost or delayed baggage. Another type of coverage to look for is financial default—that is, when your trip is disrupted because a tour operator, airline, or cruise line goes out of business. Generally you must buy this when you book your trip or shortly thereafter, and it's only available to you if your operator isn't on a list of excluded companies.

At the very least, consider buying medical-only coverage. Neither Medicare nor some private insurers cover medical expenses anywhere outside of the United States (including time aboard a cruise ship, even if it leaves from a U.S. port). Medical-only policies typically reimburse you for medical care (excluding that related to pre-existing conditions) and hospitalization abroad, and provide for evacuation. You still have to pay the bills and await reimbursement from the insurer, though.

Another option is to sign up with a medical-evacuation assistance company. A membership in one of these companies gets you doctor referrals, emergency evacuation or repatriation, 24-hour hotlines for medical consultation, and other assistance. International SOS Assistance Emergency and AirMed International provide evacuation services and medical referrals. MedjetAssist offers medical evacuation.

Expect comprehensive travel insurance policies to cost about 4% to 7% or 8% of the total price of your trip (it's more like 8%–12% if you're over age 70). A medical-only policy may or may not be cheaper than a comprehensive policy. Always read the fine print of your policy to make sure that you are covered for the risks that are of most concern to you. Compare several policies to make sure you're getting the best price and range of coverage available.

■TIP➡ OK. You know you can save a bundle on trips to warm-weather destinations by traveling in rainy season. But there's also a chance that a severe storm will disrupt your plans. The solution? Look for hotels and resorts that offer storm/hurricane guarantees. Although they rarely allow refunds, most guarantees do let you rebook later if a storm strikes.

Insurance Comparison Sites
Insure My Trip.com (☎800/487–4722 ⊕www.insuremytrip.com). **Square Mouth.com** (☎800/240–0369 or 727/490–5803 ⊕www.squaremouth.com).

Medical Assistance Companies
AirMed International Medical Group (⊕www.airmed.com) **International SOS** (⊕www.internationalsos.com). **MedjetAssist** (⊕www.medjetassist.com).

Medical-Only Insurers **International Medical Group** (☎800/628-4664 ⊕www.imglobal.com). **Wallach & Company** (☎800/237-6615 or 540/687-3166 ⊕www.wallach.com).

Comprehensive Travel Insurers **Access America** (☎866/729-6021 ⊕www.accessamerica.com). **AIG Travel Guard** (☎800/826-4919 ⊕www.travelguard.com). **CSA Travel Protection** (☎800/873-9855 ⊕www.csatravelprotection.com). **HTH Worldwide** (☎610/254-8700 ⊕www.hthworldwide.com). **Travelex Insurance** (☎888/228-9792 ⊕www.travelex-insurance.com). **Travel Insured International** (☎800/243-3174 ⊕www.travelinsured.com).

▌ VISITOR INFORMATION

The main tourist resource is the Fiji Visitors Bureau. Individual offices are not prompt or reliable in returning e-mail or providing information over the phone, though the Visitors Bureau in Nadi International Airport is quite helpful. The bureau's Web site has a lot of useful information, including a list of overseas offices. It also features general island information, accommodations listings, and activities, as well as frequently asked questions, arrival/departure information, and tour operators. The site is designed to promote and sell Fiji as a tourist destination, but travelers can find useful information here as well.

The South Pacific Tourism Organization also has a general travel site for all the South Pacific countries that provides good overall information.

Contacts **Fiji Visitors Bureau** (✉Colonial Plaza, Suite 107, Namaka, Nadi ☎672-2433 ✉5777 W. Century Blvd., Suite 220, Los Angeles, CA ☎800/932-3454 ⊕www.bulafiji.com). **South Pacific Tourism Organization** (⊕www.spto.org).

ONLINE TRAVEL TOOLS
There's a variety of helpful Web sites that can help you plan a safe and fun trip to Fiji. Your first stop should be the Fijian government's official Web site, which provides information on visas, immigration, public holidays, government departments, Fijian culture, and, perhaps most important, updates on the current political climate.

Fijilive, the local news Web site, is useful for getting a feeling for modern-day Fijian culture, current headlines, and daily goings-on.

All About Fiji **Fiji Government** (⊕www.fiji.gov.fj). **Fijilive** (⊕www.fijilive.com).

INDEX

NOTES

NOTES

NOTES

ABOUT OUR WRITERS

Robert Brenner began his travel writing career on a sub-zero January day in Chicago's Chinatown while a student of Northwestern University's Medill School of Journalism, and dreamed the numbness would one day pay tropical dividends. Stops along the way ranged from the bowels of Panama City to the alleyway pool halls of Japan and were often inspired by his mother, who "decides where she wants to go, then takes four books out from the library." A contributor to *Conde Nast Traveler* and Australia's *The Age,* he currently balances his time between what he calls the "greatness" of New York and the "goodness" of Melbourne, Australia. He wrote the Viti Levu, Yasawa & Mamanusa, Lomaiviti, Vanua Levu, Taveuni, and Kadavu chapters.

Carrie Miller is a travel addict who found her way from Minnesota to the National Geographic Society, where she was a writer/researcher for *National Geographic Traveler Magazine.* After an assignment to New Zealand, Carrie returned to D.C., packed up her desk, and moved to the land of the Long White Cloud. She found New Zealand to be the perfect diving board for exploring the South Pacific, and when she isn't traveling, freelancing, or watching dolphins from her front porch, you can find her in the gym, training for her first amateur boxing match...which seemed like a good story idea at the time. She worked on the book's Travel Smart Fiji section.